WRITE FASTER, WRITE BETTER

David A. Fryxell

WRITER'S DIGEST BOOKS

CINCINNATI, OHIO   WWW.WRITERSDIGEST.COM

Visit our Web site at www.writersdigest.com for information on more resources for writers.

To receive a free weekly e-mail newsletter delivering tips and updates about writing and about Writer's Digest products, register directly at our Web site at http://newsletters.fwpublications.com.

08 07 06 05 04   5 4 3 2 1

Library of Congress Cataloging-in-Publication Data

Fryxell, David A.
   Write faster, write better / David A. Fryxell.—1st ed.
     p. cm.
   Includes index.
   ISBN 1-58297-286-9 (alk. paper)
   1. Authorship. I. Title.

   PN151.F83   2004
   808'.02—dc22   2003066076
                                                                        CIP

Edited by Michelle Ruberg
Designed by Terri Eubanks
Cover designed by Lisa Buchanan
Production coordinated by Robin Richie

Dedication

For my mother, Lucy Dickinson Fryxell (1919-2003),
who taught me to love the language.

About the Author

David A. Fryxell is the former editor-in-chief of *Writer's Digest Magazine* and Writer's Digest Books and has been a columnist for *Writer's Digest Magazine* since 1994. He's the author of two previous books of writing instruction, *How to Write Fast (While Writing Well)* and *Elements of Article Writing: Structure and Flow*, as well as a book of humor, *Double-Parked on Main Street*. His teaching and lecturing on writing includes creating two courses for Writer's Online Workshops, serving on the faculty of the Maui Writers Retreat and Maui Writers Conference, and speaking to groups including the Southwest Writers Conference, the Society of Professional Journalists, the American Society of Journalists and Authors, and many more.

Fryxell is the author of more than one thousand magazine and newspaper pieces, for publications including *Playboy*, *Reader's Digest*, and *Travel & Leisure*. He's been an editor of *TWA Ambassador, Horizon, Pitt*, and *Milwaukee* magazines, features and business editor of the *St. Paul Pioneer Press*, and executive producer of Microsoft's Twin Cities Sidewalk Web site. He founded *Family Tree Magazine*, the nation's largest-circulation family history publication. His work as a writer and editor has earned more than 100 awards. He's profiled in the book *Super Searcher, Author, Scribe: Successful Writers Share Their Internet Research Secrets* and is included in the current edition of *Who's Who in America*. He lives in Silver City, NM, where he is a freelance writer and is editor and publisher of *Desert Exposure*, a regional lifestyle publication.

Table of Contents

INTRODUCTION

By Terry Brooks

David Fryxell and I have known each other now for the better part of a dozen years, a friendship that I have come to treasure. We met first when he was working at *Writer's Digest* and I was a touring author just beginning to meet some of the people in the publishing business. Subsequently, we both began teaching at the Maui Writers Retreat, David in nonfiction, myself in fiction. It was at the Retreat that I got to know him best and to see how he worked as a teacher of the craft of writing.

Notice that I describe him as a teacher of the "craft" of writing. I do that on purpose, because I believe writing is a craft that can be taught and not some genetically inherited or divinely bestowed mystical ability. David and I are on the same page here, as I discovered during our teaching times together. We both share a deep love and respect for the process and a strong belief that if you have it in you to be a writer, you can learn how to use the tools that will help you reach your goal.

Write Faster, Write Better is an invaluable guide to doing just that. David writes in a relaxed, conversational style—very much the way he teaches—providing easy access to the lessons of writing that he wants to impart. He approaches writing in a direct and easily understandable way, giving valuable insights into the how and why of the writing process. He understands the demands of writing for a living, and he offers sound advice on how to persevere when the pressure seems too much.

It doesn't matter if you are a writer of fiction or nonfiction, books or screenplays, the rules of the craft are the same. David has made that clear in his book, and what he has to say about organization and dedication applies to all types of writers. He takes a close look at the sorts of problems that can throw a writer off track and offers direct, sensible solutions.

I appreciate the way he interjects humorous stories and comments into his lessons, a way of teaching that avoids those didactic and mundane tomes that make you wish you had gone with the tapes and keeps you turning the pages. I like that he isn't afraid to describe himself as someone who didn't start out perfect and had to learn some hard lessons along the way. I recognize myself in some of what David has to say about his own experiences, and I think most readers will have the same response.

I am a firm believer in reading what any writer has to say about the craft. I think all of us have something to offer, and David is no exception. His book is an invaluable tool whether you are a beginning writer or a writer of somewhat more experience. Right from the first chapter, you will know you are in good hands.

Take a few minutes right now and read that chapter. You will know what I mean.

Best Wishes and Good Writing,
Terry Brooks

With more than thirteen million books in print and fifteen consecutive *New York Times* bestsellers including *Sword of Shannara, Running with the Demon, A Knight of the Word* and, most recently, *High Druid of Shannara: Jarka Ruus,* Terry Brooks is America's largest-selling fantasy novelist.

CHAPTER 1

PLANNING TO WRITE FASTER AND BETTER

You know the old joke about how there are two kinds of people in the world—those who believe there are two kinds of people in the world, and those who don't? Well, I do believe that there are two kinds of writers in the world. I'm not talking about fiction and nonfiction writers. Any notion that these are two fundamentally different species was pretty much demolished by the "literary journalism" movement and the many fine authors who've effortlessly crossed back and forth. The advice in this book, in fact, will apply equally to fiction and nonfiction writers, and we'll see examples of writing faster and better from both.

I'm not talking about published versus unpublished writers, either. An unpublished writer is just someone with a few more things to learn—like a student who's still a couple of courses shy of graduation. Or an unpublished writer may be every bit as polished as many published authors (or even more so), but simply someone whose best ideas haven't yet found a home. Getting published is as much a matter of matchmaking as it is quality of writing—meshing your ideas with the needs of a publisher. This book will help you generate publishable ideas more quickly and make your "matchmaking" process more efficient, so you can get on with writing more and publishing more.

I'm not even talking about the difference between good writers and bad ones. Learning more about the basics of the writing craft and mastering some of the habits of focus and organization that this book will explain can rapidly erase that line. So can simply sitting in your chair and spending time each and every day working on your writing. To borrow a line from another old joke, the way to become a good writer is a lot like the way to Carnegie Hall: "Practice, practice, practice."

No, I believe that the two kinds of writers in the world are the organized and the disorganized. By "organized" I don't mean merely that they have no sloping, sliding piles of papers on their desks; organization is not synonymous with neatness. "Disorganized" writers are not necessarily sloppy, either, though slovenly work habits can certainly be a symptom of equally sloppy thinking.

It's simply this: Organized writers have a plan. Disorganized writers don't. The plan may be painstakingly written down on index cards, methodically entered into a computer program, or merely held in the writer's head. But organized writers know where they're going and more or less how they'll get there.

An organized mystery novelist, for example, may not know from chapter one "whodunit" at the end of the book. But if not, she will have carefully assembled her characters so that the conclusion, when it does arrive, is as inevitable (if nonetheless surprising) as if she'd planned it from the first word. Organization is not the same as outlining your book or article—though this book will attempt to convince you that outlining is a valuable tool toward getting organized. It is rather a habit of mind that approaches the craft of writing as serious work. So the successful mystery novelist who lets the killer reveal himself as she writes doesn't plunge into her book willynilly, with an opening scene ("Dead. The woman was dead, no doubt about it. . . .") and no more notion of what comes next than her readers have. The writer who tries that will wind up at a dead end as surely as a detective who can't keep track of his clues.

The Hard Road to Easy

It's not just book-length projects that demand organization, however. Early in my career, I spent three years working in the writer's dream job of roving newspaper columnist—sort of like CBS's "On the Road" correspondent Charles Kuralt with a word processor (and a very primitive word processor it was, as this was in the early 1980s) instead of a television camera. But that job could have been a nightmare instead of a dream come true, and not because it was in the unlikely Eden of Dubuque, Iowa. My job description was simple: Write 3 feature columns, each about 20 inches long, every week. That meant 3 columns a week, 52 weeks a year—156 deadlines to make, 156 bullets to dodge each year, more than 3,000 inches of copy per annum. Each individual piece may have been relatively short, but a disorganized writer would be eaten alive by such a "dream job."

By the time I left Dubuque, I was writing 4 columns a week. I had learned, if I hadn't already known, how to organize my writing—how to write faster. But I also did some of the best writing of my life. Under deadline pressure, under the constant demand to meet my weekly quota, I was forced to develop the habits that helped me write not only faster, but better.

And, no, I didn't craft elaborate, computer-finessed outlines in multiple colors and faultless "I-A-1-a-i" form, either. In fact, it would have been tempting, given the unrelenting pressures of cranking out columns, to have decided I just didn't have time to plan my writing at all. Dive in, start typing and let the semicolons fall where they may. But that would have been a disaster: It's only by investing time upfront in planning your writing, however roughly and crudely, that you can zip through the actual writing and make it look easy.

Like most things in life, making writing look easy is the result of a lot of hard work. In my frantic cranking out of columns in Dubuque, for example, actually sitting down in the newsroom and starting to peck away at the keyboard was the end of my creative process, not the beginning.

I learned that I had to turn the story around in my mind on the drive home from the interview or whatever I was reporting on. Ideally, the process worked best if my subconscious could noodle with the topic overnight and while I was doing something else—taking a shower, mowing the lawn—though I didn't always have the luxury of that "percolation" time. Then I'd go through my notebook, numbering the pages and highlighting quotes and facts I was pretty sure I'd use in the article. Next, I'd scribble out an outline on a yellow legal pad—nothing fancy, nothing I'd want to show my fifth-grade teacher who taught me about outlining. Arrows would indicate second thoughts about where a key fact ought to go. Scratch-outs marked things that didn't really belong in the story, after all. I learned pretty quickly that any story whose salient points couldn't fit on a single sheet of legal paper was too long for the space the newspaper typically allotted my column. Finally, I'd go back through my notebook and code my outline with the page numbers where the facts to flesh out each line in my plan appeared. Only then would I sit down and start to write.

We'll go into more detail on this and other simple ways to organize your writing in chapter ten, and show how an actual story grows from the bare roots of a such an outline. For now, the point is that I took the time to figure out where my story was going before setting it loose to start heading there. Just like the mystery novelist who might spend weeks assembling her cast of characters before revealing the first corpse, I did my homework.

Once I sat down at the keyboard, sure, it looked easy; the hard work was already done.

The truth is, though, it *is* easier, overall. Maybe not as easy as it might look to someone who doesn't see all my sweating over that legal pad, but still easier than if I dived right in and started typing. I never suffer from "writer's block," because when I'm actually writing I always know where my story's going and how I'll get there. I never have to stare at a blank screen for hours, hoping somehow words will magically materialize there. Yes, I work harder before I sit down to write, but that investment of time pays dividends many times over in the actual labor of putting one word after another.

Developing (ugh) Discipline

Ironically, "making it look easy" comes down to learning discipline. You have to make yourself follow the path of an organized writer until it becomes second nature, until you can't imagine writing any other way. As screenwriter and time-management/creativity consultant Kenneth Atchity puts it, "Discipline is the key . . . the bedrock of productive writing. Talent is not a rare commodity. Discipline is."

I realize that "discipline" is not a word you hear bandied about much in writing circles—it's neither as fashionable nor as highfalutin as talking about your "muse" or inspiration. But you need to look at your writing as a job that takes the same day-to-day commitment you'd put in to earn a paycheck at a factory. The rewards of writing—both financially and psychically—may ultimately be greater than punching a time clock, but before they come, you need the discipline to get the job done.

Elizabeth George, the bestselling author of such mystery novels as *A Place of Hiding*, says, "Writing is 10 percent inspiration and 90 percent endeavor." She adds, "It's a job and has to be approached as a job. Writers write—they don't wait for it to be fun. I have fun skiing. But I don't require my entire life to be fun. I don't wait for something to inspire me."

"Writing is work," concurs Dorothy Allison, who was nominated for a National Book Award for her autobiographical novel *Bastard Out of Carolina*. "This is not joy. This is not pleasure." When Allison teaches at workshops, she admits that she has a reputation as a tough teacher, because she insists that her students put it on the page—it's not enough to hear them merely talk about their work, about what they *intend* to write. The problem she sees with many students is that "no one has taken them seriously" and told them that writing is a long, demanding process. "Writers who say, 'It just came to me' are lying sacks of shit. This is not genius. This is hard work."

But the good news, Allison adds, is that you *can* do it. It's not a matter of whether you have some elusive spark of genius. "Work will trump talent," she insists. "Hard work will trump a gift every time."

That's because, as Pulitzer Prize-winning poet Archibald MacLeish once noted, "any art is first and foremost a craft." You need to master the craft of writing in order to have any hope of producing art. And how do you do that? You guessed it: As MacLeish put it, "All art begins and ends with discipline."

MacLeish went on, "We have gone far enough in the road to self-indulgence now to know that. The man who announces to the world that he is going to 'do his thing' is like the amateur on the high-diving platform who flings himself into the void shouting at the judges that he is going to do whatever comes naturally. He will land on his ass. Naturally."

If you're willing to get organized as a writer, to approach the art of writing first as a craft that demands (ugh) discipline rather than just doing whatever comes naturally, this book can show you how *not* to land on your ass. Instead, you'll be ready to tackle the high-diving platform and really make a splash as a writer.

Why Bother To Get Organized?

By this time, however, you may be asking yourself, "Okay, but is it worth it?" Why not just keep stumbling along as a disorganized writer, dealing with writer's block and the terror of the blank page but at least unburdened by the need for discipline? Write when the muse strikes you—and, well, if that's hardly ever, at least you'll collect fewer rejection slips.

In other words, you're probably wondering, "What's in it for me?" Fair enough. Let's talk first about the most obvious benefit of getting organized: Writing faster. When you can get from first sentence to "The End" in less time, you have more time to:

a. write more
b. sell more of your work
c. get your message across to the readers of the world
d. veg out in front of the boob tube without feeling guilty that you're not writing
e. all of the above

Despite these obvious benefits, writing fast has never been particularly admired—except by those (teachers, editors, publishers) who actually need the writing done. Indeed, rapid writers have always been looked down upon in arty circles. If you write quickly, without spilling blood, sweat, and tears onto the manuscript page, the results can't possibly be any good—or so the thinking goes. Quality of writing ought to rise in direct proportion to the time invested in creation, right? A novel "knocked out" in six months can't possibly compare to a work agonized over, written and rewritten, for the better part of a writer's career. Can it?

The folks in these arty circles have a word for fast writers: *hack*. I maintain that a better term for a writer who works efficiently and consistently meets deadlines is *professional*.

If you've ever written for a living (or as a dedicated pastime), you know what I mean. While this book will also help you write better—yes, yes, I'm getting to that part!—the brutal reality for most working writers is that it's at least as important to strive to write faster: to slice the time between the thrill of getting an assignment and the joy of slipping a completed manuscript into a manila envelope, licking the flap, dropping it into the mailbox, and counting the days until the check arrives. For many writers—*professional* writers—writing faster is simply a matter of survival. Writing faster can mean the difference between making a go of a challenging career as an author versus going back to your old job as an accountant or asking "Smoking or non-smoking?" down at Bob's Big Boy. Writer's block, you might even say, is a luxury that *real* writers can't afford.

Breaking the Speed Limit

Still dubious? Let's look at some well-known and not-so-well-known authors who've set the pace for the rest of us when it comes to writing faster—just to show what a writer can accomplish when you really set your mind to it.

We have to start with one of those not-so-well-known authors: According to the *Guinness Book of World Records*, Englishman Charles Harold St. John Hamilton (1876–1961) is the most prolific author in history. Under the pseudonym of Frank Richards, he wrote the adventures of "Billy Bunter." At his prime, from 1915–1926, Hamilton would often bang out 80,000 words a week—almost the length of this book—for a trio of boys' adventure magazines. Over his lifetime, says Guinness, Hamilton produced about 75 million words.

The fastest female writer was a South African woman, Kathleen Lindsay

(1903–1973). During her lifetime, Lindsay somehow penned 904 novels under three married names and eight pen names. Please note: She died just before the advent of the PC and word processor, so librarians can only shudder at the thought of what she might have produced if fully armed with modern technology.

Neither Hamilton nor Lindsay nor any of their army of pseudonyms may ring a bell with today's readers, and it's true that their prodigious output is unlikely to find a spot (it'd have to be a darn big spot) in the annals of great literature. But swiftness of writing isn't strictly the province of what some might call "hacks." Yes, many great authors have been painfully slow at their art, creating only a handful of laboriously crafted works in their careers. But many other famous writers throughout history have proven that, unlike fine wine, good writing does not have to be produced slowly.

Often the greats of the literary past were driven to rapid productivity by the same forces that may inspire you: the need to pay bills, to simply make a living. Samuel Johnson (1709–1784), for example, wrote his "philosophical romance," *Rasselas*, in a single week in order to pay his mother's debts and the costs of her funeral. Honoré de Balzac (1799–1850), one of the most prolific authors of his day and a master of the novel, literally wrote his way out of the garret. Even when he had achieved some literary success, Balzac continued to labor 16 hours a day, starting at midnight after a few hours of sleep and continuing into the next afternoon. Fueled by countless cups of black coffee, he created the masterpiece of *La Comédie Humaine*—a tapestry of some 2,000 characters in nearly a hundred novels, written over 20 years. Literature is lucky that Balzac was a terrible investor, losing his shirt time after time in get-rich-quick schemes that forced him back to his writing desk to keep ahead of the bill collectors.

Not only the debt-ridden in the literary pantheon knew how to write fast, however. Many of the elite created at an impressive pace, blessed with a muse that worked overtime, perhaps, or simply a solid share of discipline. The Spanish playwright Lope de Vega (1562–1635) wrote several of his plays overnight, and penned more than a hundred of them in no more than a day apiece. Though "only" about 500 of de Vega's works survive, he's believed to have written more than 2,000—an output that caused an envious Miguel de Cervantes to dub de Vega "a monster of nature." Sir Walter Scott (1771–1832), it's said, dictated his novels so rapidly that his secretaries could barely keep pace; he wrote 2 of the novels in his Waverly series in just 3 weeks. And Alexandre Dumas (1802–1870) once won a wager, the story goes, by writing the entire first volume of his *Le Chevalier de Maison-Rouge* in only 72 hours.

More recent writers have kept up the pace. In fact, some have called Perry Mason creator Erle Stanley Gardner (1889–1970) "the world's fastest writer." Gardner once worked on seven novels simultaneously; at 140 books, though, he falls a few million words short of the "most-prolific" title. (He must have taken a lot of vacations.) Fellow mystery writer John Creasey (1908–1973) could probably have given Gardner a run for his money, speedwise: Creasey once cranked out 2 novels in a single week. It's worth noting that Creasey collected what's likely a world-record 743 rejection slips before publishing the first of his 564 books—and went on to write more than 40 million words in about 40 years, including the Baron and Toff series. Georges Simenon (1903–1989), the French mystery writer and creator of Inspector Maigret, also topped 500 books. Before settling down to work, Simenon would have a complete medical exam—it slows one down to keel over the typewriter, *n'est-ce pas?*—and then lock himself in a room to write. Precisely 6 days later, he would emerge with a completed novel. (And on the seventh day, one presumes, he rested.)

Like mystery writers, science-fiction authors have a tradition of doing even their best work in almost no time at all. Lester del Rey (1915–1993), a great editor as well as an accomplished writer of novels such as *Nerve*, could knock out a 6,000-word story for the pulp magazines of his day in only two hours. Del Rey once rolled a sheet of paper into the typewriter after breakfast, wrote all day, and dropped a 20,000-word novelette into the mailbox that night.

The speed record for science-fiction writers, though, is surely held by Isaac Asimov (1920–1992), author of *I, Robot* and the *Foundation* series among many others. In the first decades of his career, Asimov wrote ten hours a day; he managed 5 books in 1957 alone. By 1979, when he celebrated his 200th book with the publication of *Opus 200*, he had already written 15 million words. That total included Asimov's much-praised nonfiction books, most of which he said he wrote in less than 3 days apiece.

Many humor writers seem able to be funny at a frantic pace. This, too, takes discipline, though that probably sounds contradictory to the whimsical world of humor. P.G. Wodehouse (1881–1975), the creator of Jeeves and Bertie Wooster, planned his frothy entertainments with almost military precision, relying on many pages of notes to make sure his jokes fired at the right time and place. Once a novel was strategized, Wodehouse would start work at 7:30 in the morning, 7 days a week, and write 2,000 words a day. This regimen allowed him to produce a finished book in three months.

Today, most of our funniest writers—Dave Barry, Calvin Trillin and PJ O'Rourke, to name only a few—work in newspapers and magazines, where no sooner is today's or this week's chuckle put to bed than the demand arises again: Make somebody laugh tomorrow, or next week. Somehow, column after column or issue after issue, these writers manage to turn out not only some of the funniest writing in America, but some of the best. Inspired by their incessant deadlines, with no time to agonize and over-analyze ("Is this really funny or does it just seem funny because I wrote it?"), they find humor all around them.

But today's genre writers don't have a monopoly on speed. Probably the best-known prodigy of production among contemporary literary novelists is Joyce Carol Oates, author of *We Were the Mulvaneys*, who'd written 33 books and three plays by age 40. Critics often chide Oates for producing too much, on the dubious supposition that her work would be better if there were less of it. Despite her output, Oates is not, in fact, a model of authorial efficiency: She rises at dawn and works until mid-afternoon before having breakfast (so much for "the most important meal of the day"), writing in longhand. She rewrites some pages more than a dozen times, and has even revised some stories after publication, before they are gathered into a collection. Imagine what Oates could do if she learned to type those first drafts and to leave well enough alone after the second revision—and imagine how the critics would harp then!

Not to pick on a remarkable writer, but Oates is a good example of the folly of slavish imitation of successful authors' writing habits. You, too, could start writing right through breakfast time, abandon your computer for a pen and pad, and rework your words until you can barely read your own scribbling. But it would not make you Joyce Carol Oates, and it certainly would not boost your productivity to match hers. Some writers are able to turn out a great deal of work *despite* their writing habits, not because of them.

Better instead to emulate an author such as Bob Mayer, author of 23 books including the Area 51 series, who has more than 2 million copies in print. Mayer describes his writing strategy in *The Novel Writer's Toolkit*, published by Writer's Digest Books. For Mayer, writing is a job and he approaches it like one—as should you, if you're serious about writing faster and better.

Knocking Out a Novel

Wouldn't it be lovely, though, if we could just imitate the habits of a writer and get the same results? This temptation is what Francine du Plessix Gray, author of *Lovers and Tyrants* and regular *New Yorker* contributor, once called "the wisdom of the keyhole": If only you knew how such-and-such a successful writer worked, and copied his tools and techniques, surely you could write that way, too.

Why not? George M. Cohan, "the man who owned Broadway" whose career was captured in *Yankee Doodle Dandy*, used to rent an entire Pullman car and travel until he finished whatever he was working on, hammering out 140 pages a night to the rhythm of the rails. Ah, if only the great days of rail travel were still with us! You could rent a Pullman car, start writing, and arrive as a Yankee Doodle Dandy! Right?

The technique, the secret of their success, doesn't have to be so elaborate or stylish to tempt emulation. Rudyard Kipling could write only with pitch-black ink—mere blue-black, he said, was "an abomination." Maybe that's it! Maybe you're using the wrong color ink! Balzac wore a favorite dressing gown as a sort of authoring good luck charm; perhaps a trip down to Wal-Mart for a new bathrobe would cure your writer's block. Joan Didion (*Play It As It Lays, The White Album*) has to sleep in the same room as her manuscript-in-progress. Move the office into the bedroom! Gore Vidal (*Burr, Myra Breckenridge*), as blunt-spoken as ever, has said that he cannot summon his muse without coffee and then a bowel movement. Crank up the Krups and . . .

Well, you get the idea. It's only natural to hunger for some magic trick, some easy alternative to discipline and hard, steady work that will energize your writing. And of course that may be why you picked up this book in the first place: "Here's some simple stuff I can do to speed up and improve my writing. Maybe he'll tell me to use pitch-black ink instead of that abominable blue-black . . ."

Sorry. Writing doesn't work with a magic wand. But before you toss this book back on the shelf in favor of *How to Cure Writer's Block with One Trip to Wal-Mart*, let me be quick to tell you what you can learn from the masters, or from anyone who's found some success as an author: Writing happens one page at a time.

Wait, wait, come back—Wal-Mart isn't open right now, anyway. Of course that sounds obvious—writing happens one page at a time, *duh!*—

but it's an eye-opening realization once you let it sink in. Think of it as simple mathematics: If you write 1 page a day—just 1 page—in a year you'll have written 365 pages. That's a decent size novel.

Or take it to the next level. Jack Warner, a veteran newspaper writer who covered most of the big stories in the South for UPI and then the *Atlanta Journal-Constitution*, never thought he could write a novel. Sure, he was a fast writer—he once wrote two breaking stories at the same time, switching back and forth as the news unfolded. But he was used to writing fast and short, and the sheer length of a novel daunted Warner until he realized: A novel is just one scene after another.

"Suddenly that made it seem manageable," Warner recalls. "So I started writing one scene at a time and found it was very easy, the writing went very quickly. I wrote the first third of my novel in a week."

That novel, *Shikar*, went on to capture the attention of star literary agent Richard Curtis, who sold it to an imprint of St. Martin's Press. If Warner had never realized that a novel is just one scene after another, that success would never have happened.

You can do the same thing. You can "knock out a novel" in a year—or in three months, for that matter. You don't need a new bathrobe or a different color of ink. You just need—here it comes again—the discipline to organize your writing and then to write a page or two a day, a chapter a week, or whatever it takes to add up to your goal.

From Faster to Better

That's another secret of writing faster, in fact: Getting organized clears your way to write. So the choice often isn't between writing fast or slowly; it's between writing and not writing, at any speed.

For the writer in a one-person wordsmith's shop, productivity is every bit as important as it is for a gigantic factory churning out widgets instead of words. And it can be just as challenging: Between you and each finished manuscript lies an obstacle course of psychological traps, phone calls from hectoring editors, interruptions from spouses and children, and—worst of all—your own morass of notes and files, threatening to overwhelm the kitchen corner or basement cubbyhole you laughingly call your office.

This book is your step-by-step guide through that obstacle course. From generating workable ideas to maximizing your research results, from efficient interviewing to organizing your notes, from opening to revision, from creating characters to making your way through the labyrinth of plotting, you can learn to write faster.

You can also learn how to write better, and this book will teach you that, too. (See, I told you we'd get there.) For writing faster and writing better are not, as those snooty arty types mentioned earlier would have you believe, mutually exclusive. Quite the opposite: The same techniques that will make you a faster writer will make you a better writer. That's because the secret of speeding up your writing is learning what makes good writing and doing it right the first time.

The late *New Yorker* reporter A.J. Liebling used to boast, "I can write better than anybody who's faster, and faster than anybody who's better." Once I heard that line, I immediately adopted it as my personal credo. And as I learned from my Dubuque experience, the faster I wrote, the better I began to write.

But how do you get from here to there? How do you start getting organized so that you can start writing faster (or simply writing instead of being "blocked")—and better? You need a fundamental approach to organizing and accelerating your writing. A way of thinking more clearly about the writer's task. A method of arranging both the physical resources of your writing—your notes, reference books, and interview materials—and the dynamics of your story, from start to finish and all the twists and turns in between. A system.

Yes, no less than the widget works across town, you need a system to manage your work as a writer. Some of it can be picked up from reading interviews with writers and forewords to books, that "wisdom of the keyhole." For my own career, reading the introduction to *The John McPhee Reader* gave me a framework for organizing and thinking about my writing, a framework that I've since adapted to my own needs and thought processes. Learning how McPhee, the gifted *New Yorker* reporter, approached his work helped crystallize my own thinking about the process of writing. But it wasn't the arrangement of his office or the color of paper he used that I borrowed from McPhee; it was his sense of a system.

I know, a system sounds inimical to the mysterious art of writing—much less magical than finding the right color of ink, renting a Pullman car, or drinking coffee until either your muse or nature calls. "Did Flaubert have a system?" you ask. Balzac had a bathrobe, but did he have a system?

The point of developing a systematic approach to your writing, however, isn't to turn you into a keypunching version of those assembly line robots you see in automobile plants: Insert Verb A into Sentence B, then punctuate. Just the opposite: By getting organized—by wresting order out of the chaos of your writing process—you will be freed (to borrow a phrase) to be all that you can be as an author. Once you have a system that lets you find and plan where a story is going and how you'll get there, it's a lot easier to pay attention to the scenery en route.

In other words, with a system instead of a wishful-thinking magic wand, you'll be able to write faster—*and* write better.

Exercises

1. Keep a diary of one of your typical days in fifteen-minute segments. Especially make note of any time that you're "wasting" on activities, such as watching television, which you could instead use for writing.

2. Set your alarm clock to get up an hour earlier tomorrow and spend that "extra" time working on your current writing project. How much did you get done?

3. No matter what else you have to do today, make the time to sit down and write just one page of your current writing project. How long did it take?

CHAPTER 2

ORGANIZING YOUR WRITING LIFE

Being a writer, screenwriter Lawrence Kasdan (*Raiders of the Lost Ark*) once observed, is like having homework for the rest of your life. There's always some "assignment" to do, whether from a publisher or self-imposed. If you asked my mom what I was like as a kid, she often mentioned that she never had to bug me to do my homework. Somehow I developed, early on, an internal taskmaster that made me get my homework finished; today, that taskmaster still nags me to finish the "homework" of being a writer.

But it's not that I'm a workaholic. Right now, for instance, it's a sunny Sunday afternoon and I'd really rather be outside disregarding the advice of America's dermatologists and soaking up those rays, not writing. What keeps me from grabbing my sunglasses and zooming out to the waiting hammock is the nagging realization that if I don't work on this chapter today, I'll start to fall behind on my plan to get this book completed. And my commitment to that plan—in the previous chapter, we called it "discipline"—is even stronger than the lure of that hammock. Just barely, but stronger.

It was Aristotle who observed that the most characteristically human activity is planning one's life. He may have been right, but it's also all too characteristic of most of us to put off such planning—preferring, say, the characteristic activities of a sloth. Even when we do finally get busy, too many of us approach life without a plan. We plunge forward in a frenzy of activity—like a bouncy puppy unleashed in a roomful of doggie toys—and then, when we're exhausted, look with dismay at the mess all around us and wonder why nothing was accomplished.

Too many writers, in particular, rely on the fickle lightning bolt of inspiration instead of planning their time and their work. But writing faster and better comes from following your own inner master, not from waiting for the Muse to strike. If you wait to write until you feel inspired, you'll get in a lot of hammock time, but you won't get much writing done. If you write only when the Muse deigns to visit, the writing—what there is of it—isn't yours at all; it belongs to the Muse. So you must become your own Muse. You must nurture an inner inspiration you can summon for half an hour before you catch the morning bus, for a spurt of writing during your lunch hour, or even when you'd really rather be catching a few rays out back.

The 10-Minute Novelist

Let's start with organizing your time, since many writers never get over this basic hurdle. How many people believe they could be great writers, if only they could find the time? How many working writers spend their entire careers under the gun, unable to do their best work because they have one eye on the clock? (And how many, unable to master their own time, fool themselves into thinking they "work best under pressure"? In fact, that's the only time they work at all!)

If your problem is finding time to write, it means you're losing time: The pieces of your life that could be spent writing are being lost instead to watching television, sleeping late, and sitting around thinking about being a writer instead of writing. Mystery novelist Elizabeth George advises, "Evaluate how you're using your free time every day for a week—talking on the phone, reading the newspaper, watching TV, listening to the radio. All these things are bleeding away from your writing time, thinking time, preparation time. You have to structure your life to allow yourself to write."

Yes, modern life is hectic, but that's all the more reason to take control of your time and stop losing it to minutiae. As Marcel Proust observed, "The time which we have at our disposal every day is elastic; the passions that we feel expand it, those that we inspire contract it; and habit fills up what remains."

We've already seen in the previous chapter how a commitment to writing one page a day, or one scene a week, can add up to completing a book project. The key to keeping to that plan—your self-imposed "homework"—is of course to force yourself to find the time to write, even if it's only long enough to write one page. How long do you need? An hour? A day? How about just 10 minutes? The French chancellor D'Aguesseau, it's said, once noticed that his wife was habitually 10 minutes late coming down to dinner. He decided to make use of those 10 minutes (3,650 minutes a year, or more than 60 hours). While he waited for dinner, D'Aguesseau wrote a three-volume book, which became a best-seller when it was published in 1668.

Or maybe your successful writing career simply needs to start with your alarm clock. Anthony Trollope (1815–1882) spent most of his life working as a postal clerk, but he would get up at five o'clock each morning and write three thousand words in the three hours before beginning with the mail. If Trollope finished penning a novel before it was time to go to work— and he finished nearly 50 books this way, among them *Doctor Thorne* and *He Knew He Was Right*—he'd simply begin another. Trollope also knew when to quit: "Three hours a day will produce as much as a man ought to write," he said in his autobiography.

Do you take public transportation to work? How much writing could you get done on the bus or train? The British crime novelist Michael Gilbert (1912–) managed to write 23 books, such as *Smallbone Deceased, Death Has Deep Roots* and *The Danger Within,* during his daily fifty-minute commute to his "real job" as a solicitor.

For you, finding the time to write might mean staying up an hour later each night, closeting yourself with the typewriter one night a week, or tapping on a laptop computer on airplane rides. Even just an hour a day can add up to a solid first draft of a novel in a little over 3 months. (If that pace—say, 750 words—sounds like more than you can possibly manage in an hour, well, you haven't read the rest of this book yet.) At 4 books a year, you'd match Anthony Trollope's output in not much more than a decade.

These mundane mathematics are exactly how many renowned authors found the time to create their masterworks. Irving Wallace (1916–1990), author of *The Chapman Report)*, early in his career, used to keep detailed records of his output to spur himself to greater productivity if he started lagging behind his self-assigned quotas. Even when the words won't come, it's important to keep to your schedule: "Force yourself to sit four hours at the table," *From Here to Eternity* author James Jones (1921–1977) advised. "Sometimes you get nothing. But the self-discipline is good for you. Somewhere inside, you'll be working."

Of course, like anything else, finding the time to write becomes easier once it becomes a habit. If you can make yourself jog or spend time on the Nautilus machine every morning, you can make yourself write. The former will make you live longer; the latter will give you a reason to live.

Moonlighting in a New Light

Most writers—like the hardworking Trollope and Gilbert—hold down full-time jobs even as they labor to create careers working with words. Even many successful authors will never earn enough from their writing to completely support themselves. Your writing "job" is likely to be a moonlighting one, with all the time-juggling challenges other moonlighters face.

It's not just a matter of finding ten minutes or an hour a day to actually hunker down at the keyboard. If you're working nine to five, when do you make time to do your research? Especially if you're a nonfiction writer, how are you supposed to arrange interviews, work the phone or hunt down sources while holding down a steady job? On the flip side, while charging long-distance calls for your writing to your regular employer is obviously out, how much can you take advantage of the access and expertise afforded by your job without putting that weekly paycheck at risk?

Successful and less stressful moonlighting as a writer starts with being smart about what writing projects you tackle. I juggled a freelancing career and a nine-to-five career (well, sometimes it was more like eight-to-seven) for almost twenty-five years, and kept my sanity by knowing my limits.

The ideal moonlighting project, of course, requires hardly any research at all. Drawing on your own life experiences and expertise for articles, short stories or novels makes it easy to combine writing with regular work. Writing your memoirs, obviously, is the ideal project for a moonlighting author to tackle.

But you don't have to stick quite so close to home. Maybe you have a field of deep expertise that you can tap, whether for a book or a flurry of feature articles. What subject do you know so well that you can write about it off the top of your head? (For nonfiction writers, a side benefit to this approach is that your in-depth knowledge makes it easier to spot hot stories before the popular press picks up on them, and likewise makes you more attractive to an editor.) If you know model trains better than any normal person ought to, consider queries on topics in the model-train world. If your passion is Civil War history, mine that for your novel instead of diving into something you've never researched before.

The same goes for geography: Write what and where you know. If you're a moonlighting nonfiction writer, explore your immediate region for article ideas before banging out queries about Bali (unless of course you live in the South Pacific). A non-Manhattan address, so remote from the heart of the publishing world, may actually be an advantage: Does that magazine you long to write for have somebody covering your neck of the woods yet? If you live in New York City, the competition's thick; if Lexington, Kentucky is home, however, you may have a large area all to yourself.

If a regular job squeezes your research hours, set that novel someplace you already know intimately, make up your setting, or do a bit of both. When Jack Warner was writing his novel *Shikar*, for instance, he was still employed full-time at the *Atlanta Journal-Constitution*. So he decided to set his novel, about a man-eating tiger loose in America, in northern Georgia, an area he didn't have to research. To make his moonlighting even easier, he wrote *Shikar* about a mythical Georgia county—what he didn't know, he could simply invent.

Your regular, nine-to-five job can actually help you gather raw material for your writing. Think of those hours you spend at the office as research. Whatever you do, whether it's insurance adjusting or pharmaceutical sales, there's surely a trade magazine devoted to it. Depending on your job, you may also be on the cutting edge of a subject with more popular appeal. A psychology teacher might popularize her knowledge in self-help articles for *Self* or *Parents* magazine. A biologist could craft convincing Michael Crichton-style "science run amok" thrillers.

Be careful when mining your job for your writing, however. Don't reveal company secrets—even in fiction. Don't write anything you wouldn't want your colleagues—or, worse, your boss—to read; they have lives outside the office, too, remember, and might see your story. If your regular job also involves writing, for heaven's sake, don't write for the competition.

Other types of writing projects also seem ideally suited for the evening and weekend freelancer. These stories either let you pick the time for research, or they naturally involve research during hours you don't have to be at your desk.

Reviews of all kinds fit well into a writer's inflexible schedule. Consider product reviews in some field where you have special know-how—not only book reviews, but evaluations of quilting equipment, computer software, kitchen gear, or whatever else you know well enough to talk about.

For example, I wrote regularly for years for a publication called *Link-Up*, which covered online and other databases. I've been going online since the days of 300-baud modems, and I know something about research needs from my writing and reporting work. So I could craft a meaningful review of almost any database, however esoteric the subject. The around-the-clock availability of such online offerings meant I could explore them when my schedule permitted. As with most reviews, not much interviewing was required; what questions I did need to ask, I could usually handle by e-mail.

If your interests lie more on the stage than in cyberspace, maybe you can write theater reviews for a local paper or magazine. Almost anything arts- or leisure-related—music, dance, nightlife, even sports—makes a good target because, by its very nature, it's likely to happen when you (and most other nine-to-fivers) can take part.

Similarly, any subject spinning off shopping—whether it's haute couture or the annual "best of" stories that are the bread and butter of city magazines—can usually be researched during non-working hours. If the stores are open, you can fill your notebook.

Restaurant reviews can be another wonderful writing opportunity—and you get to dine out on somebody else's dime, too. Among my first freelance assignments were several regional restaurant roundups for *Travel & Leisure* magazine, all researched in the evening in the pleasant company of my new bride. The only downside was that those assignments almost spoiled me for anything else! If you want to pursue restaurant reviewing, try to develop some proof of your proficiency and the quality of your palate. Take some courses at a local cooking school. Or maybe you worked your way through college at a restaurant—not, please, the cafeteria. Whatever you do, though, don't say in your query, "I don't know much about restaurants, but I love to eat." Innumerable applicants for a restaurant-reviewer position I once filled used that line; all went instantly into the reject pile.

Travel is another field well suited, almost by definition, to the moonlighting writer. Whether your trips require a vacation from your day job or you can plan weekend getaways, use them as opportunities to gather research for travel articles. If you're a fiction writer, of course, you should plan your vacations around places where you want to set your stories.

As you spread your writing wings, however, inevitably you'll want to tackle some projects that require in-depth interviews, phone research, and in-person investigation. Sometimes these stories can still be done during your off-hours. If your subject is busy and finds it hard to squeeze in an interview during the day, volunteer to go to his or her home. A bonus of this approach is that you get to see your subject in less-guarded surroundings, and the subject's home offers details that can illuminate his or her character. (Avoid falling back on "let's do lunch" or dinner interviews, however—successful interviewing can be challenging enough without the added burden of handling a knife and fork.)

Other projects will require you to spend a precious vacation day. You shouldn't be too quick to take on a writing assignment that costs you hard-earned vacation, but the math may make sense: If you can make $1,000 for writing an article that absolutely requires you to use up one vacation day, unless you make more than about $250,000 a year ($1,000 per workday, 5 days a week, 52 weeks a year), it may be a worthwhile tradeoff. Of course, you'll need to devote more than a single day to all your writing and research, but there you're spending your unpaid time, evenings and weekends, not your precious paid vacation. A plum assignment may even be worth taking a day or two off from your job without pay, as long as that doesn't sound alarm bells with your employer.

When you do devote vacation time to an assignment, make the most of it. Do all your secondary research beforehand, on your own time, so that you get everything else you need in just one in-person experience. If you must travel to an interview, shoot for a Friday or Monday appointment so you can make half the journey on the weekend. Or get up early and take the red-eye home, so you can do it all in one very busy but very productive day.

When I interviewed a number of business tycoons for a magazine series on American success stories, for example, I had to take off from my regular job to fulfill the assignment. But each profile cost me just a single vacation day: I did all my homework in advance, planned all my questions, jetted in and jetted out on the same day, and, throughout, kept uppermost in mind the exact angle and theme of each assignment. All the advance research and all the subsequent organizing and writing was done on evenings and weekends. Since the magazine paid pretty well, the interview days seemed like a good investment of my vacation time.

But such assignments can be intermittent and undependable, and freelance work doesn't earn you any paid vacation days. So I offer one more piece of advice for the moonlighting author: Don't quit your day job. After all, as we've just seen, you don't have to.

Writer, Interrupted

However and wherever you find time to work on your writing, you probably feel it's no good if you're constantly interrupted. How can you do any quality writing if the phone rings every five minutes? Who could write a best-selling novel with the kids screaming at you every time "SpongeBob SquarePants" takes a commercial break?

You can. Trust me on this: I never dared to count, but at my last job I'll bet that some days I got interrupted a dozen times an hour. Every five minutes or so, the phone rang or someone stuck a head in my door to ask a question or get help with a problem. The interruptions were usually important, as important as whatever I might be writing at the time, but they were interruptions nonetheless. My train of thought got broken, if not derailed entirely.

It's not much better at home. I can't write for more than a few minutes straight without the phone jangling, the cat jumping in my lap and demanding to be petted, or the latest household crisis erupting ("Dad! I can't find my shoes!"). Pretty soon my brain is getting more conflicting inputs than a television set with its channel changer stuck on "surf."

Sound familiar? To write, it seems, is to be interrupted. How can you keep putting one sentence after another and keep them all making sense if the world beyond your keyboard insists on intruding?

The first step in coping with interruptions, of course, is to minimize them. Realistically, you can't shut out your family or your co-workers (though I may try shutting out the cat). And becoming a hermit stopped being a viable lifestyle choice several centuries ago. But you *can* try to organize your writing life to give yourself more concentrated blocks of keyboard time.

Take that annoying telephone, for example. Stop letting its ringing rule your life: Get an answering machine and learn to resist that almost irresistible impulse of modern life to pick . . . (ring!) up . . . (ring!) the . . . (ring!) phone. Plan to return phone calls in a batch, rather than dealing with them scattershot. Organize your own phoning—research calls, for instance, or pestering your agent about whether he's sold your novel yet—in blocks. If you write best in the morning, set aside the afternoons for making calls.

E-mail can be as distracting as the telephone, if you let it. If you have a constant Internet connection (through an office network, for instance, or via a cable or other high-speed modem), set your e-mail program to retrieve messages only manually; otherwise, the "ping" of automatically fetched e-mails and that little envelope icon in the corner of your screen may be too much to resist. If you dial in to check e-mail, limit your e-mail action to before and after writing sessions. It's too easy to spend the whole day reading and writing e-mail, rather than stories.

While you can't become a hermit, you can arrange your writing life so that your keyboard time comes when you're least likely to be interrupted. One novelist I know does all his writing after midnight, when outside distractions are at a minimum. If you're more of a morning person, get up an hour or two before the rest of the household, à la Trollope. Or, if most of your family can't miss "Must See TV," schedule a writing session on Thursday night when everyone else will be glued to the tube instead of interrupting you.

No matter how well you try to insulate yourself against interruptions, however, they will find you. Phone solicitors will call when you're the only one in the house, and you have to pick up the phone because what if it's one of the kids and they're having car trouble? The UPS guy will deliver, or the gas company will pick your quietest, most concentrated writing time to read the meter.

The secret to dealing with interruptions without letting them permanently interrupt the flow of your writing is to organize your work in small chunks. You need to break your big jobs into tasks small enough that you can finish them between interruptions, or at least keep all the elements of the current task fresh in your mind while you're signing for that UPS delivery.

Why? Think of your writing challenge like one of those plate spinners who used to entertain on *The Ed Sullivan Show*: If you're keeping a dozen plates in the air and suddenly someone throws a bowling pin at you—an interruption—you're bound to have broken crockery. But if you're spinning only one plate at a time, you have a hand free to deal with distractions; then you can get right back to what you were doing.

The trick, then, is figuring out how to approach your writing chores piecemeal, rather than juggling a dozen concepts, problems, and article elements at once. If you're giving your brain all it can handle ("OK, remember, this paragraph will have to go after that one, but before this one . . ."), it's too hard to get all the pieces in place again, all the plates spinning, after an interruption. When you're marching through an article or a chapter one chunk at a time, one small challenge after another, it's easier to pick up where you left off.

Fortunately, the organizational approach we'll be exploring, step-by-step, in this book also happens to be ideally suited to coping with interruptions. To organize your work into small chunks that can better stand interruption, you need to know where your writing is going and how you'll get there. Strewing your notes all over the room and simply diving at the keyboard, confident you'll somehow figure it out as you go along, won't work. Trying to keep all the connections in a piece of writing straight in your head is asking for interruption disaster.

Living With Deadlines

Now all you've got to do is meet your deadline. Inevitably, deadlines seem to be the, er, death of most people who take up the challenge of calling themselves writers. And yet many writers feel they work best (or solely) under the pressure of what Kenneth Atchity calls "end time." William Saroyan, for example, wrote his classic *The Human Comedy* in only a few days because he had a deadline to meet. Why are deadlines so difficult to meet, and why do so many writers need one to fire up their creative juices?

First of all, contrary to what you might think, chronic deadline-missers are seldom simply lazy. The writers I've had working for me who suffered the worst trouble meeting deadlines were often the hardest workers on my staff. They'd spend long hours at the library, conduct in-depth interviews and laboriously transcribe them, and write all weekend. Yet somehow their stories never arrived at my desk on time. By contrast, I would start on a story at the same time, edit other stories and do a ton of administrative work in addition to my writing assignment, and go home promptly at five o'clock. To an outside observer, I was the lazy one—but my stories were always finished a couple of days early, giving me plenty of time to listen to my staff writers moan and make excuses.

The point of relating this isn't to pat myself on the back. The point is that I organized my time; the other writers didn't. They finished their stories in a deadline-fueled adrenaline frenzy; I rarely missed my bus home.

It's easy to be glib about "organizing your time." Throughout this book, however, I'll be giving you specific techniques you can use to better organize your writing time—as well as a whole philosophy that will link organizing your time to the way you organize your work as a writer. For now, I just want to concentrate on organizing your time as it relates to meeting those dreaded deadlines.

In working with writers as an editor, I've found that the most common trait among deadline-abusers is that they really have no idea how long any given writing task will take them to complete. Oh, they *think* they do: "Sure, I can get that to you in three weeks." But the gap between self-expectation and reality is almost total. I've had writers, typically with a story already late, blithely assure me, "It just needs one more good afternoon of work." A week later, I'd pop my head in to check on the story, which is still missing in action: "Oh, it just needs one more good afternoon of work," the writer will insist again. "You'll have it by tomorrow at the latest."

These writers are not lying to me or to themselves. They are utterly sincere. They are also utterly in the dark about the path their work must take and the speed they can travel. They lack an inner measuring stick by which to gauge the complexity of a subject, how much research it entails, and how long a story will take at the keyboard. They begin a project the way Columbus set sail for the Indies: without a map and with no concept of the journey's duration, only a firm faith that they'll get there somehow. Is it any wonder that so often they wind up late, and at the wrong destination? (Columbus's discovery of the Americas may have been a boon to history, but it was not, after all, his assignment. Editors who want spice from the Indies will lose patience if you keep sending them surprises from the Americas.)

The solution, once again, is this: You must have a map. Remember my writer who perpetually thinks his story needs only one more afternoon of work? If he had a plan for his story, with his notes carefully tagged to each portion of the plan, he would know darn well how much ground he had yet to cover. Writers who miss deadlines also, ironically, are always turning in copy that's too long. Both the lateness and the wordiness are symptoms of the same problem: If you're writing a 4,500-word story and you don't know where it's going, no alarms go off in your head when you hit 3,500 words and the story's not yet half done. You *don't know* it's not yet half done. For all you know, you could be steaming toward the conclusion.

With a map—not only for the actual writing, but for all the steps that come before—you can plan your work routine from day one till the deadline. With a map and a little experience, you'll know when you must wrap up your research and start writing. You will learn to work under the pressure of many small, intermediate deadlines, instead of in the panic of "end time." And if your challenge is "finding time," you will see how the bits and pieces of time you find for writing can add up, for each one represents a clearly defined step along the road to completion. Like D'Aguesseau, who wrote while waiting for his wife to come down to dinner, you'll get there, one bite at a time.

Beyond the Messy Desk

But before we turn to the grand issues of organizing your themes and ideas—creating your "maps"—I want to say a few words about the mundane issues of organizing your desk and your files. Again, in my experience, writers who miss deadlines and can't manage their time are almost inevitably, well, slobs. Dare to peek in their offices when they are in the throes of creation, and you'll run to call 9-1-1: Surely some catastrophe has taken place here! Files and photocopies lie about the floor like the aftermath of an avalanche. Books (half of them overdue from the library) rise in Babel-like towers. Yellow sticky notes cluster ten-deep on the desk, like bees that have chanced upon a particularly rich vein of clover.

Remember Oscar Madison, the sloppy half of Neil Simon's *The Odd Couple*? He was a writer, of course. Typecasting.

But I don't mean to sound like Felix Unger, the fussy neatnik coupled with Oscar Madison. You don't have to be prissy to get organized as a writer. You don't even have to have a clean desk.

In an article I did once about the links between the look of executives' desks and their efficiency, the experts I consulted concluded that the optimum approach was Aristotle's Golden Mean. Too much chaos wastes time; an excess of neatness is counter-productive. These experts advocated, instead, what are called "organized piles." Most of the truly efficient people I know practice this technique, whatever they call it. To a visitor, the desk might appear a bit messy, with small piles of work here and there, but to its occupant, the desk has a place for everything, and everything is in its place. Those piles of papers are meaningful, not random, and any item on the desk can be retrieved in a flash.

As I write this, to be honest, for the past several weeks my own desk has been more than a bit messy. But between a recent move halfway across the country, diving into a pile of can't-wait projects and buying a new computer—while still needing to keep the old one set up just a bit longer, eating up my prime "get organized" flat space—my desk has devolved to a state best described by the word "strewn."

Yet I haven't missed a deadline on any of those due-yesterday projects. I know exactly what I need to tackle next and where those research materials are hiding. Most important, I know who's paid me and who hasn't.

I really will get around to straightening up one of these days. But in the meantime, I've had to prioritize. That means, while some cosmetic details might slide, the key elements for managing my writing business must be kept straight, no matter what.

If you're not always as neat as you should be—or if you make Felix in *The Odd Couple* look downright slovenly but your writing life is still a mess—try these techniques for getting organized on the things that count:

Start an electronic tracking system. Face it—relying on sticky notes and backs of grocery lists to keep track of your projects is a system doomed to failure the first time a gust of wind blows across your desk. One reason my messy desk doesn't matter is that my most important bits of information reside on my computer, where I can find them in a flash.

Your digital tracker doesn't have to be fancy and you don't have to invest in the latest software bells and whistles. I use a simple spreadsheet. One worksheet keeps track of writing projects, with columns for Client, Assignment, Contact Person, Deadline, and Fee, plus columns at the end to log when I completed the assignment and sent an invoice and whether I've been paid. A second worksheet in the same file (I can click back and forth with tabs at the bottom) records queries: Client Queried, Contact, Topic, Date Sent, and Status. If you're submitting fiction manuscripts instead of article ideas, you could readily adapt my tracker to log Publisher/Publication, Contact, Story Title, Date Sent, and Status.

You don't have to use a spreadsheet program; you can create much the same thing with tables in your word-processing program. You can even let the subscription WritersMarket.com Web site track queries and submissions for you, over the Internet.

The keys are keeping your tracker simple enough that you'll actually update it, and gathering all your most vital project information in a single place. You could do one file for queries and a separate one for assignments, or separate book and magazine projects—but I think two trackers is the maximum. You want to be able to see everything at a glance to know what you need to tackle next.

This doesn't mean you shouldn't also create sub-trackers for major projects, such as a novel or nonfiction book you're writing. Whenever I start a book project, I make a spreadsheet that lists the chapters and my estimated word count for each, along with intermediate deadlines. I fill in the actual word count as I knock out each chapter, which not only gives me a satisfying thrill of completion but guarantees I don't arrive at the final chapter unwittingly either way over or way under my contracted length. And those intermediate milestones? I enter them on my main tracker, so I can see how other projects must weave in with work on the book.

Use electronic file folders. Another way in which your computer can help you tame pile pandemonium is to take advantage of that handy "New Folder" command. Store everything related to a project—from the initial query or "what if?" idea to downloaded Web pages to the final draft—together in a properly labeled folder on your hard drive.

When I started a recent story about Spain and Portugal, for example, I created a "Spain&Portugal" folder within my computer's Documents folder. As I found useful pages on the Web, I'd copy and paste portions (with their accompanying URLs so I could return if necessary) into word-processing files within that folder, one each for Spain and Portugal. Valuable pages got saved entirely, right into the folder for later reference.

Back up everything. These electronic systems, of course, are only as good as your faithfulness in backing them up. If your hard drive goes on the fritz or you hit an unintended delete key, you'll wish you'd done everything on good, old-fashioned paper—messy desk and dead trees be damned. Just as you must get in the habit of keeping your tracker up-to-date, you've got to develop a backup routine and stick to it. Even if supper's burning on the stove, let it smoke until you've completed your backup regimen.

At a minimum, back up your tracker and every work in progress at the end of your working session, and back up your entire active file system at least weekly. That's not enough to completely prevent hiccups in case of disaster, but it reduces your risk. And don't rely on a single backup medium: I copy all my documents to a Zip disk, then also copy completed pieces (as well as larger works-in-progress) to a floppy; periodically, the whole shebang gets burned to a CD for good measure. (I use regular, one-time-only CDs, which cost pennies, then throw them away as they get outdated; rewritable CDs tend to be flaky and unreadable in any other machine, which is a problem if your PC or Mac dies.) Don't forget your e-mail inbox—I keep a lot of key info in e-mail, so that gets backed up, too.

Throw everything in a (paper) file folder. Yes, you are allowed to use paper—just don't let loose pieces accumulate in random piles atop your desk, floor, and sleeping pets. When you start a project, follow the same routine for paper items that you do for digital ones: Label a manila folder and religiously stuff anything related to that project—research notes, clippings, photocopies, your original query letter, the editor's assignment letter, whatever—into that folder. Don't worry about organizing within the folder, unless it gets so fat you need to break into sub-folders. At most it might take you five minutes to find what you need in any given manila folder, even if it's stuffed to the breaking point. The point is to make sure everything's there for you to find when the time comes.

That's the important thing—how quickly you can lay your hands on material you need—not how neatly the labels on the folders are calligraphied. You need a folder for each writing project, labeled specifically and clearly enough that you'll recognize it a few years from now. For most projects—an article assignment, for example—one catchall folder is probably enough. For big chores—a novel or a nonfiction book—it makes sense to subdivide your files into multiple folders; you'll probably need about one folder per chapter.

When I started my first book, for example, I ran out and bought several packs of large, ruled index cards, two dozen manila folders, and a plastic file box to keep it all in. I labeled each folder with the name of a chapter (plus a few for "Misc.") and taped the description of the chapter, from my book proposal, on the front. As I took notes and thought of things I wanted to say in the book, I scribbled them down on index cards. Whenever I got a small handful of finished cards, I'd file them by chapter. When I was ready to start writing, I picked up the folder for chapter one and sorted the cards into a logical sequence. And bit by bit the book materialized.

That was back in the dark ages of computing, of course, when printers were "dot matrix" and the Web was something a spider wove. But even today, plain old paper and manila folders come in handy. Sometimes, for example, even when dealing with research on the Web, it's simpler to hit the print key. With that Spain and Portugal project, I realized I had so much online info that copying and pasting was becoming too time-consuming. So I loaded a fresh ream in the printer and just printed like crazy. Everything went into the "Spain&Portugal" manila folder, so it was all at my fingertips when I sat down to write. Not a fancy system, but one that even the most disorganized writer can stick to.

Finally, when your story or other project is done, file a printout of the completed manuscript in the same folder. Sure, you have it saved and backed up electronically—but what if you change word-processing programs or your next computer no longer has a floppy drive? I can still read the articles I wrote eons ago on a TRS-80 computer with 5¼-inch floppy disks—because I saved printouts. Those old dot-matrix pages mean I can revive, update and recycle those story ideas even today.

Start an ideas folder. Again with the dead trees! Sacrifice another manila folder and label it "Ideas" or "Story Fodder" or the like. Then whenever you tear something out of a newspaper, rip out a page from a magazine, print an item worth saving from the Web or scribble a story-idea note to yourself, stick it in the folder. Otherwise your home will be littered with little scraps of paper and you won't be able to lay your hands on them when you're in need of an idea.

If you're an aspiring article writer, use this folder to set yourself a query-writing routine: Once a week, say, dip into the Ideas folder and pull out something that interests you. Find a market that matches it and don't let yourself get up from your desk until you've banged out and sent off a query. Whenever a submission comes back, naturally, you must send it out to the next market right away. That way, over time, you'll develop a huge inventory of active ideas. When an idea gets bought, don't retire it—figure out a different slant on the topic and start shipping it out to a new batch of markets. Don't forget to record all this query activity on your tracker—now, not later when and if you get around to it.

Keep things. This violates every rule of those organizational gurus who are forever preaching that you should toss things out. But for a writer, the stuff in those old files represents raw material for new projects. I keep old notes, photocopies of research, pretty much everything. You can even copy digital files onto a disk and toss this into the manila folder, too.

Partly this is a question of prioritizing time. When I've finished a story, I can either spend time weeding through its accompanying folder, or I can stick the whole dang thing in a file cabinet and spend my time pitching or writing something else. As long as the storage space holds out, I'd rather move on to the next project.

Besides, when a piece is freshly completed, you don't yet know what's worth keeping and what can be safely tossed. What if the editor calls, wanting fact-checking information or an address (or a rewrite—don't toss those notes!)? What new ideas might you later tease out of this topic for different markets? How might that short story later wind up fitting into your novel? You might find yourself incorporating research from old projects into new ones in ways you couldn't anticipate. For example, a feature I wrote for *Kiwanis* magazine, years ago, on finishing what you start—aimed at a general audience, not at writers—gave me valuable material for tackling the same topic in chapter fourteen of this very book.

So I figure it's most efficient and safest to hang onto everything until you run out of filing space or you move. Then it will usually be obvious at a glance what can go in the trash: That piece on the booming buggy-whip business? Toss it. The interview with the CEO who died six years ago? Probably just as past tense. The epic poem you wrote to help you get a handle on one of your ancient Greek characters? Let's not even go there. You can often throw away whole folders at this point, rather than wasting time picking through them.

For now, save everything. Just make sure it's all together in a folder and filed away rather than stacked in a teetering pile on your desk.

As you get your physical materials organized, you'll begin to see that these simple systems of folders and such go hand in hand with organizing your time. The project takes shape one piece at a time, index card (or whatever) by index card. So, too, your time is organized, taking one step at a time, one folder at a time, one writing session at a time. Ultimately, the organization of your writing itself follows the same pattern: sentences into paragraphs, paragraphs into scenes, scenes into a completed work. That's the process we'll begin in the next chapter.

Exercises

1. Based on your results in exercises two and three from chapter one, make a plan for completion of your current writing project (or the project you've dreamed of writing if only you had the time). How many pages a day would you need to write? How much time would you need to find each day?

2. The next time you sit down for a writing session, put a pad and pen beside your keyboard. Each time something interrupts your work—a phone call, an e-mail, a conversation with a colleague or family member—make a quick note on the pad. How often are you interrupted? What are your most common sources of interruptions? Use the tips in this chapter to minimize and group these interruptions.

3. Using a spreadsheet or word-processing program, set up a basic project-tracking sheet as described in this chapter. Your sheet should include columns such as Client, Assignment, Contact Person, Deadline, and Fee.

4. Building on your tracker from number three, set up a similar file for tracking queries and proposals. Your file should include columns such as (for nonfiction) Client Queried, Contact, Topic, Date Sent, and Status or (for fiction) Publisher/Publication, Contact, Story Title, Date Sent, and Status.

5. Start your ideas folder. Take a plain manila folder and keep it handy for any time you scribble a note or cut out possible story fodder from a newspaper or magazine.

CHAPTER 3

THE SECRET OF STRUCTURE

Organizing your actual writing isn't so different from organizing your writing time or the folders, index cards and papers of your writing work. Think of the problem of the messy desk in the last chapter: The key to working through the clutter was prioritizing what was really important, and concentrating on those top-priority tasks. In much the same way, whether you're writing a 500-page blockbuster novel or a 1,500-word article, the key to organizing your writing is deciding what's really important about the story you have to tell or the point you want to make. Everything that contributes to your goal goes into your writing; everything that's extraneous gets swept away.

This sounds easier and simpler than it is. Obviously, whatever doesn't fit your story should be jettisoned in favor of what's important. But this process of finding and sticking to your focus turns out to be many writers' biggest hurdle; it's why novels don't get written, memoirs stall and that 1,500-word article sprawls into a 20,000-word monstrosity no one will print.

Your focus must come first. Once you've found your focus, you can discover the secret of structure: how easily you can build a story on the foundation of that focus.

Just ask Tolstoy—he knew: "The most important thing in a work of art is that it should have a kind of focus, i.e., there should be some point where all the rays meet or from which they issue. And this focus must not be able to be completely explained in words. This indeed is one of the significant facts about a true work of art—that its content in its entirety can be expressed only by itself."

Or ask any astronomer. If you've ever peered through a backyard telescope, you know how quickly—and unsteadily—the stars sweep through your field of view. Bump the telescope and your chosen constellation is lost;

breathe too hard and the stars shake before your eyes. It's easy to spend a whole night squinting through a telescope at the immensity overhead and never really *see* anything.

The skilled astronomer, however, knows the secrets of seeing with a telescope, how to use its power to narrow the universe and bring a piece of the heavens down to earth. With practice and training, you too could learn to steady a big telescope and aim it, not just at the stars in general, but at one particular twinkling light. A planet, perhaps. With still more fine-tuning, you could concentrate your view on the features of the planet—Jupiter, let's say—and see clearly enough to learn something from what you see. You could discover, for example, whether the roiling surface of Jupiter still shows any effects from the impact of the comets that struck it so spectacularly back in the mid-1990s.

Imagine that you went through all this, and on the walk down the hill from the observatory someone asked you, "What did you see?" You would have an answer—one very specific answer about what happens when a comet meets a giant planet. That's a long way from the amateur's "Oh, I saw some stars."

What the astronomer learns is *focus*. Presented with a whole universe to study, he chooses to focus on some part of it and accomplish something, rather than to merely marvel at the twinkling lights.

Focusing Your Idea

Similarly, when readers wonder, "What is your story about?" a writer must have an answer—a very specific answer, albeit one, as Tolstoy notes, that can't necessarily be fully explained apart from the work itself. To appreciate the answer, readers must read the work; that's why you must write it.

Your writer's answer comes from focusing in on a particular part of the "sky," from making conscious choices not only about what to write but also about what *not* to write. It's just like the process of prioritizing the tasks on your messy desk; you can't do everything, so you must choose. As William Zinsser put it in *On Writing Well*, "Every writing project must be reduced before you start to write it."

You start with the universe. Every story idea can be spun out dozens of ways, just as a telescope can take in any slice of the sky; what makes your story unique is your particular focus, the angle that you take on the subject.

Take the writing of a simple magazine article, for example. "An article is not everything that's true," noted writing expert Gary Provost, "It's every *important* thing that's true." Some years ago, I got an assignment to interview and write a profile of Malcolm Forbes, the colorful founder of the magazine that bears his name. Forbes' life and career were about as big and varied as any galaxy: editor, entrepreneur, author, motorcyclist, collector, balloonist, politician . . . As a result, however, the task of writing a single, 1,500-word article about Malcolm Forbes at first seemed akin to that of an astronomer tackling the Milky Way. I could easily have written 1,500 words just on Forbes' collection of Fabergé eggs.

In fact, that would have made a pretty good magazine article. Why? Because it concentrates on a specific piece of the multifaceted man—in short, it has a focus. The "hook" of such an article could have gone something like this: "Not only is Malcolm Forbes one of America's best-known magazine editors and a self-proclaimed 'Capitalist Tool,' he is also one of the world's great collectors of one of the world's rarest creations: the Fabergé egg." Such an article wouldn't begin to say "everything that's true" about Malcolm Forbes, Renaissance man, but it *would* manage to say what's important about Malcolm Forbes, Fabergé egg collector. By choosing to leave out 99 percent of what might be said, this approach would make a focused, readable article on the remaining 1 percent.

But that wasn't the focus my editor wanted, and the editor, being the customer in the freelance-writing transaction, is always right. No, the editor wanted an article on Malcolm Forbes as an example of the American Dream in action. You can think of the Fabergé-egg article as a very thin slice of the possible Forbes stories, like a geologist picking up one particularly interesting rock from a large site. The American Dream focus was like a geologist taking a core sample: an equally thin slice that cuts through and represents multiple layers of rock. Everything I selected for my article had to support and fit within my focus; anything outside that focus got left in my notebook.

The difference between "a profile of Malcolm Forbes" and "a story on how Malcolm Forbes, flamboyant editor and self-proclaimed 'Capitalist Tool' is also the world's leading collector of Fabergé eggs" is the difference between an idea and an angle. You can almost think of it as a mathematical process: "Malcolm Forbes" is an idea; "Malcolm Forbes plus Fabergé eggs" or "Malcolm Forbes divided by the American Dream" are angles.

Ideas, like stars in the night sky, are everywhere. But, as Thomas Mann, winner of the Nobel Prize for literature, once observed, "The task of a writer consists in being able to make something out of a idea." That task begins with finding your focus, from which the structure and form of your work must evolve.

In general, the tighter the focus, the better. When it comes to nonfiction, Zinsser put it bluntly: "Every successful piece of nonfiction should leave the reader with one provocative thought that he or she didn't have before. Not two thoughts, or five—just one."

Much the same goes for fiction. Let's say you get the idea to write a story about werewolves. That's an interesting, exciting topic that's been a staple of horror fiction for decades and of myth for who knows how long. But "werewolves" is an idea, not a story; you need an angle. You could write about a werewolf, that ancient creature of legend, in the modern world—"werewolf plus contemporary big city," to use our mathematical approach. Indeed, that's pretty much the angle of the movie *An American Werewolf in London*. Or you could write about a battle between *two* werewolves (with terrified humans caught in-between, of course), much as regular wolves might contest for dominance—"werewolves divided by alpha male," you might say. You could even focus on a werewolf who turns out to be a hero; after all, who's to say that werewolves are any more "evil" than the ordinary wolves naturalists are trying to reintroduce to national forests?

Because this werewolf-as-hero focus contains an element of surprise, it could have the most appeal. Focusing on surprising juxtapositions (good-guy werewolf, Malcolm Forbes as egg collector) is often a useful way to develop an angle for a story.

Thinking Like Hollywood

To continue our horror-story theme, do you remember the horror movie *Night of the Lepus*? Bad as that film was, it's a useful lesson in focus. You see, Hollywood legend has it that *Night of the Lepus* was sold to movie moguls as "*Jaws* with rabbits." That's what's called "high concept" in the movie biz—no matter how low the actual on-screen results may sink.

The point isn't how in the world a Hollywood producer could have been so dumb as to green light "*Jaws* with rabbits." No, the point is, no matter how silly it sounds, that high-concept description communicates instantly the essence of the premise: bunnies on the rampage, terrorizing a helpless town with—well, with whatever it is that rampaging bunnies would do to a helpless town.

Even if you don't have a screenplay to pitch, thinking of your ideas in Hollywood high-concept terms can help you focus and zoom in on what you really want to write. Let's say you're tackling a book-length project. Many book authors struggle with their scope: Where does the book start? What to put in and what to leave out? After all, if you're writing a nonfiction book, theoretically it could encompass the whole world (not to mention all of human history). If you're tackling a memoir, every instant of your life— and even your parents' and grandparents' lives—could be fair game. And a novel? Well, think of James Michener, starting his blockbuster yarns with shifting tectonic plates and primordial ooze.

Tone and approach can be as challenging as scope. What's your book going to *feel* like? Will it be funny or serious or a mix? Sweeping and epic or small and personal?

Figuring out the high-concept capsule of your book can help settle these questions in your own mind. If you can focus your adventure story as "*The Perfect Storm* in an RV," you'll have a star to guide you in your journey from page one to "The End."

This doesn't mean you're going to set out to slavishly imitate these successful movies or books. Rather, think of the high-concept approach as a shorthand way to summarize a set of decisions. So if you're writing "*The Perfect Storm* in an RV," you've decided that you're *not* writing a comedy, for example. If it's nonfiction, there's an indication that you're nonetheless aiming for almost a novelization of your material.

On the other hand, if you sum up your story instead as "*Zen and the Art of Motorcycle Maintenance* in an RV," that creates an entirely different set of expectations and reflects some other decisions.

I saw how effective this high-concept technique could be in forcing writers to focus their work at the Maui Writers Retreat a few years ago, where I led a group polishing and perfecting their books. As "homework" after the first day, I assigned everyone the task of writing twenty-five words or less on "what your book is about and why anyone should read it." This proved a more daunting task than I'd expected. Capturing the essence of a whole book and all their ideas and hopes for it in just twenty-five words—not to mention explaining its audience appeal—gave my students a sleepless night.

Ironically, their ideas came together far more readily a few days later when I asked them to focus even more sharply and think of their books in Hollywood high-concept terms. Forcing them to boil down their ideas into about a half-dozen words switched on that "aha!" lightbulb in their heads and revealed what their books were *really* all about.

The most dramatic example was a former teacher, retired after forty years in the trenches. She was burning to tell her story and to show the world what's wrong with public schools and what could be done to make them right. But she couldn't get her arms around what, out of her forty years of teaching, might be shaped into a book. Then, one afternoon, as she and I sat by the shore and tried to keep from being swept away by the trade winds, the high-concept answer blew into our heads: Her book should be "*M*A*S*H* in junior high." She was a funny writer, and the analogy to *M*A*S*H* perfectly captured the sense of laughing through tragedy—whether the triage of a Korean War hospital or of eighth grade—that could let her tell her story without becoming preachy.

Inspired, we tried the technique with other students whose book ideas had been hard to wrangle into shape. There was the writer who'd moved from America to Jerusalem, where she'd built an unusual rooftop house—and gotten entangled in eleven years' worth of Byzantine (perhaps literally) Middle Eastern laws. She wanted to write about her experiences, but lacked a lens through which to focus her subject. So we seized on another movie analogy: Her book was really "*The Money Pit* in Jerusalem." (Or, for older audiences who might relate to Cary Grant better than Tom Hanks, "*Mr. Blandings Builds His Dream House* in Jerusalem.")

Another former teacher, who'd gone from a terrifying experience in the classroom to an enlightening sojourn in Bali, hoped to share the secrets of the nonviolent paradise she'd found. But she had a hard time seeing the book buried in her material until we hit on "from *The Blackboard Jungle* to *Lost Horizon*."

Not all of our efforts to boil books down to a single, clarifying phrase worked so neatly. But even the concepts perhaps not quite ready for Hollywood helped these writers get a fresh take on the core of their books. One writer's tale of self-discovery through the colorful world of poker crystallized for her when we described it, a bit awkwardly, as "*Thelma and Louise* minus Louise plus poker."

Your high-concept formulations don't have to be ready for pitching to an agent or a producer, as long as they help you write the right book.

They don't have to be inspired by movies, either. Another of our Maui writers was working on a true crime story set on the Big Island of Hawaii. She grappled with various viewpoints and possible focuses. But finally a high concept helped her hone her theme: "*In Cold Blood* on the Big Island." It worked—that book recently found a publisher.

To develop your own high-concept capsule for your book or other idea, think of a movie or well-known book that has something of the spirit, approach and tone you might be after. Try it on for size: Do you want to write more of a *Gone with the Wind* or a *Fear and Loathing in Las Vegas*? Of course, you'll put your own twist on it—that's what makes a Hollywood-style high concept. Maybe your book, at its heart, is *"Apollo 13* on a cruise ship." Or it could be you're really writing *"Paper Lion* about lacrosse." It's not that you're going to be a copycat; rather, hitting on a high concept can help keep you on track with what really belongs in your story and what doesn't. (Just stay away from bunnies, unless you're writing about Hugh Hefner.)

Headline Grabbers

Another good way to find your focus, especially for nonfiction articles, is to try to sum up your story in a mock headline or subhead. If you can't, you probably don't really know what your article is about yet—you still haven't settled on one tree to climb out of the forest of possibilities.

Let's look at a few real-life examples of magazine articles whose heads and subheads reflect a tight focus. Here's a story from *Men's Journal* on tennis. Obviously, "tennis" is an idea, not an angle. What about tennis? What's new in tennis? What's the angle? Grass courts. The article reports that grass courts, Wimbledon-style, are growing across the U.S.; since balls "bounce low and fast" on grass, players (think: readers) need to learn how to handle the action. Think of the focus as "tennis plus grass-courts boom plus adjusting your play." The actual headline and subhead? "Getting Low on Grass: A few tips on sodding the English at their own game."

Or consider a story on parenting advice from *Woman's Day*. Shelves of books have been written on how to be a better parent; to work as a magazine article, the subject has to be sliced as thin as a harried parent's patience. This one took the tack of "Children are extremely sensitive to parents' judgments about them . . . " and focused on the angle of "labeling your children." The headline and subhead perfectly captured the focus: "The Smart One, The Pretty One, The Shy One. . . . : Why labeling your children isn't such a good idea."

As these examples show, getting from idea to angle, from an expanse of stars to one object smack in focus in your authorial telescope, doesn't have to be hard. Remember these tips for focusing your ideas:

1. **Narrow, narrow, narrow.** Concentrate on a single thought that you want to communicate about your subject.

2. **Combine two ideas.** Then write only about the area where they inter-sect (werewolves and heroism, Malcolm Forbes and the American Dream).

3. **Use surprise as a selection tool.** Focus only on those elements that will seem fresh or unusual to readers.

4. **Hone your angle.** See whether you can write a Hollywood high con-cept or a headline and subhead for it.

From Focus to Form

It's pretty obvious how mastering the art of focusing can help make your writing more interesting to readers—and editors and agents—but what does it have to do with your story's structure? Like the story itself, your structure must spring from the focus that you select. Focus and form are not merely two elements of writing, features that are nice to have, like preferring floor mats and a killer stereo when you're shopping for a car. No, they are essential and inseparable, like the engine and the axle—they make your writing go.

Together, your focus and the form that arises from it make a message that is unique to your piece of writing. This is how you arrive at Tolstoy's goal of a work of art whose "content in its entirety can be expressed only by itself." Think of focus and form as a hologram, the form being the element that lifts the focus from two to three dimensions. Like a hologram, in a successful piece of writing the parts are ultimately submerged in the whole. If you cut a piece out of a hologram, the part contains all the essential information of the entire hologram; the hologram has no parts, only wholes.

Let me give you one example of how a story's form springs from its focus, and how the two are inseparably intertwined. Some years ago, I wrote a profile of Walter Browne, who was then one of the best—but not quite *the* best—chess players in the world. This was not long after Bobby Fischer's triumph in Iceland, and Browne was chasing Fischer to become the *second* American to wear the champion's crown. The similarities between the two men were striking, making more pointed Browne's failure to catch his better-known rival.

In a pure example of what we'll later see defined as the "organic" ap-proach to structuring a story (as opposed to the "mechanic" approach), I modeled my article on the alternating moves of a chess game. The story took turns between the "white," winning and successful side of Browne and the "black," dark and troubled and ultimately unsatisfied side of his life.

I opened with a scene of Browne playing a young opponent at a tournament in Lone Pine, California. It was Browne at his finest ("like playing chess with an oncoming train"), and I used this example of his take-no-prisoners style to explain his success, not only at chess, but at almost any game he plays: "Walter Browne is a Vince Lombardi dream-come-true: winning, at whatever game, isn't the most important thing—it's the only thing." At the end of the scene, naturally, Browne wins. But from that triumph I delved into Browne's background, detailing the similarities between his story and Fischer's—and his haunted, unsuccessful pursuit of Fischer. I worked my way toward a quote from Browne's wife, Raquel: "My husband, he needs *peace*." And so on, switching between Browne the ultimate gamesman and Browne the restless man.

I could have written any number of stories about Walter Browne. But my particular focus on the dichotomy of his career, once selected, led me to a particular structure for the story. I couldn't have used that structure for any other focus, any more than an astronomer focusing on the Horse-head Nebula could use a map of Jupiter.

Building Walls, Finding Fence Posts

Once you've found your focus, structuring your story is like building a wall. You don't build a wall forty bricks at a time. One by one, the bricks are mortared into place. When you're done, the whole is greater than the sum of the parts, stronger than the pile of bricks and mortar with which you began. The more carefully and skillfully each individual brick is laid, the finer the finished wall will be. Nothing is gained by rushing ahead and building the top before the lower sections are complete.

At the same time, however, nobody builds a wall without a plan. How high will it be? Where will it join the rest of the house? The individual bricks, laid one by one, can't make these decisions for themselves.

Aristotle said that the work of a writer should have structure the same way the work of a bricklayer, or a potter, or a carpenter has an underlying structure. A number of modern writers have borrowed the term "architectonics" to describe this deep, fundamental structure so necessary to their work—the ultimate sense of "getting organized" as a writer. The architectonics of a piece of writing, said Norman Sims in his book *The Literary Journalists*, is "the structural design that gives order, balance, and unity to a work, the element of form that relates the parts to each other and to the whole." In the simplest sense, it's the scheme that links and orders your index cards or scribbled notes. In the broadest sense, it's the ultimate map that guides your writing.

In any sense, it's perhaps the most difficult part of being a writer. "The kind of architectonic structures that you have to build," says Pulitzer Prize-winner Richard Rhodes (*The Making of the Atomic Bomb, Farm*), "that nobody ever teaches or talks about, are crucial to writing and have little to do with verbal abilities. They have to do with pattern ability and administrative abilities—generalship, if you will. Writers don't talk about it much, unfortunately." Fellow author Joe McGinniss (*The Selling of the President, Fatal Vision*) agrees: He says that the decision-making process about "the unity of the book" before he ever begins to write, is the hardest part of every project.

You may find the solutions to the underlying structure of your story in the subject itself—what Samuel Coleridge called the "organic" principle of organization—or you may impose them upon the subject matter ("mechanic," in Coleridge's distinction). Though admittedly far oversimplified from Coleridge's theory, these can still be useful idea-starters for two ways of structuring your story:

Organic approach: My story about Walter Browne is a straightforward example of organic architectonics, drawing its structure from the back-and-forth, black-and-white nature of chess itself. *New Yorker* writer John McPhee is a master of the organic form. His book *Oranges*, for example, simply parallels the life cycle of the fruit he's writing about; of course, there's nothing simple about the way in which McPhee weaves a world of information about the citrus industry into this organic organizational scheme. In *The Search for Marvin Gardens*, McPhee uses a Monopoly board—originally patterned after Atlantic City, New Jersey—to structure his story about the real-life, run-down Atlantic City of today. The contrast between the cardboard, megabucks game and the down-in-the-dumps reality is driven home through an imaginary Monopoly game that's played throughout the story. At the dramatic center of another McPhee book, *The Pine Barrens*, about the wilds of New Jersey, stands a chapter on the town of Chatsworth—"The Capital of the Pines," which sits virtually at the geographical center of the Pine Barrens, just as the chapter forms the center of *The Pine Barrens*.

More broadly, perhaps your story follows the classic plot patterns of Greek tragedy—an "organic" form that Aristotle once argued could not be rearranged—or the Shakespearian plots that Coleridge admired. Your structure may spring from your characters: Once you've created them, they cannot do otherwise and the story simply unfolds. For the ancient Greeks, the key was hubris—an overweening pride that brings about the fall of the hero—as in *Oedipus Rex, Agamemnon,* or *Orestes*—as surely as a tumor grows to kill an otherwise healthy body.

Looking for your organizing principles within your subject itself is a good way to start building the architectonics of your story. Think about the shapes and structures inherent in your idea. Doodle on a notepad: What form does your story suggest? Some stories are naturally linear, with a clear progression from beginning to end, and when you have such a story you should grab onto that linear structure for all it's worth. Other tales are more circular, tending back to where they began. If you're writing a novel about a race-horse, perhaps in some sense it should be circular, like the racetrack where your most dramatic action unfolds. Many stories represent intertwining of disparate forces or characters, and that intertwining should suggest your story's shape. A few stories—McPhee's Atlantic City/Monopoly article, my black-and-white chess profile—have an unmistakable structure at the heart of their subject, which you should embrace as long as you're careful not to let it become a gimmick.

"The piece of writing has a structure inside it," McPhee has observed. "It begins, goes along somewhere, and ends in a manner that is thought out beforehand. I always know the last line of a story before I've written the first one. Going through all that creates the form and shape of the thing. It also relieves the writer, once you know the structure, to concentrate each day on one thing. You know right where it fits."

We'll return to that vital last point—"It also relieves the writer, once you know the structure, to concentrate each day on one thing"—in the pages to come, as we look at how knowing where you're going banishes writer's block and speeds up your work. But first I want to look at stories that *don't* organize themselves, where some organic principle doesn't spring up out of the material.

Mechanic approach: It should come as no surprise that McPhee is a virtuoso of the mechanic approach as well. Consider his book *Encounters with the Archdruid,* a lengthy profile of Sierra Club president (and "arch-druid" environmentalist) David Brower. The mechanic form of the book is exposed in the drawing on the cover: three triangles in a row above a line, below which stands a lone, centered triangle that seems to act as a fulcrum. The three upper triangles represent the three antagonists that McPhee set out to pit Brower (the fulcrum triangle) against. He brought Brower together with, in turn, a mining advocate, a resort-development booster, and a proponent of a dam project, each at the site of their environmental conflict. These three "encounters" form the organizational plan of the book. *Encounters with the Archdruid* happens to be nonfiction, but it's easy to see how you could apply the same approach to structuring a novel.

For example, Julia Glass took a deliberately mechanic approach to her recent novel *Three Junes*, which won the National Book Award. Glass structured her book like the triptych paintings often seen as altarpieces, where a center picture is flanked by a related image on either side, almost like wings. She tells her central story of Fenno McLeod, a Scottish expatriate in New York, in first person. Fenno's story forms the second of the novel's three segments; the first and third segments—the "wings" of her triptych—are related at a greater distance, in third person.

Chronology can also require some mechanical magic. Handling chronology, whether in fiction or nonfiction, is one of the toughest tasks a writer faces. The ancient Greek dramatists came up with the notion of *in medias res* (in the middle of things), a scheme on which McPhee does a skillful riff in another book, *Travels in Georgia*. It's the story of, among other things, a woman who dines on the critters she finds squashed in the road. Yes, she eats road kill. McPhee could have begun by describing an unappetizing scene of the woman devouring road-killed weasel and muskrat, which in fact was the actual chronological start of his travels with her. But while that would certainly have been a grabber, it might have been a little strong for an opening scene, turning off as many readers as it intrigued. It also uses up one of the most powerful scenes in McPhee's tale right at the start: Where could the story possibly go from there, to top that? So instead he begins *in medias res*, with a more acceptable yet still striking anecdote of the woman eating a snapping turtle (better than a weasel). Then he goes on to visit, with his protagonist, the stream-channelization project that brought him to Georgia and this story in the first place. Only then does he take us to the actual opening scene of weasel-eating. Skipping past the snapping turtle and the channelization project, the story then proceeds in chronological order. Its mechanical structure, imposed by McPhee for dramatic and reader-interest reasons, could be charted as: B-C-A-D-E-F . . .

When should you opt for a mechanic rather than organic structure for your own stories? Certainly, if no organic structure suggests itself, it will fall to you to impose some organizing principle on your story. But the mechanical approach needn't be viewed only as a last resort. You should also impose a structure, rather than relying on something inherent in the material, if the result is a more dramatic, gripping way of telling your story. You're a writer, after all, not a camera: Your nonfiction ought to be *more* interesting than unedited real life, and your fiction must be larger and more compelling than the material from which it springs.

The choice may also depend on how your story originates. If you observe something and then deem it worthy of writing about, an organic approach may suggest itself. But if, instead, you set out to find or create a story—as McPhee did in pitting his environmentalist against three antagonists—you may wind up building a dramatic framework into which you pour the details of your story. Either approach can work; the key is to have a structure once you sit down to write.

To switch building metaphors, what you're looking for as you start making choices about structuring your story are fence posts. You're trying to identify the structural elements that, like fence posts, will hold up your story at crucial points and let it flow along forward.

How can you find your own "fence posts"? It's mostly a matter of keeping your eyes and ears open for them, of being alive to the possibilities. Is there an image that keeps recurring as you research (or imagine) the story, or some metaphor that unites all the pieces of your puzzle? Does one picture or phrase seem to sum up what you're saying, giving you that *frisson* of "Yes, that's it!"? Is there some place or some thing at the center of your story, the physical or metaphorical locus of your theme?

Don't panic if you can't seem to recognize these possibilities at first glance. Often they won't occur to you until you sit down to mull over your material, to shape what you've gathered or created into a story. Remember our notion of building a fence: You can't build a fence without first figuring out where it will go. And fence posts don't find themselves—you have to organize your material in such a way that the strongest, tallest points stick out before you ever start to write. Then the story will seem to build itself, stringing out ahead of you. Write faster? You'll have to, just to keep up.

Exercises

1. In no more than twenty-five words, write a concise description of your current writing project—what's it all about?—and why anyone should want to read it.

2. Take your write-up from exercise one and recast it as a "Hollywood high concept" description of what you're working on and/or (especially for nonfiction articles) write a mock headline and subhead for your idea.

3. If you're working on a book-length project, try writing your own promotional copy as it might appear on the back cover of your book. If you're writing a shorter piece, try writing a table of contents entry and cover line describing your work as it might appear in a magazine.

4. Try briefly outlining a short human-interest feature story from a newspaper, magazine (the "middle column" features on the front page of the *Wall Street Journal* are ideal for this), or short story you admire. See if you can summarize the key elements of the story or narrative in no more than a dozen bullet points. Are there ways you could improve on the structure of the piece you've outlined?

5. No matter the length of your current writing project, see if you can outline its key points in no more than a dozen brief phrases or topic labels. (If you're writing a book, of course, each point will need to encompass a much broader amount of material.)

6. Again in no more than twenty-five words, tell a potential reader or editor what is *surprising* about your story idea. What would someone discover from reading your story that is unexpected?

7. See if you can express the essence of your story idea as the intersection of two subjects or ideas: "My story is about X and Y."

CHAPTER 4

FINDING IDEAS—FAST

Whether you're writing a novel, a newspaper article, or anything in between, the same basic principles apply if you want to write faster and better. As we've seen, you need to organize your time, both in terms of finding the time and planning your work to meet a deadline. You need to organize your tools, from your desk to your files, from your notes to your research materials. And you need to organize your story, in the simplest sense of what comes after what and in the deeper architectonics of what it all means.

Once you get organized, you'll find—almost magically—that your writing is better. The time, the tools, and the themes will work *with* you instead of against you. Instead of worrying about meeting deadlines, finding notes among the clutter, and figuring out where your story goes next, you'll be able to concentrate on the pure act of writing. You will achieve what psychologists who study work and creativity call *flow*: that almost effortless, out-of-time-and-place unity of you and your work.

And you will write faster. You will write faster because you'll write with confidence. You'll have a "map" of where you're going. You'll be organized in your efforts to get there. No detours. No false starts.

That's the goal. Now let's take it step by step, starting with that old familiar question writers always get asked: Where do you get your ideas?

But let's rephrase that. Where do you get the *right* ideas?

Because, you see, ideas are everywhere. Your challenge is finding the ideas that you can write best, that are uniquely suited to your time, talents, background, and situation. A romance novel set in Elizabethan times might be a wonderful idea—for someone—but if you have neither the knowledge of that period nor the time to research it, that's a terrible idea for you. A hard-boiled detective story set in Omaha could make a great read—but it's probably not an idea you ought to tackle if you don't enjoy Raymond

Chandler and you've never been west of Scranton. If an idea doesn't match the writer, she won't be able to write it quickly; ultimately, the odds are against her being able to write it well. Of course there are exceptions—the elderly spinster who writes a wildly erotic best-seller entirely from her, er, vivid imagination—but writing is hard enough without bucking tides you don't have to.

I realize that some of you are still back at the beginning of the previous paragraph, agog at the notion that "ideas are everywhere." When I was writing my newspaper column, knocking out three or four stories a week, people would ask me, "Where do you get your ideas?" They would see this stream of stories, week after week, and wonder what the headwaters could possibly be like. Who has so many ideas, anyway? It was hard to explain to people not in the writing or reporting business, but the fact was, *getting* the ideas was never the problem. My first day on the job, I started a manila file folder labeled "Ideas." The pace of my column writing never caught up with the stuffing and replenishing of my Ideas file. When I left for greener pastures, in fact, I bequeathed to my successor not one, but two, bulging folders full of ideas for columns.

No, getting the ideas wasn't the challenge—and it won't be for you, either, once you get into the idea-collecting groove. The tough part was getting ideas that I could execute within the time constraints of a thrice-weekly feature column. Translating a glimmer of an idea into a doable column meant figuring out what preliminary research I needed to do and whom to interview, setting up the interview(s), and, usually, driving a hundred miles or so out to East Pigsty, Iowa, and back. Some ideas, often ones that seemed like a good idea at the time I scribbled them down or tore a nugget of inspiration out of some weekly newspaper, never could survive that leap from idea into action. I'd come across them in my file, think about how hard they would be to execute, shake my head, and flip past to something more realistic for my deadlines. I'll admit: Many of the ideas I bequeathed to my successor fell into this category, and she probably passed them along, in turn, to whoever followed her on the column.

I don't mean to say I was lazy, or to suggest that laziness is the proper approach when evaluating ideas. Rather, I want to advise against biting off more than you can chew under the circumstances. The circumstances might be your current job or writing schedule, or they might include the limits of your knowledge and abilities. If I'd been a staff writer for a major magazine at the time, for example, with only one story to do that month (or every few months, even), many of the ideas I passed over again and again as unworkable might suddenly have made good stories for me. If I had known more about certain fields—agribusiness, for example—I might have tackled some more substantive ideas in those fields, or tackled the same ideas in a different way.

Write only the stories you can write sounds like a truism, a statement so obvious and self-evident it hardly bears saying. But accepting this premise and making it a part of your approach to your work is actually a crucial step along the path to writing faster and better. If you try to write stories that, for one reason or another, you really can't write—because you don't have the luxury of time at the present or because the subject is too big for you—you'll do more than slow yourself down and waste time. Ultimately, you will injure your self-esteem as a writer. You will damage the confidence that's vital to successful, "in flow" writing. Yes, you should always stretch as a creative person. But don't try to climb Mount Everest before you can handle the hill in your own backyard. Robert Burns may have been right, in principle, when he said, "A man's reach should exceed his grasp, else what's a heaven for?"—but that won't impress editors when you can't deliver on an assignment or a book contract. ("Gee, I only took that contract for a fifteen-book series of novels set in Czarist Russia, written as the fictionalized autobiography of a Cossack, in order to grow as a writer. Can I get the manuscript to you in heaven?")

Writing only the stories you can write means you must be a lot choosier when you go looking for ideas. Since ideas seldom come ready-made with you in mind ("Inside this issue of *The New York Times*: Three story ideas just right for Jane Wordsmith"), however, you'll need to learn to see ideas in different ways, to turn them around and adapt them to what you can write.

Cutting Ideas Down to Size

One way to take an idea from the "intriguing but impossible" pile and turn it into something you can write is to narrow the focus. At the time I was columnizing in Iowa, for example, farm debt was a big problem. Farmers were going under right and left, and there were serious questions about the long-term survival of the family farm. So, naturally, I thought about doing a big story on farmers and debt—the ultimate "Will the family farm survive?" story. Interview a few dozen farmers, government experts, economists and bankers. Chart the course of farm debt over the past century. Talk to some more experts to see how farm debt relates to the national economy. Visit several family farms as well as large, corporate-owned farms. Go to farm-implement dealers and small-town businesses, to see how the sagging agricultural economy has affected their sales. . . . Before I knew it, I had a story that would take months to accomplish—a story that, frankly, was probably beyond my ability to intelligently research and, just as important, that went deeper than my own interest in the subject.

I could have just tossed my couple of newspaper clippings on farm debt into the "intriguing but impossible" section of my file, and moved on. Instead, however, I thought about how I could narrow the focus of this idea. How could I make it a story that I could write? And how could I make it a story that I would *want* to write, all the way to the finish? Often, narrowing the focus is as simple as moving from the general to the particular, from the sweeping to the specific. Instead of writing the ultimate round-up story on farm debt, I would write about *one* farm family in our area. I would bring this big, complex subject home to newspaper readers by showing how it affects some folks pretty much like them. Then, to put my specific farm family into the broader picture, I would include some basic statistics on the scope of the problem, quote a few experts, and compare the family's situation to the national average.

That was a story I could write. Incidentally, it was also a much better and more interesting story than my first take on the idea. It was human; it was real; it was about faces instead of abstractions. I think readers learned more about the crisis confronting the family farm from my little story than from any big story that I, at least, could have written. I wrote the story I could write and did my best with it, instead of attempting something that was bound to fail and trying to sell my editor and my readers on the results.

The same principle applies to fiction. Maybe you aren't really up to writing the ultimate World War II novel—and besides, Herman Wouk has beaten you to it. Instead of spending a decade or two trying to outdo *The Winds of War* and *War and Remembrance*, maybe you should write a novel inspired by your mom's experiences living near a camp for German POWs. Or perhaps you visited a small French town that would be a perfect setting for a romantic story of the Resistance. You don't have to include every shot fired from Pearl Harbor to Hitler's bunker, particularly not if this is your first novel.

With every idea that you attempt, narrow it until you know you can do it right. Test every project against the rule: *Write only the stories you can write.* If it doesn't fit, narrow the focus until it does.

Similarly, fit the idea to the task, instead of expanding the assignment to try to encompass some grand idea. Don't try to make a magazine feature out of a 10-inch newspaper story, or a book out of a magazine feature assignment. Don't try to make a novel out of a short story. Don't play Cecil B. DeMille with a one-act, two-character play, turning it into an epic of Biblical proportions like DeMille's movies. Find the story you can write, and concentrate on writing it right.

I Know Nothing!

A second way to transform an unworkable idea into a story you can write is to turn your ignorance to your advantage. If the first technique is a question of focus, this (continuing the camera metaphor) is a matter of *angle* or *viewpoint.* I've done a number of stories on businesses or industrial operations—from inside a cheese factory to how Rolls-Royce automobiles are made. For me to attempt to learn everything there is to know about the chemistry of cheese making or the fine points of internal-combustion engines was clearly impossible. (And it would have been a waste of time, since few readers would sit still for a lecture on cheese chemistry or engine design.) Instead, I simply tackled the stories as a skilled observer: Hey, folks, here's what cheese making looks, sounds, and smells like. Here's what you would see if you got a guided tour of the Rolls-Royce automobile plant, as I did. Few readers have ever been in a cheese factory, and fewer still have ever gone to England and watched Rolls-Royce cars being made. But everyone's eaten cheese and everyone knows the cachet of Rolls-Royce—so I could take a certain modest level of reader interest for granted. Then I approached these stories from the same viewpoint as most readers: a basic curiosity about where familiar things—cheese, famous cars—come from, about what makes them the way they are.

No, you won't learn how to make cheese or how to build a car from reading my stories. But you'll learn what I did (at least the most interesting parts), see what I saw, and come away knowing something more about the world. I wrote these stories simply by keeping my eyes open, asking questions, and trying to keep in mind what the average reader would want to know.

The ultimate example of this ignorance-is-bliss approach, for me, was my first visit to a dairy farm. I grew up in South Dakota, so people always assume that I know my way around a barnyard. But, in fact, I was a city kid, the offspring of college professors, not farmers. I grew up thinking that milk came from the grocery store, and the hardest work I associated with milk was struggling to open a carton without ripping the spout. Cows were something to sing about ("e-i-e-i-o").

So one day, as a newspaper writer in Iowa, I decided to write about dairy farming. Now, it would have been as ludicrous for me to write an in-depth report on the dairy business as for me to explain general relativity. (Indeed, relativity might have been an easier assignment; at least I'd studied physics in school.) That was not a story I could write—not and meet any of my other deadlines for a few months. The story I could write, instead, was the story of a city kid getting his hands (and shoes) dirty on a dairy farm for the first time. By *using* my ignorance—my honest amazement, in fact—about the hard work that puts milk on my table, I could bring the world of dairy farming alive. Readers who, like me, had little experience with dairy farms could see something new through my eyes; readers who knew dairy farming could enjoy my greenhorn's discovery of something familiar to them.

I don't mean to suggest that all idea problems can be solved by playing George Plimpton. But Plimpton's amateur's-eye-view (in *Paper Lion* and other books) does point out the power of having a fresh angle, of picking a viewpoint appropriate not only for the story, but for the writer. Experts often know too much about a subject to communicate it effectively (or interestingly!) to a lay audience. Open eyes and an open mind can be potent tools for a writer looking for the fastest and best way to turn an idea into a story.

Much the same principle can be applied to ideas for fiction. Suppose you want to write a spy novel, inspired by the literate espionage sagas of John le Carré. But of course le Carré writes from the inside looking out, based on his firsthand experience of the shadowy world of British intelligence. For you to learn enough to write credibly from that viewpoint would be impossible (particularly with this secret subject!). So perhaps your protagonist ought to be an ordinary citizen—like you—who unwittingly falls into the world of espionage, as in Alfred Hitchcock's *North by Northwest*. You could probably learn enough about the spy game to keep one step ahead of your hero, and your readers. Part of the story then becomes the unfolding of this secret world, paralleling the discoveries you make in your research.

Any time you consider a complex subject, think about whether it's worth your while to become an expert before writing about it. Maybe you can write a better, more engaging story just by learning more than your readers know. Try on a new viewpoint and see how your story looks now. Remember: It's the angle from which you approach an idea that makes for a story you can write.

Finding Your Audience

A third technique for turning ideas into fast stories—assuming you're a freelancer and not a staff writer—is changing the intended audience. (Obviously, staff writers are stuck with their publication's given audience.) This is a variation on the shifts in focus and viewpoint: You change the story you have to write by changing for whom you're writing it.

For example, suppose you have an idea to write about nuclear power. As always, the next step is to find the story that you can write. You might find that there's a terrific market for an up-to-date textbook on nuclear power, but—unless you have a degree in nuclear physics or engineering—that's probably not something you can write. So you could aim instead for a general audience, attempting a popular-science book on nuclear power, or possibly a thriller set inside a nuclear-power plant. But again, unless you have some background in this field, either would be daunting to undertake.

Take the idea one step further in the hierarchy of audiences: How about a children's book on nuclear power? Or a visit to a nuclear power plant for a young people's science magazine? Those ideas might be doable given your current knowledge of the subject and some quick research. Best of all, actually doing such a story could give you the additional expertise necessary to then pitch the idea for a general adult audience.

The same kind of hierarchy applies to local, regional and national stories. Suppose you have an idea on quilting—say you've noticed that several younger women you know have taken up quilting. The first and fastest story you might write could be a trend article for your local newspaper, based on the people you already know plus a visit to local stores that sell quilting supplies. Then you might try to broaden the story for a regional audience: Take what you already know and do some research in neighboring cities, then pitch the story to a state or regional "shelter book" (*Sunset* or *Midwest Living*, for example). Ultimately, you might even be able to write and sell a national story ("Quilting Boom Sweeps U.S." or "Quilting: It's Not Just for Grandma Anymore"). Or you'd be ready to launch your series of mystery novels with a detective who runs a quilt shop.

The important thing is to try walking before you sign up for the Boston Marathon. Write the fastest version of the idea first, then look for ways to write it for a different audience. Each subsequent treatment of the original idea will be faster to write because you've already done at least some of the homework.

Look at every idea with your mental writer's time clock in mind: How can you translate this idea into something you can write quickly? Narrow the focus, change the viewpoint, and alter the intended audience. Every idea has a hundred, a thousand permutations. In each idea, there is a story that you are uniquely suited to write.

Shaking the Idea Tree

But hold on a minute. Haven't we put the cart before the proverbial horse here? We've been talking about how to evaluate ideas, how to turn them on their heads and twist them inside out to create fast stories. What about *finding* the ideas? You have an empty head and a bunch of empty file folders; the heck with evaluating ideas—how do you get them in the first place?

You've forgotten that finding ideas is the easy part. Without any framework for what to do with them, you could wade out into the ocean of ideas and come back with a net so full, you'd spend all your time sorting through your catch. Before you go fishing for ideas you can write, it's best to know something about what your prey looks like, its habits, and where it hides.

Once you know what you're looking for, you'll start finding ideas everywhere—in the newspaper, for instance, or from an hour or two surfing the Internet. You'll catch yourself clipping the magazines you subscribe to until they resemble the fixings for papier-mâché, and keeping a notepad by your comfy TV chair so you can scribble ideas you glean from the nightly news.

Let's flip through a typical Sunday newspaper, just to get the idea. You'll likely find the front section among the less-rich sources of story ideas, particularly for nonfiction; much of the front-page news is too ephemeral to turn into "timely" articles many months down the road, when your query might actually become a printed magazine piece. Besides, what you're looking for is not the who-what-when-where-why of breaking news, but the ideas and trends lying between the lines.

For a certain breed of fiction writer, of course, tomorrow's ideas start with today's front page—think of all those "ripped from the headlines" television dramas that somebody has to write (why not you?). The trick here is not to simply reproduce the day's crimes, changing a few names to keep the lawyers at bay. Put a twist on the ideas you "rip from the headlines," or combine two true tales to create a fresh idea. A memorable episode of the television series "Law and Order," for example, was taken from the fall 2002 sniper shootings in the Washington, DC area. Though moving the action to New York City, it roughly paralleled the real-life suspects' case— at first. But instead of merely making the shooting suspects a troubled drifter and a young compatriot, the episode blended in other headline-making cases where young kidnap victims bond with their abductors, coming to believe the kidnappers are actually parents. The writers cleverly played "What if?" with their original idea from the headlines: What if the sniper was the young man, acting in a misguided effort to protect his father? And what if his father was really his kidnapper, not his father at all?

Writers of other genres may need to look deeper than the front page to start harvesting fruitful ideas. Suppose you come across one of those endless news stories about the latest study of this or that: "Study Ties Educational Gains To More Productivity Growth." Better-educated workers, you learn as you read on, are more productive workers—something employers have long suspected, but that's never been so fully documented. To transform that study into your own article, try asking the question: "What's next?" (not unlike the fiction writer's "What if?"). Presumably, employers will start looking more seriously at employee-education programs; your article could help them get the most bang for their bucks. What companies have experiences in employee education worth emulating? What do experts in this field recommend—and warn against?

Some further research, plus the study from the newspaper cited high in your query letter, could lead to a sale to *Inc.*, your regional business magazine, or even one of the in-flight magazines that caters to executive fliers/readers. Or you could flip the "What's next?" on its head and write from the employee's standpoint. An article on "How extra education can make you a more productive—and marketable—employee" might land, for example, at a magazine aimed at working women.

Or suppose, a few pages further on, there's an article on sleep disorders affecting long-distance truckers. The question to ask here is: "What else?" That is, what other jobs might be affected by sleep disorders and body-clock mix-ups? Maybe you could write a popular-science article about work and the body's internal clock, taking off from this timely research to discuss related findings about night-shift workers, air-traffic controllers, and others. If your bent is science fiction rather than science fact, you could extrapolate what you learn about sleep deprivation into a story: Perhaps they've invented a drug that lets people do without sleep, reclaiming all those "wasted" hours of every day, but it turns out to have certain side effects . . .

But let's skip ahead from the front section to the Sunday-only parts of the paper that concentrate more on trends and explainers—gold mines for the idea prospector. Here in *The New York Times* is a piece on "blogs," the Web-based diaries/link lists that so many Internet surfers are using (or so it says here) as a new means of personal expression. Has your local newspaper or city magazine done a feature on bloggers in your area? Pitch it before somebody else does! How about a blogger story on niche sites for your favorite hobbyist magazine ("Model-Train Bloggers Ride the Web's Rails for You").

Another *Times* story carries the headline, "Why Science Loses Women in the Ranks"—practically an invitation to you to profile one or more women who've gone against the grain and succeeded in science. Or, if fiction is your preference and you're looking for a protagonist, perhaps she could be a scientist struggling to stick it out in a male-dominated profession.

All these ideas exemplify asking the question, "What could I add?" What local spin could you add to a national craze? What human face could you add to a statistical phenomenon?

For trend spotting, your favorite newspaper's business and arts sections, though seemingly on opposite ends of the spectrum, are both useful barometers of social and cultural forces beyond their topic boundaries. Look here to see what will be timely when your articles reach print, to spot waves about to crest.

If the business section brings yet another a story on "road warriors," those high-flying executives who spend hundreds of days a year traveling, for example, try asking yourself, "What's the flip side?" A women's magazine might snap up an article on the wives of road warriors, and how they keep their marriages intact. Does absence really make the heart grow fonder? And what about the men who keep the home fires burning while their wives rack up the frequent-flier miles?

When the arts and entertainment section previews the summer crop of movies, look for coming cultural boomlets. The last time movies based on comic books were hot, for example, I turned my adolescent fixation with superheroes into a timely think-piece on superheroes and society for an in-flight magazine and a fun comics quiz for *Playboy*. You can imagine how fast I hauled out those old notes when the papers reported the plans for the

X-Men, *Spider-Man*, *Daredevil*, and *Hulk* film adaptations. Like "What's next?" or "What could I add?," asking yourself what else might readers want to know is a good way to spin ideas off pop-culture trends.

Take these nuggets from the newspaper—or from *Newsweek* or your favorite Web site—and tug at their margins. Turn them on their heads. Spin them forward and ask, "What's next?" Put on your fiction-writer's cap and ask, "What if?"

You may never read a newspaper in quite the same way again—and you'll never pick up the paper without a pair of scissors by your side. The ideas really are everywhere, if you know how to see them and what questions to ask about them.

No Place Like Home

But fast ideas don't come only from faraway sources like *The New York Times* or CNN. As Dorothy learned in *The Wizard of Oz*, there's no place like home—and that's true in the idea chase as well. Start with what you know, what's close to home. (No, I didn't know anything about dairy farming, to pick up on an earlier example, but it was certainly close to home. The ignorance-is-bliss approach to an idea doesn't make much sense if you can't get ready access to the subject. Sure, you'd like to take a fresh approach to Tom Cruise, but will he let you?) Not only does the adage "write what you know" speed up your writing; it also adds to the authenticity of the finished product. In the case of fiction, your make-believe will be more believable if you're not making it *all* up. Consider giving your protagonist the same job that you, a friend or a relative actually hold. Think of the success suspense-novelist Dick Francis, a former jockey, had writing books set in the racing world, such as *Reflex* and *Longshot*. Or Elizabeth Peters—an archaeologist in real life—and her series of archaeology-based thrillers, such as *Crocodile on the Sandbank*. And don't set your whole story in a land or time period that's utterly foreign to you. Why do you think horror writer Stephen King sets almost all his nerve-wracking novels in his home state of Maine? Peters, again, can afford to set several of her books in and around the tombs of Egypt—because she's been there and worked there.

As we saw in the section on moonlighting, your job, if you have one other than writing, is a fine source of ideas; if not your job, then your hobbies. Information in trade journals in your field or specialized hobby publications can often be turned into stories for the general public. Here you already have the inside track on the necessary expertise.

The next step into the circle of what's familiar and fast might be friends, neighbors or relatives, their vocations and avocations. Years ago, I got the idea for a story on Tupperware, for example, from a neighbor who kept inviting my wife to her Tupperware parties; one night I accepted in my wife's stead, and wrote a man's-eye-view of this mostly female institution. That was a lot easier, I might note, than pursuing the story the other way around: deciding to write about Tupperware and then trying to track down a party somewhere.

Finally, your own community is another good place to find workable ideas. If you live in a town of any size, you probably have a small army of people ready, willing, and paid to supply you with story ideas: the public relations staffs at colleges and universities, hospitals, local conventions and visitors bureaus, and various corporations. While many of their ideas will be dull, or too obviously self-serving, these PR people do have a font of information and expertise at their fingertips that you can tap. The more experienced among them are savvy media professionals, used to pitching ideas to editors and can help you identify salable stories. By making friends with your local PR staffs and by asking a few smart questions, you can benefit from their legwork and resources. Get on PR mailing lists. You'll throw out most of what you get, but what you cull from that chaff could be ready-made stories. The PR department of the university I used to work at, for example, produced an ongoing series of feature-idea "tip sheets"— capsule story descriptions, complete with phone numbers to call to follow up. Many of these could be instantly translated into queries: the campus Ghostbusters, for example, or the world's top expert on how homing pigeons find their way home. Others needed only an infusion of a few other experts from around the country to round them out into major trend pieces.

Other story-starters will simply find you, once you know how to keep your eyes open in your community. Elizabeth Peters says she gets ideas from odd signs in shop windows, street names, and fillers in her local paper. When I was writing my newspaper column, my wife used to scan the classified ads for me; that's how we found, for example, a woman whose business was raising canaries—in her home. It also pays to follow the national media for tidbits about your community that might not be known right under your nose. For instance, when I was editing *Milwaukee* magazine, *The New York Times* had an item about the growth of baseball in Australia, and happened to mention that the only Australian currently playing professionally in the U.S. was a Milwaukee Brewers farmhand. Bingo! There was a potential story for my magazine. I soon discovered, in fact, that the Brewers had one of the major leagues' most active recruiting operations Down Under.

Finding your ideas close to home doesn't mean they have to be mundane or parochial (witness our leap to baseball in Australia). Even science fiction, that haven of far-out ideas and exotic locales, usually starts with the familiar: *Nine Princes in Amber* author Roger Zelazny once said he used the Yellow Pages to generate ideas. He would flip through the phone book, noting the first half-dozen or so entries he spotted, then try to project those businesses into the future. Or he might shift some familiar enterprise to another planet, or make its customers aliens. A bait and tackle ad led to Zelazny's award-winning futuristic "fish story," "The Doors of His Face, the Lamps of His Mouth."

Starting from the known and projecting into the unknown is a lot easier than trying to imagine an utterly fictional reality with no grounding in the familiar. That's partly the secret of the science fiction writer's favorite question, "What if?" What if the South had won the Civil War (*Bring the Jubilee* by Ward Moore, *Guns of the South* by Harry Turtledove)? What if you could make yourself invisible (*The Invisible Man* by H.G. Wells, *The Murderer Invisible* by Philip Wylie)? What if an asteroid came too near the earth (*A Torrent of Faces* by James Blish and Norman L. Knight) or what if we earthlings ran out of room for our trash and began using asteroids as extraterrestrial landfills (*Garbage World* by Charles Platt)?

Trying Ideas on for Size

Once you get into the habit of looking around you for ideas, trust me, you really will find them everywhere. You'll start to recognize that "fit" between an idea and your own abilities, interests, and resources. Your mind will seem to work on overdrive, calculating the ways in which you and only you could put a particular spin on an idea.

Instead of groping for stories you really can't write and setting impossible goals, you'll discover a wealth of speedy, doable stories virtually at your own front door.

That doesn't mean, of course, you can't find fast ideas whenever you travel. Every weekend getaway, every vacation, or business trip, is fodder for several stories. If you took the trip, after all, someone else might want to follow in your footsteps (or tire tracks)—and you can guide them. But travel doesn't have to be limited to ideas for travel articles per se: You can set a scene of your novel in your destination, or use examples from there in a round-up article.

The key to turning travel experiences into story fodder is to be a pack rat. Grab every brochure, flier, handout, map, guidebook, and pamphlet you can get your hands on. They're valuable not only for the written facts and figures, dates, and names, but for the photographs that can jog your memory and add colorful descriptions to your copy. You can also take photographs yourself, of course. It doesn't matter whether you're a terrific photographer or not, as long as your pictures are in focus. Always take *color* snapshots, so you'll know later whether that quaint old inn you're describing is red or blue. Take an extra suitcase if you have to, just for your research goodies, or mail a package back home to yourself. Also tote a notebook, to supplement the published materials with insights and observations of your own. Don't count on remembering the details of even the most memorable vacation; you might not use some of this raw material for months or even years. Then, once you get home, devote a file cabinet or a box in the closet to all your travel materials—labeled by destination so you can find them when you need them. The result is a resource collection not even the biggest library can match, and a trove of story ideas almost as doable as those found right around the corner.

But don't be a pack rat for no purpose, whether on the road or at home. Try each idea on for size before you start devoting time and energy to developing it. Your goal should be to know in advance what to do with the ideas you find, whether to pursue them or ignore them. Otherwise, you'll waste a lot of time and energy clipping and considering ideas you can't realistically write. *Gee, wouldn't it be great to write a profile of Julia Roberts?* you might think, and then start making a file on this big-time movie star. But unless you have some reasonable expectation of being able to interview Julia Roberts, you'll be wasting your time. Ideas are cheap; your time isn't. Part of learning to write faster is learning to concentrate your efforts on the art of the possible.

Once your inner "radar" gets attuned to doable stories vs. unlikely ideas, you'll be a smarter scanner for ideas. You will start to see an immediate match between your knowledge and skills, and any would-be story that floats across your horizon. As Robert Payne, author of *The Dream and the Tomb*, put it, "The ideas get you." Then you can really start writing faster and better.

Exercises

1. Pick several stories from a magazine you enjoy and reslant them so they might be sold to any or all of these other magazines: *Modern Maturity, Glamour, Men's Journal, Seventeen*. Keep in mind the audience of each magazine.

2. Take the basic idea of one or more of these classic novels, whichever you're most familiar with—*Huckleberry Finn, Moby Dick, Emma, A Tale of Two Cities*—and write a brief description of what the novel might be like if, instead, it were:
   a. a children's book
   b. a science-fiction novel
   c. a movie aimed primarily at teenage boys

3. Recast your description of your writing project from the exercises in chapter three so that the focus is narrower ("cutting it down to size"), or you're approaching the topic from the viewpoint of a novice or new-comer ("the ignorance angle").

4. Rewrite your twenty-five-words-or-less description of your idea and why readers should care about it (chapter three, exercise one), changing your intended audience. How might your idea be reworked for children? Young adults? Readers of the opposite sex? An academic audience? Readers of grocery-store-checkout tabloids or cheap paperbacks?

5. Go through a Sunday newspaper and clip items or articles of any length that might be fodder for stories (fiction, nonfiction or a combination). Write one-sentence or one-phrase descriptions of at least ten story ideas inspired by your clippings.

6. Go through the Ideas folder you started in chapter two (exercise five) and write one-sentence or one-phrase descriptions of at least five story ideas inspired by your clippings and notes.

7. For each story-idea description in exercise six, write at least one additional story idea inspired by the *same* clipping or note. Try changing the focus, the angle or the intended audience, to come up with your alternative ideas.

CHAPTER 5

THINKING LIKE AN EDITOR

Now that you've seen how easy it is to find ideas—and not just any old ideas, but ones you can tackle with confidence—you should be eager to start writing. Before you head to the keyboard, though, there's one more secret you need to know, especially if you're writing nonfiction: Don't write that story until you find a place that will print it! Otherwise, you'll waste all the time you've saved, writing articles with the wrong slant for an audience that doesn't exist. You'll fill up your files with orphaned stories and have no time left to write for results.

If you want to write and sell nonfiction, you need to write query letters first. Don't charge ahead and write the article, thinking that its sheer wonderfulness will sweep an editor off her feet; it might indeed be wonderful, but it still might not be right for the editor's publication. (If you're a beginner without a fistful of clips, you may have to write "on spec," without a guaranteed assignment, but you should still get an editor's interest and input before you write.)

But it's not just article authors who can benefit from getting inside the head of those at the other end of the submission process. Trying to sell a book, either nonfiction or a novel? You'll need to be able to boil down your idea—and why you're the one to write it—into a single page, sometimes called a "one-sheet," that you can use to make your pitch to editors and literary agents. Sure, you hope they'll read your whole outline and sample chapters, but you can't count on it. You may have just that one page to convince them your novel is their next best-seller.

Not only does that one-sheet or that query letter have to effectively distill a publishable idea—you have to identify somebody who might publish it. That's the other half of the idea-hunting equation for efficient writers: As you comb the vast universe of story ideas for ideas that you can readily write, you should further select only those stories that you can write *for somebody*. Look at what kind of books are selling and at who's publishing what. You might yearn to write true-confession novels set in the world of sports—but does anyone want to publish them? Think of what magazines you want to write for, markets you have a reasonable chance of cracking, and keep them in mind as you look for ideas. Play editor: If you were the editor of *Midwest Living*, would you be interested in a hard-hitting exposé of corruption in Kearney, Nebraska? After all, Nebraska is in the *Midwest*, and these corrupt guys are, well, *living*—right? Wrong. *Midwest Living* focuses on travel, home, food, gardening, and other service topics—the good life in the Midwest, not the seamy underside of living there. What about a query on antiquing throughout Indiana, drawing on your own travels and hobby of collecting antiques? That might be worth a shot.

Like finding doable stories in the first place. Success at pitching ideas to publishers has less to do with *finding* ideas than with evaluating them and applying your creativity to them. The key is the spin you put on an idea (our old friend the angle), and how closely that fits the approach of the magazine, book imprint, or other market. This part of the writing game is as much about matchmaking—pairing your idea with the right market for it—as it is about writing and creativity. That means you need to learn to think like an editor.

What Do Editors Want?

Sometimes it feels like you have to be a mind reader to be a successful freelance writer. You study the markets, frame your queries and proposals, send them out—and then some inscrutable editor passes judgment on your ideas. Who knows what the editor is thinking? Maybe he got up on the wrong side of the bed that morning, or maybe she doesn't like the cut of your stationery. All you know is you get a rejection letter instead of an assignment. And your idea never gets the chance to bloom.

Thinking like an editor—understanding the kinds of questions that editors ask themselves, consciously or unconsciously, when evaluating an idea—can take some of the mystery out of querying. Sure, some editors' decisions will always seem arbitrary, their motivations a puzzle. And some decisions really do get made because the coffee was cold at the editor's breakfast that morning, or because the editor just can't abide off-white letterhead. Go figure—people are funny beasts.

But if you learn to test your ideas against the same questions an editor asks—*before* you fire off that submission—you can save yourself headaches, heartaches and, of course, *time.* By following the fine-tuning that your answers suggest, you might also make a sale you otherwise would have missed. Sometimes fixing an idea to better answer editors' questions means rejiggering it; other times, it just requires tweaking how you present your idea. Here are some key questions to ask yourself in evaluating how well your idea matches its intended market:

- **Does it fit?** Editors first test your idea against their mission and audience. This question is the one most queries flunk, and the one from which there's least likely to be a reprieve. It's why so many rejection letters say something like, "not quite right for us."

Testing whether your idea "fits" can indeed feel like trying to read the editor's mind. But you can find clues if you follow what's probably the oldest freelance-writing advice there is: Study the market. I know—you're tired of hearing that. Writing magazines and teachers have been doling out that lesson since the days when manuscripts were in cuneiform. But it's still true. To get a feel for the editor's notion of his mission and audience—to read his mind, if you will—study a magazine's contents page (which we'll talk more about later in this chapter) or zoom in on the book imprint's catalog. Regardless of what the stories and books might actually deliver, what does the editor want to achieve? What are her masters in marketing pressuring her to churn out? Try to do a little reading between the lines, a bit of telepathy.

If you're writing fiction, you've likely already written your story and are looking for a market to submit it to, rather than to query. But that doesn't relieve you of the "Does it fit?" rule. Your hard-boiled detective thriller doesn't fit Brown Skin Books, a publisher of erotica for women of color, any more than your bodice-ripping historical romance matches the needs of the Nautical & Aviation Publishing Co., which wants "naval and military history fiction and reference." (No, that word "history" doesn't open the door, any more than if your hero happens to be an admiral!) For short fiction, try the contents-page test: Can you really see a blurb for your "Gunfight on the Chisholm Trail" coming right after "10 Secrets for Lips That Really Shimmer"?

Does it fit, or do you have to squeeze? Don't rationalize that "Well, my idea doesn't exactly fit, but they might like it for variety"—either it fits or it doesn't.

- **Who cares?** This question sounds harsh, but it's shorthand for an essential characteristic of successful stories: Do they compel somebody to read them? Do they have some powerful "hook" that can grab readers' attention? You'll have to answer the "Who cares?" question to write your actual story, so you might as well make sure of the answer when formulating it. Think of "Who cares?" as "Why should readers care?" or "How is this relevant to readers?"

The answer may be as simple as telling readers what's in it for them—that's the essence of service journalism. Articles on the best restaurants, the hottest products or the most alluring getaways, promises of making readers smarter, sexier, or wealthier—all have a huge head start on answering "Who cares?" Self-help books have a similar sure-fire appeal, as long as the problem those "selves" need help with is compelling enough. If you can convince an editor that your topic is something readers care about (saving for their kids' college tuition; yes, keeping their iguanas' scales shinier, probably not, unless you're querying *Lizard Life* magazine), a service or self-help pitch almost always passes the "Who cares?" test.

Human beings also love to read about other human beings, real or fictional. Do you have characters that readers can care about? If everyone in your story seems like a robot, the answer to "Who cares?" will likely be "Nobody!"—even if you're writing science fiction.

- **Is it interesting?** Here the answers get even more subjective, but that doesn't mean you can't help an editor arrive at the "right" answer. Think about that broad, vague question as the sum of several smaller questions, which variously apply depending on the subject:

Is it big? Something that involves a million people, a billion dollars, many products, or industries is usually more interesting than something small, limited in scope and minor in impact. Think of the interest in "blockbuster" novels and movies: Imagine *Gone with the Wind* if Margaret Mitchell had focused on the burning of Newton, Georgia, instead of Atlanta. Would *Armageddon* have been as gripping if only a remote, uninhabited island had been at risk, instead of the whole planet?

Is it important? Obviously subjective, but you can try to show that a subject is important—and therefore interesting—by rolling out credentials (a Harvard study seems more important than a breakthrough from Sunny Valley Tech), pulling rank (cabinet secretaries over small-town mayors, movie stars over radio DJs), and spotlighting superlatives (number-one of anything seems more important than number-six).

Is it a trend? Even if your subject isn't big and important yet, if it's *becoming* big and important, that makes it interesting. Think of Michael

Crichton's nanotechnology thriller, *Prey*, written before most of us had ever seen nano anything. Anticipate the "Is it a trend?" question by offering evidence that your topic is growing, spreading, gaining credence—"ahead of the curve," in trend jargon.

Is it dynamic? By "dynamic" I mean all those things that make for good headlines as well as good drama: changing, surprising, charged with conflict. Dynamic is the difference between a mountain and a volcano, between dog-bites-man and man-bites-dog, between love and a love story.

Then there's timing. Ask *Is it new?* and *Is it timely?* Your subject doesn't have to be both, but it helps if the answer to at least one is "yes." A new idea beats an old one. Editors are always looking for the newest thing, not because they are fickle but because they know their readers want to know what's new (otherwise they wouldn't need to buy magazines or books!).

Timeliness can even mean the difference in answering that "Who cares?" question. For example, I once bought a feature on the sport of curling (you know—brooms, ice, big rock) for the online city guide I was editing. Normally, a curling feature would have had a steep "Who cares?" hill to climb. But the idea was timely because curling was about to make its Olympic debut at the games in Nagano, Japan. That idea was also a good "fit" since it promised to tell readers not about curling in Japan but about how to see and even try curling right here in their hometown (also helping to answer the "Who cares?" question). Was it interesting? Well, curling was "big" enough for the Olympics—making it automatically "important." And its rise to Olympic prominence made it, at least arguably, a trend. You could even spot a "dynamic" element in the surprising contrast between a humble, elderly-man's sport (seems like shuffleboard on ice) and the quest for a gold medal.

When an idea racks up the "yes" answers like that in an editor's mind, it's likely that you too will get a "yes"—and an assignment. But remember that in *this* test, it's not cheating to know the questions in advance.

Getting to Yes

Despite the blizzard of rejection slips that writers paper their workspaces with, most editors are really dying to say "yes." Saying "yes" to a writer means an editor has solved a problem, whether it's *What the heck am I going to put in the next issue?* or *What's going to be my blockbuster novel next fall?*. Saying "yes" to your idea means an editor has fed the idea monster with at least one idea he didn't have to come up with himself. Giving you an assignment or accepting your submission may even mean an editor can, for once at least, leave the office before 6:00 and maybe eat something besides Chinese takeout for a night.

As you play matchmaker with your ideas, keep in mind these four secrets most editors wish you knew to make their jobs easier—and to make it easier for them to say "yes":

- **Copy the formula.** Most successful magazines have a formula. They might prefer to think of it as a "mission statement," but it's the essential appeal of that publication—what makes it sell, what readers expect from each issue. Not every article in every issue will perfectly embody this formula, but these are the articles that editors are most hungry for. For a magazine aimed at teen girls, the formula might be "how to get boys to like you"; for certain sizzling women's magazines, it's "how to have better/more sex." One travel magazine might be selling the cachet of undiscovered, even unattainable exotic dream vacations; another might emphasize slightly less dreamy trips on a budget. Even fiction-focused magazines have a formula: There's a world of difference between *Analog Science Fiction and Fact* and *The Magazine of Fantasy & Science Fiction*, not to mention between *Analog* and *Ploughshares*. And you can analyze book imprints the same way, if you're aiming to pitch longer works.

  Look for patterns in whatever you're targeting, then try to come up with ideas that mimic the most common themes. A "healthy gourmet" magazine that regularly runs features on "10 Sinfully Rich Low-Fat Desserts" and "Chocolate Without Fear," for example, would probably love your query on "Cheesecake Without the Guilt—or the Fat." If every issue of the men's magazine you long to write for has articles along the lines of "Great Outdoor Gear" and "Mountain-Climbing Must-Haves," your pitch on new gizmos for backpackers might be a winner.

- **Don't ask editors to take chances.** Think of this as the converse of the previous point. While an article on quilting equipment might be a wonderful way for the readers of that men's magazine to get in touch with their feminine side, don't expect the editor of *Macho Outdoorsman* to take a flier on your query. Your erotic fiction might really wake up the religious readers of *Guideposts*, but don't ask the editor to risk her career on you. Editors cringe when they read queries and cover letters that begin, "I know you don't normally run stories like this, but . . ."

Great editors will take risks—but don't expect them to gamble on you or your idea if they've never worked with you. Don't pitch human-interest stories to how-to magazines, or collections of humorous essays to textbook publishers. Yes, those editors may occasionally buy something in that vein, but these ideas aren't what those editors are looking to say "yes" to.

• **Sell yourself.** Give editors an excuse to say "yes" to you. Most editors would love to find another talented, dependable writer with expertise in their subject area. You think the editor of *Modern Moth Farmer* magazine doesn't die a little bit each day he comes to work and has to grapple with the near-impossibility of finding freelancers who know moths *and* the English language? Help him out! Cite your qualifications, clearly and concisely, in your query. Include clips—not just any clips chosen at random, but published samples that prove your ability to handle similar material. (Never published anything about flying insects but have a clip from *Dromedary Life*? That's a better bet than your published poetry or book reviews.)

Don't hide your light under the proverbial bushel. If you're pitching a novel set in the seamy inside world of Hollywood and you worked as a movie-makeup artist for ten years, for heaven's sake mention that credential in your one-sheet. Or consider the author I once met who wanted to write a biography of a leading figure in the Black Panthers of the 1960s. Not until about ten minutes into the conversation, after some serious prodding, did this author happen to mention that he was the prominent Black Panther's attorney for all those years!

Again, this starts with identifying ideas you can do. If you're stretching too far beyond your competency, you'll be able to tell from your strained query—and so will the editor, as she reaches for the rejection slips.

• **Present yourself like a pro.** A prime reason editors say "no" to new writers is the fear that this cure may be worse than the disease of having nothing for the next issue or the next catalog. What if you blow the deadline, write five thousand words when the assignment calls for five hundred, or can't compose anything coherent longer than a query letter? Then the editor has *real* problems: He's counting on you to fill a hole, and instead he gets a black hole.

So do your best to assuage the editor's lurking fear that you may be her worst nightmare instead of her next find. Make your submission package impeccable. Use only black ink on white paper. Opt for the understated in your letterhead and resist the temptation to put "Freelance Writer" under your name. Include clips, but not your entire oeuvre, and make them neat photocopies, not a collage or something that looks like a ransom note. Don't threaten to call "in a few days" just to make sure the editor got your letter.

Should these things matter if you're truly talented and have a great idea? Of course not, but why put obstacles in the way of an editor discovering your genius?

Reading Between the Lines of the Contents Page

Still having trouble thinking like an editor? If your primary target is writing for magazines, let me share two more tricks for getting inside a magazine editor's head—fast.

The first is simple: Study the magazine's table of contents page. With a little practice reading between the lines, you can tell whether the story you're contemplating has a chance to wind up on that contents page someday.

Now, it's true that contents pages don't always get the respect they deserve in the magazine world. Too often the responsibility for writing them gets shuffled off to someone near the bottom of the masthead, an editorial assistant who tackles this assignment in between photocopying chores.

But on the magazines I edited, I usually wrote the contents page myself. The contents page, after all, is a magazine's front doorstep, the place where readers enter into the magazine (or decide they wouldn't feel at home in its pages). At its best, a contents page is the purest representation of a magazine's personality. Good editors use its brief blurbs to "sell" the rest of the magazine to newsstand browsers, as well as subscribers who, if not properly enticed, may lay this issue aside and never pick it up again (and, eventually, never renew their subscriptions). Those blurbs, because they contain the distilled essence of how the editor sees the articles (and how he or she wishes readers to perceive the contents), may even be a more accurate measure of the editor's mind than the articles themselves. After all, if the article didn't turn out quite as the editor hoped, at least the blurb can be perfect!

Even at its banged-out-by-an-editorial-assistant worst, a magazine's contents page represents a snapshot of the publication's soul. Think about what goes into the making of a contents page: Months earlier, an editor or editors begin sifting the stories that wind up listed on the contents page. Some stories are dropped along the way; others are postponed to a future issue, for reasons of balance or space. Many of the articles on that contents page started as an editor's idea, being parceled out to trusted freelancers or staff writers. The rest were ideas that succeeded on exactly the path that you want to take—from query to assignment to acceptance. Each issue's contents page is a snapshot of what works at that particular magazine. Because the contents page represents the issue as a whole, it's the clearest single representation of the editor's mind.

To see what I mean, let's take an actual article from a magazine (I won't tell you which magazine—yet) and try to fit its contents-page teaser into alien contents pages. Suppose this is our story in a nutshell: "Raising Kids in a Wired World: An age-by-age guide to getting the most from surfing the Web." Imagine that this blurb is a summary of a query, and you'll see immediately the importance of targeting your queries and scoping out the contents page before you lick that stamp. All articles are *not* created equal, and those that don't fit stick out in the contents page like a *National Enquirer* in a rack of slick fashion mags.

We'll make this easy—and, I trust, obvious. But keep in mind that editors see stacks of submissions every day that miss the mark as widely as we'll be doing here. A little contents-page scrutiny can make sure yours isn't one of them.

An easy place to start pitching "Raising Kids in a Wired World" ought to be—what else?—computer magazines. But take a look at a couple of contents-page teasers from *PC World:* "Microsoft's next operating system, code-named Longhorn, is still a couple of years away, but a leaked pre-beta version reveals some details," "CD copying crackdown looms; is TIA DOA?" Are you getting the idea that this magazine might be a tad more advanced than the idea we're pitching? For one thing, its readers already own computers. For another, though *PC World* readers might be parents, they're not looking to this magazine for help in their role as savvy child-rearers.

Let's try another approach. With all the talk lately about men becoming more involved parents, a magazine for men might welcome an article aimed at dads. Better yet, men's magazines often cover technology. So how well does our "guide for phobic parents" fit with this typical contents-page blurb from *Esquire?* "The New Phone Sex: It's late. You're all alone. And Victoria Principal is looking really hot on QVC . . ." (Well, at least it's sort of about technology . . .) Okay, maybe not. But let's flip ahead to the departments, where a service piece might be more at home: "The Bald Truth About Hair: How do you stop losing it? How do you make the most of what you've still got?" Like our computer guide, this article promises to be informative and helpful, and the tone of the teaser—like ours—suggests that the editor welcomes writing with a touch of attitude, a breezy style. But again, this is not a match made in heaven, because of why readers (even dad readers) come to *Esquire*. And the contents page is the perfect place to examine this magazine's basic appeal: It's the magazine about "Man at His Best" (not "Father Knows Best"), a mix of hard-hitting journalism, breezy trend stories and service pieces aimed at men qua men. *Esquire* readers are looking to be entertained and to learn something that helps them cope as men in our changing society. All of which leaves out our idea.

What might work for *Esquire* instead? First, ditch the kids. Second, rev up the technology and the macho appeal: "More Power: Hot computers are to the 21st century what hot cars were to the 20th. Read our guide to today's muscle machines and you'll never again have to worry whether your hard drive is big enough."

For our parents-oriented idea, though, we obviously need a magazine that appeals more equally to men and women, perhaps even one a little more earnest, a tad less flip, so it might match our idea's underlying helpfulness. Hey, picking the right computer for your kids is serious business.

How about *The Atlantic*? It appeals to men and women—*older* men and women, more likely to be parents—and it's certainly serious. Here are some items from an *Atlantic* contents page: "The New Downtowns: The author, an architect and a social historian, looks at the past and present of the shopping mall, a widely maligned institution in which he finds more than a little to admire." "Tokyo—Fine, Thank You: The Japanese economy has been repeatedly depicted of late as being deeply troubled. Look again."

Sorry, wrong number! Here the mismatch is partly subject matter (not much about parents and kids here, except perhaps in a sociological or psychological context), partly tone (way more serious!), and partly approach (*The Atlantic* is not a place for service pieces). A story on computers, parents and kids that might make *The Atlantic* would be something like: "Computing in the Classroom Reconsidered: The author, an educational theorist, looks at the effects of the widespread introduction of computer technology on American education, which he finds fails to live up to its promise."

We need a magazine whose formula boils down to "here's help being a better parent"—one where parenthood is at the core of the mission, not on the periphery. Might our idea fit into the magazine with these contents-page lines? "Here Comes the Sun: Protect your child from potentially dangerous rays." "Quiz: What's Your Mothering Style? Are you a 'Sergeant Mom' or an 'Earth Mother?' Find out here." That's *Parenting* magazine, where our sample story—written by Anne Reeks—actually ran.

Just as *Esquire* aims to help its readers be better men, *Parenting* clearly promises to help its (upscale, slightly guilt-ridden) readers be better parents. Just as a parents' guide to Web surfing wouldn't fit any of the other magazines we considered, the contents-page descriptions from those other publications would seem out of place here. "The New Phone Sex" or "The New Downtowns" in *Parenting*? Not a chance.

Cheating by Clicking

The second trick for quickly figuring out what editors might be interested in your ideas—and how to angle your queries to best appeal to them— involves a bit of, well, cheating. And a confession: With my daughter now in her 20s, I don't get *Parenting* magazine any more. So how did I scope out its contents without making a trek to the newsstand or the library? I used its Web site, of course.

Magazines create Web sites for different reasons, none of which have anything to do with making it easier for writers to query them. Many just feel the need to stake their claim in the cyberspace gold rush, and aren't quite sure what to put online besides their latest cover and table of contents. That's fine by us writers, because that's exactly what we're looking for.

Other magazines create whole online editions, duplicating and sometimes extending their print versions. If they want to give away what we'd otherwise have to pay for, so much the better. Best of all are sites that reproduce not only the current issue, but back issues, preferably searchable—a writer's dream come true. Want to see if *Smithsonian* magazine has already run a feature on the history of bicycles before you waste your time and postage on a query? Just search www.smithsonianmag.si.edu, which has linked tables of contents for back issues dating back through 1995. You can also get a sense of what articles the editors are buying and then query with a fresh twist on a proven theme or approach. (If they've done bicycles, maybe next they'll want roller skates . . .)

Still other magazines have transformed themselves into "portals" or other Web-centric critters, leaving barely a trace of their print heritage. They may not even have the same name as their print counterparts, such as www.epicurious.com, which is the online incarnation of *Gourmet* and *Bon Appétit* magazines. You may need to root around through such sites to find anything at all about the original magazines, even just a table of contents. Click on anything that says "Current issue," or follow the links as though you're trying to subscribe.

Whatever the site's approach, you should be looking for the same things. Your needs are very different from those of regular readers, so you'll have to do some clicking around and reading between the pixels. When studying a magazine's Web site, look for:

- **Tables of contents,** current and past.

- **Article archives or indices,** for more ideas about what the magazine is buying and to check for overlaps with your own topic. Thinking about querying *Men's Health* about feet? You can search issues since 1996 at www.menshealth.com. Though you have to pay to read the full text of any hits, no fee is necessary once your search turns up "10 Ways You're Probably Abusing Your Feet." Move on to the next market, the next Web site.

- **Writers' guidelines and contact information.** These may take some digging, and many magazines don't even post their guidelines online. But it's worth checking for an online masthead, an address at minimum, and possibly more goodies hidden under such fine-print links as "Contact us" or "About us."

- **Story ideas.** Take advantage of sites that offer more than just "repurposed" print content and surf these extra goodies for hot topics that might be repurposed right back into print. For example, besides highlights of the current issue, some magazines offer message boards where readers share and sound off: Your next query idea might be lurking in those message boards. Over at www.modernbride.com, you won't find much about the print *Modern Bride* magazine, but if you want to write for it, you might want to sign up for the free e-newsletter.

- **Tone and approach.** Because it's easier to change than a print magazine, a Web site usually reflects the latest thinking and ambitions of the forces behind a magazine. It can give you a glimpse of where the magazine wants to go, even before the print product gets there.

You can find magazines' Web site addresses in their listings in *Writer's Market* and in clickable form on the subscription www.writersmarket.com Web site. Despite the Web-ification of almost everything, the proliferation of Web sites through magazine publishing varies widely. Some of the best-known magazines have little or no Web presence; other, little-known titles have rich, sprawling sites.

The popularity and usefulness (for writers, that is) of magazine Web sites also varies by category. Some print categories that are attractive to freelancers are almost completely missing in action online—such as in-flight magazines, where the point, after all, is to entertain readers on an airplane, not those sitting at home in front of their computers. Women's magazines seem particularly prone to the site-as-portal approach, popping up lots of stuff—even daily—that's only tangential to their print version.

On the opposite end of the spectrum, not surprisingly, are technology titles. Though these, too, favor the portal approach, magazines such as *PC Magazine* and *PC World* reprint their entire contents online (at www.pcmag .com and www.pcworld.com, respectively) and let you search their archives for free. Many science magazines are similarly forthcoming online, even if their subject matter is as unwired as, say, *Archaeology*, which has many articles and a back-issue index at its www.archaeology.org site.

Literary, political, and other highbrow titles often have rich sites as they seek to spread the word beyond their sometimes-smallish circulations. A big-title exemplar is *The Atlantic Monthly*, whose wonderful site at www.thea tlantic.com lets you read much of the magazine online for free, if you can stand the eyestrain. Fiction writers, please note such sites of magazines that also buy fiction can be as useful for you as for nonfiction query-writers in scoping out what kind of stories they typically buy. Got an H.P. Lovecraftish horror tale? Hmmm, not seeing anything like that at the *Atlantic* site . . .

On the flip side, the Web can be a great way to research smaller titles, which may be hard to find at your local newsstand. The same goes for regional magazines. If your newsstand doesn't carry *Arizona Highways* but you have a great idea with an Arizona slant, you can find the current TOC at www.arizonahighways.com.

Should you always try to follow up this preliminary Web research with a gander at the real thing? Sure. Is that always possible or practical? No. So go ahead, take advantage of the Web, the world's largest newsstand.

Looking Forward

You need to know one more thing to start thinking like an editor, to efficiently turn ideas into successful queries: Editors live in the future. In my various incarnations as a magazine editor, for example, I always had a hard time getting into the spirit of the season around Christmas time. Others would get in a frenzy over tinsel and lights, baking (building? forging?) fruitcake and quaffing eggnog until they got scrambled. But I was a Scrooge. No "Bah! Humbug!" intended—it's just that I'd already had my holidays, months ago, at the magazine. Depending on the magazine, I might first ponder Christmas in early summer, when sunburn—not Jack Frost—was nipping at my nose. That's typically when my rolling story lists would roll into the December issue. I'd assign those stories in July, edit them in September, and proofread the galleys as the leaves turned outside my office. By the time that issue finally hit the stands and the rest of the world caught up with my holiday spirit, I would have long ago moved on. If this is December, it must be time to brainstorm summer travel stories . . .

Because of the tyranny of production schedules, color deadlines, press timing, and newsstand cover dates, magazine editors must work in a time warp. To avoid pitching out of season—wasting not only time but perfectly good ideas—you, as a writer, must zap into that time warp. In fact, what you really need is to get a jump even on the fast-forward-thinking of magazine editors: If an editor is assigning stories for the June issue in, say, January, your query on perfect summer picnics needs to arrive in the mail along with the Christmas cards and the complimentary chocolates from the printer. Conversely, your heartwarming short story about the true meaning of Christmas should arrive with summer sunscreen stains on the envelope.

But your challenge goes beyond timing a holiday crafts idea, a spring-prom short story or a fall-colors travel piece. As we've seen, magazines strive to be timely (a magic word in publishing)—so editors look future-ward for ever more of their story ideas. Even if a story is not overtly seasonal, editors still prefer to peg ideas to the calendar—so a baseball idea fits better in April (or October, at World Series time), an education story slides more readily into a September issue, and tales of love and marriage fit better in Valentine-inspired February or matrimony-mad June. Less predictably, editors aim at the moving target of trends: What will be "hot" next fall, or next year?

Ironically, the best strategy for warping into the future starts in the past (which means there's no time like the present to get started). You need to build a solid file of recent-past ideas to draw on about halfway through the calendar cycle. At Christmas time, start clipping articles that have the nugget of a idea you can develop, stories you can rework with a fresh twist, tips, and facts you wish you'd known to make your own holidays brighter or less stressful. What stories happen only this time of year? Think of Salvation Army bell-ringers, schools for Santas, packages in prison. You may need to research some of these stories as they're happening, so you can write them in time for next year. Then, six to eight months *before* Christmas comes around again, haul out your holiday file and start querying. It's a "wait till next year" strategy when "next year" is only a few months away.

But this approach isn't limited to the same old seasonal stories. Other parts of the calendar are just as predictable as Christmas and the Fourth of July. Consult almanacs and history books for anniversaries (those ending in zero or five) of important, offbeat or interesting events that will come up in the next twelve months. Add these to your growing "tickler file." Is next year the anniversary of the invention of Twinkies or the rubber band? Maybe we'll be marking the anniversary of the making of an important movie, the publication of a seminal book or the death of a rock star. Your novel set against the background of the first moon landing in 1969 will be more appealing to publishers in 2009—but that means you'd better pitch it about 2006. Shorter-term, don't forget one-year anniversaries, which offer the opportunity for updates on stories that recently dominated the news.

Editors—good ones, at least—are planning ahead by looking backward and scouting for trends, but (don't forget!) they're only human. An overworked editor can't keep up with everything. Particularly, if you cultivate some areas of semi-expertise, where you know a bit more than the average lay reader, your odds of hitting the time warp an instant before the editor are excellent.

And editors will respond. It's not easy for them to dream of a white Christmas while the rest of the world gets a tan, after all, so they welcome writers who can think ahead, too. Your timely story idea will seem like an unexpected Christmas present to the editor who's feeling future tense.

Who's Who on the Masthead

So you're finally ready to spring your great idea on the magazine world—if only you could figure out whom to send it to. Flip open any leading magazine, find the page of tiny type with all the staff names listed and, being a writer, you'll instantly wonder: Who the heck are all these people on the masthead? And which one do you send your query to?

You don't have to be flogging nonfiction to run smack into masthead madness, either. Whether you're sending short stories to genre magazines like *Analog Science Fiction and Fact* or *Alfred Hitchcock's Mystery Magazine*, or hoping to fill one of the precious fiction slots at a *Redbook* or *Playboy*, the litany of editorial names can give you pause.

Look at *Woman's Day*. It's got an Editor-in-Chief; a Managing Editor; a Senior Editor, Articles, *and* a Senior Editor, Features, *plus* a Features Editor (the difference being . . . ?); an Assistant Editor *and* an Editorial Assistant; and so on. Which, in this zoo of blue-pencil creatures, would be the proper recipient of your query letter? If you send it to the Features Editor when it really should have been addressed to the Senior Editor, Features, will your idea wind up in the trash instead of in a future issue?

But *Woman's Day* is a model of order and simplicity compared to the editorial hierarchy over at *Esquire*. Maybe a magazine for men requires a more complicated pecking order to assuage delicate male editorial egos: Editor-in-Chief, Managing Editor (a woman—so much for that theory), Deputy Editor, Executive Editor, an Articles Editor and a Features Editor, a Literary Editor, a passel of Senior Editors and Associate Editors, Assistant Editors and Editorial Assistants, Contributing Editors and the intriguing "Special Assistant to the Editor-in-Chief" (if anybody can get through to the top guy, it's the Special Assistant to the Editor-in-Chief, right?).

Faced with this profusion and confusion of editorial titledom, the would-be writer might be paralyzed at the very top of a query, unable to get past the address. And by the time you sweat your way through to the envelope— well, maybe you should just forget the whole thing and take up something easy, like brain surgery.

The arcana of magazine mastheads springs partly from the various func-tions necessary to put out a publication every week or every month—and partly from the fact that magazine editors, by and large, don't make a lot of money. Sure, the top editors do all right, and the paychecks even further down the masthead at big, glossy magazines are pretty good. But the average editorial underling can only dream of a bank balance as fat as his cousin the plumber's. Love of the language and—more to the point here—ego motivate magazine editors more than money.

Hence the proliferation of titles. Imagine you're the publisher of a middling, sometimes struggling, magazine. You call one of your Associate Editors into your office for her annual salary chat: "I'm afraid I can only give you a 1 percent raise, Sally," you say quickly, speeding ahead to the good news: "But I'm delighted to be able to promote you to *Senior* Associate Editor."

Sally, thrilled by her meteoric rise in the industry, leaves in a happy haze of ego gratification, momentarily forgetting that her rent is three months late. Next year, if she really applies herself, she might make *Executive* Senior Associate Editor.

The lesson magazine publishers learned long ago is: Titles are cheaper than money. Title inflation and the natural hierarchy of duties have com-bined to create a rough, generally understood pecking order throughout the publishing world:

- The top editor is usually just the Editor (status through simplicity), often the Editor-in-Chief, sometimes the Executive Editor (though this title may also land several rungs lower). If the top editing title is combined with a business-side title, such as Publisher and Editor-in-Chief, you're probably aiming your query too high there—somebody a niche or two down is doing the real work of getting the magazine out.

Sometimes you'll also see an Editorial Director at the summit of the staff list. Magazine groups that publish a number of periodicals may have an Editorial Director who is responsible for the whole magazine line, with individual Editors under the Editorial Director who are assigned to each magazine. It's a rare Editorial Director who reads query letters; better to target your ideas deeper down in the trenches.

At smaller magazines, the Editor-in-Chief or Editor or whoever's at the top of the actual editorial heap may actually be the person who handles "over the transom" manuscripts and queries (also known as the "slush pile"—unsolicited submissions). When I was Editor of *Milwaukee Magazine*, I read all the queries myself. On the other hand, when I was a Senior Editor of *TWA Ambassador* magazine, with an Editor and Managing Editor above me, it wasn't the Editor who read queries—it was me. You can't outguess these situations; if the masthead has a half-dozen names or fewer, go ahead and address your query to the name at the top (excepting again Publisher hybrids and Editorial Directors).

At more amply staffed magazines, keep looking down the masthead . . .

- In a classic publishing hierarchy, the second in command is the Managing Editor (excepting at Time Inc. titles, where this indicates the person in charge). That's almost universally the case at newspapers, as well as at many magazines. But the Managing Editor's role is usually making the trains run on time, more so than making decisions about content. (In some structures, the Executive Editor takes on this "executing" role, like the executive officer on a ship.) Aim your queries either higher or lower than the "M.E." level.

- Larger magazines typically have an Articles Editor or some variation on this title at the third or fourth tier of the masthead. If so, here's your clearest shot for a query. The Articles Editor is the top person responsible for the real work of finding, planning and selecting the main stories for the magazine—in short, the person you'd most like to get to know.

- Similarly, if you're submitting fiction and the magazine has a Literary Editor or (in a rare burst of clarity) a Fiction Editor, target that person rather than whoever is at the top of the masthead. This is the gal or guy that the Editor is counting on to winnow the fictional wheat from the chaff, while the Editor dreams up big cover stories, does lunch and negotiates for a bigger clothing allowance.

- A magazine may have one or more Senior Editors arrayed on one side or the other of the Articles Editor and/or Literary Editor. Unless these Senior Editors are clearly identified as in charge of an area you want to pitch (the Senior Editor/Columns would be the person to query about a new column idea, for example), skip this rung on the ladder. Senior Editor can mean almost anything in magazine masthead-ese. It can even mean the person is a *writer*: At *Milwaukee Magazine,* my Senior Editor was a columnist and star feature writer, and did no actual editing at all. (Of course, at *Ambassador* I was at one point a Senior Editor in full blue-pencil mode, and when I was effectively editor-in-chief of *Horizon* my title was Senior Editor. Go figure. But if you're playing the odds, Senior Editor is still not prime query quarry.)

Here, or at the end of the list, you may also find Contributing Editors. Definitely skip them: These are regular contributors who are rarely even at the magazine's offices. I'm a Contributing Editor to *Writer's Digest*—but the magazine's mail goes to Cincinnati and I'm in New Mexico, so please don't query me!

- Below the Senior level, the established order of things gets clearer, mirroring the academic hierarchy of Associate Professor, then Assistant Professor. So next usually come Associate Editors, then Assistant Editors. An editor at this level is unlikely to wield much clout over the magazine's main features, but may be a valuable contact (and foot in the door) for departments. Some magazines helpfully credit the Associate or Assistant Editor in charge of each standing department, giving you a name to aim your two-hundred- or five-hundred-word idea at. If in doubt, address your query to "Editor—" and the name of the regular department.

These lower-level editors can be crucial to breaking in to a magazine. While a magazine might be reluctant to risk a cover-story assignment on somebody entirely new to its pages, a brief or one-shot column is less of a gamble. Once you're regularly and reliably meeting the magazine's needs with shorter pieces, you become a candidate for greater things.

When I was freelancing regularly for *Travel & Leisure,* for instance, most of my work went to an Associate Editor; he ultimately recommended me for assignments in the main "story well" of the magazine. Similarly, as an Assistant Editor at *Ambassador*, I "discovered" a number of authors who went on to become regular columnists and feature-story writers for us.

- Editorial Assistants dwell at the bottom of the editorial food chain. These may be experienced junior editors with some content duties—or they may be interns or secretaries. (Remember, titles are cheaper than money.) Your query may be bucked down to an Editorial Assistant to handle, but that doesn't mean you should start there.

Picking the right editor for your submission can be a hit-or-miss proposition, even with this knowledge of masthead mysteries. But don't panic: While it's always better to address your idea to an individual—the *right* individual—missing the target isn't fatal. Most magazine staffs have routines for rerouting misaddressed queries, and eventually your envelope will land in the right In basket.

Efficiency aside, though, one reason for making the effort to find the right editor is to create a good first impression—and to avoid making a bad one. Worse than picking the wrong editor is addressing an editor who hasn't worked there for a couple of years. This *faux pas* signals the current staff that you're not studying their magazine closely, the ultimate sin in conscientious querying and submitting. (It's also off-putting: How would you like to keep getting mail for the family that used to live in your house?)

Is it all right to telephone to find the right editor for your idea? Yes—but limit your calls to the receptionist or low-level editor who first picks up the phone. Just ask, "Can you please tell me the name of the editor in charge of the Bits and Briefs section?" or whatever. (And *do* ask for the right spelling.) Don't try to speak to the editor in question to bounce the idea off him or her over the phone or to ask if it's "all right" to send your query. At best you'll get a noncommittal answer; at worst you'll be remembered—but as a pest.

Once you do establish a relationship with an editor at whatever level on the totem pole, by all means cultivate it. An occasional substantive phone call or note in between submissions is all right—but again, err on the side of discretion. If you begin to suspect that the editor is ducking your calls, back off. Don't become a stalker.

Keep in mind that facile, lively writers who meet their deadlines and allotted word counts are hard to find. Every editor on the masthead is looking for you and your ideas—if only you can prove that you're one of that rare breed. What you're striving for, over time, is to turn the tables and reach the point where the right editor on the masthead is calling or writing *you*, pitching assignments. Then the ideas *really* will find you.

Exercises

1. Pick a magazine you'd like to write for and study the contents page without first looking at the coverlines. How would you write five coverlines from that contents page to appeal to potential newsstand buyers?

2. Take one of the stories from the first exercise in the previous chapter and write a query letter pitching it to the editor of the magazine in which it appeared.

3. Study the masthead of the magazine in number two. Which editor would you address your query to?

4. Take the same article and write a query letter pitching it to a *different* magazine, such as one of those listed in exercise one in chapter four.

5. Select one of your story ideas from the fifth or sixth exercise in chapter four, either fiction or nonfiction, and come up with a list of at least five publications it might be targeted to. Find the Web site of each publication and check whether a similar idea has recently been published there.

6. Take the contents page of a favorite magazine and try to rewrite at least five of the titles and blurbs to create new, different (but not *very* different) story ideas for that magazine.

7. Try to write a one-sentence (or one-phrase) mission statement that expresses the essential appeal of the magazine whose contents page you looked at in number six.

8. Who's the publisher of your favorite novelist? Using the publisher's Web site, an online bookseller or *Writer's Market*, find at least five other authors from the same imprint. How are they similar? Try to write a mission statement for that imprint.

CHAPTER 6
STRATEGIES FOR RESEARCH AND INTERVIEWING

Let's face it: Despite the popular notion of the "joy of writing," the truth is that sitting your butt down at the keyboard and grinding out one word after another, one page after the next, can be hard, lonely, even painful work. One of the goals of this book—presumably, one of the reasons you bought it—is to minimize that pain and maximize your results.

On the other hand, the *preparation* for writing can be fun and exciting, or at least mighty addicting for those of us who grew up spending way too much time among the library stacks and who now can't resist clicking on just one more Web page. If your research requires interviewing people, you can get out of the house, and you have an excuse for meeting with colorful, interesting, even famous folks. Or maybe you need to travel before you can write—a trip to Scotland, say, to prepare yourself for that romance novel set in the Highlands, or a junket to Jamaica for your next travel article. (Why do you think people become travel writers, anyway? It's the perks!) There's a certain appeal, too, in hunting down information in the library or ferreting out facts online—almost like being the detective in that mystery novel you'd write if only the research didn't eat up all your time.

Because that's the problem, isn't it? The trap it's all too easy to fall into: You spend so much time getting ready to write that you never get anything written, or at least you never accomplish your writing goals because the research consumes you instead. At some point, research becomes an excuse to keep postponing the hard work of putting words on the page. Or, because you don't have a strategy to guide your preparation, you waste time better spent writing and never get the research you really need.

Worse, many writers over-research and over-interview, gathering too much material—which they then feel compelled to cram into their stories. That nice professor over at the university spent 3 hours with you; surely there's some way to include 30 pages of background on particle physics in your thriller? You've transcribed 1000 pages of interviews; how do you squeeze all that into a 2,500-word article? You read 45 books about bats; where can you show off all you now know within the cramped confines of a short story about a cave explorer? Over-researching and over-interviewing are the roots of the jungle of notes (which must be slogged through, even though only a tiny fraction ever gets used) and the morass of taped interviews (which must be laboriously transcribed—you think—even though only a few key comments will make it into the story) that bog down many writers. Too much information can be paralyzing.

Whether your problem is enjoying the preparation for writing a little too much or the paralysis of gathering a surfeit of "good stuff," the solution is the same: You need a plan. You need a strategy to guide your research and interviewing—and you need it before the first fact weasels its way into your notebook.

Getting the Right Stuff

Your research and interviewing strategy must grow out of your conception of the story: your angle, viewpoint, focus, audience. The strategy for a historical novel set during the Civil War, say, would be different from the strategy for a 2,500-word article on visiting the Manassas battlefield. But the difference is more than just a question of length and ambition. Your plan for a *Travel & Leisure* story on touring Manassas ("Visiting Where the Civil War Began," for example) would differ from the plan for a historical article for *Civil War Illustrated* ("Stonewall Jackson's Manassas Tactics Reconsidered"). The strategy must spring from your unique understanding of whatever story you plan to tell.

But don't get the idea that I'm pooh-poohing the importance of thorough, enterprising research and interviewing. Quite the opposite: As Jim Bishop (*The Day Lincoln Was Shot*) once observed, "Assuming that all authors have a flair for a well-honed phrase, the difference between the winners and the losers is research, the digging of facts." Indeed, it's precisely because good research and savvy interviewing are so crucial that you must target your efforts and not fritter away your preparation time. There are only so many hours in the day (twenty-four, last I counted), and every minute you waste on unnecessary or fruitless research is a minute you aren't getting good material—or honing your prose with actual writing. Over-researching is not good writing; it's busywork masquerading as good writing, or an excuse to postpone sitting down at the keyboard.

Nor am I saying that you can wave some magic wand and make the hard, often time-consuming work of research and interviewing disappear. *Roots* would not have been the same book, for example, if Alex Haley had re-searched the ocean-crossing ordeal of new slaves just by reading about it, or if he'd relied on his imagination. Instead, Haley caught a freighter from Africa to America and spent the nights of the voyage sleeping naked on a plank in the lightless hold of the ship. Only then could he write authentically about how his ancestor must have felt. The art of the possible comes into play here, however, along with the art of writing. If you don't have the time or resources to tackle a project as ambitious as *Roots*, don't get in over your head. Sure, retracing the journey of Marco Polo might make an interesting book, but unless you have a big bankroll and prior experience trekking across Asia, it might not be the book for you. Remember: Write only the stories you can write.

Many notable works of nonfiction are the result of prodigious feats of research. John McPhee's *Travels in Georgia*, which I've already discussed, sprang from traveling 1,100 miles of Southern roads with his field-zoologist subject. For his book on Alaska, *Coming into the Country*, McPhee spent several months at a time over a two-year period touring that state's back-country. To write his Pulitzer Prize-winning *The Soul of a New Machine*, Tracy Kidder spent eight months inside Digital Equipment Corp.

But it's not just nonfiction where research and even interviews are crucial to the success of a writing project; fiction, too, requires an infusion of facts to make credible those parts that you make up. Consider the novels of James Michener (*Hawaii*, *Iberia*, and many more)—rich, complex feats of research that just happen to take the form of fiction. Or Arthur Hailey, whose novels (*Airport*, *Wheels*, *Hotel*, and so on) require months of research before the writing.

Indeed, few works of writing can be simply made up out of whole cloth. Even (especially!) science fiction, which sets its sagas in imaginary worlds, requires research: Just how much of Jupiter *is* ammonia, anyway? It might be good to know before your hero tries to land there.

So, no, the secret to speeding up your research and interviewing isn't simply to eliminate it, or even to do as little as possible. Doing too little advance work can actually slow you down once you start writing: If you don't have all the information you need, you can hit a roadblock far more serious than writer's block. By the time you've gone out and done the research you should have done in the first place, you'll have lost your "flow"—and you may have to trash some of what you've already written, to make it jibe with the newfound facts.

Rather, the secret is developing a research and interviewing strategy that captures all the facts you need—and covers as little extraneous territory as possible. That requires thinking hard about your story right from the initial idea (as we've already started to do), developing efficient ways to record what you'll later use in writing your story (but not oodles of data you'll never need), approaching your research in a way that maximizes results, and preparing for your interviews so you get the most out of the least talking time.

The 80/20 Rule

Once you've focused your idea and are ready to start planning your research and interviewing, you need to follow the rule. Not the rules, plural, but a little-known rule called the Pareto Principle. You may have heard of it as the "80/20" rule. The Pareto Principle is most often invoked in the world of business—"You'll get 80 percent of your revenue from 20 percent of your customers," for example. But it's also a golden rule for your research strategy.

The 80/20 rule is one of the more benign legacies of Italian sociologist and economist Vilfredo Pareto (1848–1923), who was a pioneer in applying mathematics to economic theory. Unfortunately, his subsequent sociological work helped provide the intellectual underpinnings for the rise of fascism. But perhaps the Pareto Principle also applies to the career of its namesake, with 80 percent of the value of his work today coming from just 20 percent of his intellectual output, his economic studies.

So what can Signor Pareto teach you about getting ready to write? First, as you begin scouting for secondary sources to supplement your original findings and to prepare you for interviews, recognize that you'll typically get most of your "good stuff" from just a handful of books and magazine articles. So don't feel that you have to take equal amounts of notes from every source you consult—expect to get 80 percent of your notes from just 20 percent of your reading. And it's important to start winnowing the useful from the not-so-useful at this stage, before useless material even makes it into your notebook (where, later, you might be tempted to use it). Be rigorous and ruthless as you tackle your research.

When I was researching a story about computers and artificial intelligence, for instance, I checked out huge stack of books on the subject. Some of these tomes were pretty technical and intimidating. But I wasn't preparing for a Ph.D. thesis, just boning up for a magazine article. So I knew I'd merely skim the more technical works, hoping to pick out a few useful tidbits. The handful of books and articles I found that were targeted at lay readers, on the other hand, got a thorough going-over and yielded most of my notes. Yes, probably about 80 percent. All sources are not created equal—that's one of the lessons the Pareto Principle holds for writers.

Similarly, all interviews are not equally valuable or equally productive— nor do they have to be. Let's say you're writing a profile. In addition to interviewing the subject of your profile, you'll want to get others' takes. You'll call up friends and enemies, colleagues, and rivals. Maybe you'll track down childhood buddies, a grade school teacher, a college roommate. But all these interviews—at least 80 percent of the people you talk to for your story (say, your subject plus four secondary interviews)—won't produce the bulk of your article. Unless you have an uncooperative profile subject, probably 80 percent of what you write will come from your interview with your main subject. The rest will represent commentary, perspective, and background gleaned from all your other interviews.

Even in a complex, multifaceted story like my piece on artificial intelligence, you're likely to get the most useful material from a couple of quotable experts, with the rest of your interviews relegated to bit-player status. And that's okay—too many equally prominent voices can confuse the reader, who must struggle to keep them all straight. Better to let a few stellar sources take the lead as you tell your story, with the rest chiming in only as needed.

Or suppose you're planning to write a Michael Crichton-style techno-thriller about a man-made plague that escapes the laboratory and threatens civilization. If you're lucky, you might find one cooperative scientist at, say, the Centers for Disease Control, who can give you a feel for what battling epidemics is really like. That interview subject might even become the basis, cleverly fictionalized, for your protagonist. It's unlikely, though, that you'll dig up five or six researchers who will all be equally helpful, and you shouldn't make yourself nuts looking for them. Part of a savvy research strategy is knowing when you've struck gold.

The Pareto Principle is also worth keeping in mind when you're actually doing those interviews. Think about the interviews you've done, and about who did how much of the talking. Did you talk almost as much as your subject? Remember that, as much as you aim for a conversational tone in your interviews, an interview is not a conversation. You're there to ask questions and to listen to the answers—so much of the art of the interview lies in knowing when to shut up.

If your interviews tend to be close to 50/50 conversations, you need to apply the Pareto Principle. That magic 80/20 rule turns out to be a good guideline for how much your subject should talk during an interview versus how much you should chime in. Discipline yourself to keep your side of the interview to only about 20 percent; let your subject do 80 percent of the talking. Rules are made to be broken, of course, and there will be times when you need to talk more simply to coax your subject along. But be careful not to always be the first one to pipe up when there's "dead air": Those slightly uncomfortable silences can pressure an untalkative subject just as they make you want to say something, anything.

From Focus to Strategy

To show how to develop a research and interviewing strategy, and how that planning speeds up your work, let's look at two examples—one, the researching of a "round-up" article and the other, a personality profile. In both cases, I'll use articles I've written—simply because I know the story behind my own stories best. But the same sort of approach, in the case of the round-up, would apply to planning your research for the setting of a novel, for example. Preparing for a personality profile is very much like strategizing any interview-intensive research, especially when your subject can spare you only a little slice of time (that real-life ship captain, say, for the chapter in your novel set on the high seas—but he's setting sail tomorrow).

The round-up article was an assignment for *Express*, a magazine published for Federal Express customers. The nature of the magazine made the roundup a little unusual and quite a bit more difficult: My job was to write fifteen hundred words on the horse-breeding industry—specifically, including how horse breeders and sellers rely on (you guessed it!) FedEx to get their business done. You might encounter a similar situation in tackling fiction: Say you have a chapter—not a whole novel, so you can't spend too much time on this chunk of research—involving a horse race. But you need to zoom in on a highly specific aspect of that subject: How the tote boards work, so your main character can pull off a gambling scam and get the big score he needs for the next chapter.

My particular challenge boiled down to this: A very specific angle, which would guide and channel my research and interviews. A relatively brief word count, which meant I didn't have to learn everything there is to know about the thoroughbred world (but also that I'd have to be highly selective, since whole books have been written on this business). A few not-very-useful (as it turned out) leads on Federal Express customers in the horse trade. And, oh, by the way, a deadline only a couple of weeks away.

I quickly developed a handful of major goals, based on the kind of information I knew I'd have to gather to get the job done fast:

1. Get a quick, general overview of the thoroughbred business.
2. Get some historical background and a feel for why the business is now so fast-paced and high-pressured that it needs Federal Express.
3. Find some specific examples of different ways in which horse breeders and sellers rely on overnight delivery.
4. Get some quotes from actual FedEx customers that I could use to highlight points one, two, *and* three. (I wouldn't have time to waste talking to generic experts for quotes relating to points one and two; my interviews would have to concentrate on actual customers, once I found them, and get the overview material at the same time.)

With that basic strategy in mind, I started at the library with the *Encyclopedia of Associations*. There I found the Thoroughbred Owners and Breeders Association, to which I placed a quick call for help. Without going into a lot of detail, I simply asked for an introductory kit—brochures, back issues of their magazine, photocopies of news stories, or whatever they could send me—that would help give me an overview, as well as leads to potential FedEx customers. At the library, I also found a book, *The Horse Traders* by Steven Crist, that I scanned both for a feel of the business and (as it developed) three pages of specific notes. Sure, I could have checked out a dozen books on horses—but, remember, this was only a 1,500-word article. I didn't need to become an expert or fill a dozen notebooks with information I'd never use. The most important part of my story (don't forget the angle!) wouldn't come from books, but from interviews.

I got another seven pages of notes from the materials sent by the thoroughbred association—including the addresses and phone numbers of the largest horse auction sales companies. I called Fasig-Tipton Co., then the second largest such firm, on the theory that number two might be trying harder, and thus, more eager for publicity. Sure enough, eventually I got a phone interview with a charming senior vice president at Fasig-Tipton, who confessed (to my delight and relief) that the firm was "an extremely heavy user" of Federal Express. Thanks to my planning, I was able to get him to talk quotably on the industry in general, why it was now so fast-paced, and, of course, how the firm uses overnight delivery for its sales catalogues and other key materials.

A few more interviews, following up on leads from Federal Express and on phone numbers from the association, and I was ready to write. In all, I took just twenty-one pages of tightly focused notes. And, yes, I turned in the story in time to make the deadline.

My fast thoroughbred story is an example of how to efficiently cut a specific slice out of a very big pie, how to cover a far-flung and distant subject without traveling except by phone lines, and how to maximize a minimum number of interviews. The approach fit the assignment—that's why it worked. If the task had been instead, say, a five thousand-word travel article celebrating the charms of Kentucky's thoroughbred country, the goals and strategy would have been entirely different. I still might have called the thoroughbred association and read a background book or two, but I would also have had to travel to get a notebook-full of visual details. I might still have interviewed the VP from Fasig-Tipton, but it would have been in the context of a walk-through of his operation.

More broadly, this example also shows some general tactical lessons you can apply to almost any story you undertake, whether you're researching your next novel, a magazine article or anything in between. Here are some key steps to keep in mind:

1. Develop a list of major research goals, a list that flows directly from the specific focus of your story.
2. Break down your goals by likely sources of information. Wherever possible, combine your efforts to get the most out of a single library visit or interview.
3. Cast the widest net with the information sources that require the least effort on your part—like my simple phone call to the association. I didn't waste a lot of time, making their job easier by narrowing my request.
4. As you tap each information source, be prepared. Make sure you get what you came for. *Then* explore whether this source might also be helpful in addressing any of your other research goals,

and whether this source can, in turn, open doors to other efficient information resources.

5. Make your own luck. I called the number-two auction house because I figured they'd be more eager to talk. Lucky me, they also turned out to be a FedEx customer. If I'd gone down the list to number forty-five, however, that firm might have proven too small to do much FedEx business.

Cooking Up a Plan

Another way to think about developing your strategy is that it's like having a quick-and-dirty triage in mind for every aspect of your fact-gathering: If that book at the library were slowly smoldering, what would you need to glean from it before it caught fire and was consumed? If you knew your interview subject would be called away by an emergency in fifteen minutes, what questions would you absolutely need to ask? If you plan for the worst-case scenario, you know you'll be able to get at least the bare minimum you need to start writing. Anything beyond that is just gravy.

A good example of story-preparation at its most pressurized is the celebrity profile. Whether the "celebrity" in question is merely local—your interview with the mayor—or of *People* magazine proportions, you likely have several strikes against you going in:

- Your subject has been written about before, so you need a fresh and clearly focused angle.
- Your subject has been interviewed before, so you'll need to break through his or her tendency to fall back on stock answers.
- Your subject is busy, so you won't have much time.

On the plus side, you should be able to find plenty of secondary material to jump-start and supplement your interview. But a pile of paper research can also be a problem—you have to wade through it, and without clear goals it's easy to get writer's cramp from note-taking before you even meet your quarry. Still, you can use that secondary material to help narrow your focus and compensate for your tight interviewing time. Figure out what your story's going to be about, then plan what questions you *must* ask— because the answers aren't found in previous articles, Web sites or press handouts about your celebrity.

Again, your subject doesn't have to be world-famous, and you don't have to be writing a profile-style article. The key here is interviewing time—you don't have a lot of it—and planning ahead to make the most of it. If the pilot who rescued your biography subject is ninety-five years old and can stay awake for only thirty-minute stretches, you need a strategy before you start talking to him. When the carnival-ride operator you want to chat with (for that scene in your novel where the Ferris wheel goes haywire) can spare you just his fifteen-minute break, you'll want a plan.

In my case, it was celebrity chef Rick Bayless, who I profiled for an in-flight magazine. I was familiar with Bayless' cookbooks and his Frontera line of Mexican-food products, and I longed for an excuse to eat at one of his acclaimed Chicago restaurants.

My first step was to contact his publicist at the restaurants (which I found by "Googling" his name plus "Frontera restaurant"), get a press kit, and start the wheels turning to try to schedule an interview. The biographical information in the press kit would be vital to my strategy: I wouldn't have to waste a lot of precious interview time getting the basics of his career.

Next, I hit the Web for more articles and background. A little Web surfing revealed that Bayless was about to premiere a second season of his public-television series. This gave me a timeliness factor and one line of possible questions. It also led me to get his book based on the series' first season. As I read his introduction to the book and more articles, a focus for my own piece began to develop: This guy wasn't just the Emeril of Mexican food; he cared more about the food than the fame. Here's how that theme ultimately found expression in the article's head and subhead:

Beyond the Taco

Rick Bayless—Chicago chef, cookbook author, Frontera food entrepreneur and now TV host—is on a mission to spread authentic Mexican cuisine north of the border.

I began to plan my questions to concentrate on Bayless' passion for real Mexican cooking:

- How did he become so fascinated by food?
- Why have Americans been so slow to embrace Mexican fare "beyond the taco"?
- How does he see himself and his "mission"?

This planning became more urgent when my actual interview got scheduled: I'd have less than an hour, and it would have to be over the phone; by the time I could get to Chicago, Bayless planned to be in Mexico, shooting television episodes.

Readers would want some background on Bayless to put the answers to my questions in context, of course, as well as details on his restaurants, cookbooks, and television shows. So I made those points the target of my secondary research, which in turn helped determine where I'd look. I already had a good deal of biographical info, but as I came across other articles about him, I made sure to note anything new about Bayless' life and career—things I probably wouldn't have time to ask him. I hunted up restaurant reviews, not so much for the reviewer's opinion, but for specifics about the restaurants' menu and ambiance. I got all of Bayless' cookbooks. His publicist sent me three tapes of his television shows, which our local PBS station hadn't aired.

When the time came for my phone interview, I was able to lead the conversation in exactly the direction I needed to supply what I didn't already have. It's not just a matter of preparing your questions; you also need to know what answers to follow up on. I don't tape-record most interviews (if I did, I'd spend a lot of time transcribing when I'd rather be writing), so it's also important to have a notion in advance of what to write down and what to let slide as unlikely to wind up in my article anyway. (This also speeds up the writing and keeps you out of the too-many-notes morass: If you didn't write it down in the first place, you don't have to agonize later about leaving it out of your story!)

Remember the key points I knew I'd have to cover? I got on-the-money quotes about starting to work in his parents' restaurant before he was ten, and about how Americans' love for melted cheese on tacos and such has kept us from graduating to the "crunch, variety of textures, and brighter flavors" of authentic Mexican food. I zeroed in on his "mission" and whether he sees himself as the next Emeril, which became this section of the actual article:

> "That would mean I'd have to co-opt my mission. Look at Emeril—he started off doing Cajun food; he hardly ever does Cajun food any more.

> "I look at TV only as a medium to achieve my mission, which is to share things with American viewers about Mexico and about food that will enrich their lives," Bayless goes on. "I have a very clear notion of my mission—that's what the restaurant is about, what my writing is about. TV lets me reach a much broader audience."

The completed story ran twenty-five hundred words; my entire interview notes totaled just over one thousand words. But they were the *right* words— precisely targeted to fill in the blanks from what I could gather with other research. Without a strategy, I might have wasted a lot of secondary research on topics that never had a chance of making my article; worse, I might have skipped some of the details I did need, such as information about his restaurants. Lacking a plan, I could have spent the first twenty minutes of my interview asking biographical facts I could get on paper—and then had just ten minutes for the "good stuff" that would bring those dry facts to life.

I did finally get to eat at one of Bayless' restaurants, by the way, and thanks to a schedule change the chef himself was there after all. He came over to our table and chatted for a moment. That lucky break gave me my opening paragraphs:

> Rick Bayless isn't even supposed to be here. He's supposed to be in Mexico, filming another 13 episodes for his PBS television series, "Mexico One Plate at a Time," the second season of which airs this fall. He's just back home in Chicago for the weekend, really. But he can't help himself.
>
> So here he is, gliding almost unnoticed—if not for his white chef's jacket—between the gilded formality of Topolobampo, his fine-dining restaurant, and the south-of-the-border bustle of his famed Frontera Grill, next door. Caught, recognized from his TV appearances—not only on his own series but on the "Today Show," "Good Morning America" and the like—and his shyly smiling book-jacket photos on four award-winning cookbooks, Bayless stops to say hello.
>
> At 48, he's still boyishly handsome. Round glasses frame Gulf of Mexico-blue eyes above a fuzzy suggestion of beard and moustache. He wears his fame a bit uncomfortably. But get him talking about Mexican food—the real thing, not the cheesy pretenders Americans have been hawked by talking Chihuahuas on TV—and his voice tightens with excitement like a teenager on a big date.

Could I have written the story without that serendipity? No doubt about it. Though I wove a wealth of background about Bayless into the context of a little scene, only the bit about him "gliding almost unnoticed" and stopping to say hello actually depended on our lucky visit to the restaurant.

The television series information came from the Web and his publicist; the list of morning shows and the cookbook count, from his bio; ditto his age; the description relied more on his book-jacket picture and publicity photo than from meeting him in person. His enthusiasm for Mexican food, of course, came from our phone interview.

So, sure, sometimes you get lucky. But it's best not to bet on luck—plan your research and interviewing to get what you need in a worst-case scenario. Anything else will be a bonus, for you and your readers.

What other lessons can you draw from my "Beyond the Taco" experience for your own projects? Here are four that occur to me:

1. Don't be afraid to get material the easy way, from secondary sources and PR people. Never plagiarize, but don't go out of your way to reinvent the wheel: Facts are facts, wherever and however you find them. If you're researching for fiction, attribution of sources is less of an issue, so you can take information wherever you find it—don't be shy!
2. Prioritize. Get the most important answers early on. If you're interviewing an ex-WWII submarine commander at a nursing home for your military novel and your key question is "What did it feel like inside that sub?," don't wait until he starts to nod off to ask it.
3. Choreograph your interviews in advance, not only to ask the right questions, but to know when to follow up.
4. If you get lucky, don't be shy about taking advantage of it.

And, of course, fit the strategy to the story. From the racetrack to the restaurant kitchen, the basics of efficient research and interviewing are the same: Get your angle. Develop a strategy that flows from your angle. Focus your efforts on achieving your strategic goals.

Finding Instant Experts

What if the source you need for your story isn't as ready-made as a corporate honcho or celebrity? If you're tackling an article about the new gizmos put out by Gizmatic Corp., finding someone to interview is pretty straightforward: You call the PR or marketing department at Gizmatic Corp., and they hook you up. But if you're writing a think piece about the impact of technology on society, the designated talking head at Gizmatic might not be your best bet. For that sort of article—or, say, background for your science-fiction novel—you need an Expert.

We live in the Era of Experts. From talking-head television shows to your next writing assignment, experts are the meat and potatoes of the information feast that daily fills our heads. You may have a notebook full of facts and your own opinions about a topic, but most editors want somebody else besides you—no offense—to say the things in your story. Editors and readers alike want experts.

The right expert can also speed up your writing and save you a lot of wasted motion in your research plan. Pretty much by definition, an expert on a subject is somebody who has spent years learning about it. By asking an expert, you're tapping those years of knowledge in just a few minutes. If your questions are planned and pointed enough, you can quickly extract what an expert thinks are the most important things you (and your readers) need to know about his or her field. Think of an expert as a very smart, very flexible computer database; you can't get information any faster than through a good interview.

Experts also add credibility to your writing. When you make an assertion or even when you state facts and figures, you're just some writer. But when an expert—with credentials—says the same thing, readers sense the voice of authority. Of course, the expert has to match the subject matter: A mycologist (someone who studies mushrooms) would add weight to an article on morels, but won't lend much credibility to a story about spaceflight.

Seasoning your writing with experts also has a halo effect: Because you clearly consulted experts who know what they're talking about, readers give you more credit for knowing what *you're* talking about. After all, you talked to the experts! Even in paragraphs that don't cite an expert source, your writing has an aura of credibility. Presumably, those statements not attributed to an expert represent your synthesis of information from the vast array of experts you consulted. And why do you think novelists like Greg Iles, author of *Spandau Phoenix*, list a bevy of experts in the acknowledgments in the back of their books? It's partly to say thanks, of course, but also to let readers know that the author knows what he's talking about.

Of course, credibility is more than mere appearances: Your writing really *will* be better informed if you've consulted a range of experts, rather than relying just on your own brainpower. Iles' novel *Dead Sleep*, for example, which deals heavily with the FBI, wouldn't have the same aura of verisimilitude if he hadn't consulted four real-life agents in two different locales.

Your writing will also be more readable, in part because of another asset experts add: the human factor. If readers wanted just the facts, they'd curl up in an easy chair with the *Statistical Abstract of the United States*. No, you need living, breathing experts to make your copy readable, to bring your story to life, to add flesh and blood to the bare bones of facts and figures. Particularly in direct quotation, experts enliven stories with personality, colorful turns of phrase, controversial statements, humor, drama, and deeply felt emotions. You need experts in your writing for the same reason television talk shows need their "talking heads": Imagine "The McLaughlin Group" with dueling graphs instead of hotheaded political junkies, or Ted Koppel reading from *The Congressional Record* rather than grilling live congressmen. Experts add an essential element of humanity to any story. Experts are like the difference between calling up somebody and reading the phonebook.

But calling them up is exactly the trouble with experts—you have to track them down. And you can't just call anybody (otherwise your mom would make an easy, all-purpose source); you have to find somebody who knows about the subject you're writing on. You've decided to make the murder "weapon" in your mystery novel a poisonous mushroom—but where the heck do you find a mycologist when you really need one? An editor calls with an assignment on a topic that's just popped into her head—where do you start in the search for experts to deliver a story that's well researched, credible, and lively?

That was the problem I faced some time back when a computer-magazine editor (who I knew quite well) asked me to write that article on artificial intelligence (which I knew about only slightly). My list of experts in the "AI" field was as blank as a powered-down computer screen. Where to begin? It wasn't as though I could look under "E" for "expert," or even "A" for "artificial intelligence" in the Yellow Pages, or just pick up the phone and call Dial-an-Expert.

Not exactly, but those approaches are not so far off, if you know how to get the expert engine rolling.

For starters, look in your own notes. In tackling the AI story, I took more than thirty pages of notes from books, magazines, and newspapers before I even began my quest for experts. In those thirty pages was the name of the head of a major university computer center that happened to be in my own backyard; he became my first expert. As you take notes from secondary sources, keep your radar tuned for names of experts and leads to other names. Feel free to "cannibalize" the experts quoted in these articles: It's not plagiarism, since of course you'll do your own interviews and put your own spin on the story. And it's only reasonable to assume that if these experts were willing and quotable once, they're likely to do it again.

Other potential experts may not actually be quoted in your preliminary research. Look for recent historical references, citations of figures important in the field, people mentioned in anecdotes, even authors of books and articles listed in footnotes or sidebars. Don't neglect the authors of the material you're taking notes from as possible experts themselves, particularly if the source material is more technical or written for a less popular audience than the piece you plan. The author of that nonfiction book would probably be thrilled to be a source for your novel.

Keep your eyes open, too, for institutions, companies, or other organizations that may be sources of expertise on your topic. Armed with this kernel of data, you can look up the organization, "Google" it at www.google.com, call directory assistance (make sure to note the organization's location, if it's mentioned, so you can track it down with 1 + the area code + 555-1212), or use one of the many online phonebook sites, such as www.switchbo ard.com. Then you can call and ask for someone in public relations (or "public information" in some governmental or nonprofit organizations; try "marketing" if "public relations" draws a blank at a smaller company). This person can then lead you to a real live expert.

That's the strategy I followed for another artificial-intelligence source: I'd gleaned from my research the name of a company engaged in AI. I called the company in California and let myself get passed around from one desk to another until I found a senior scientist who was both highly qualified and willing to talk with me. I didn't know his name when I started, but I had a name—a corporate name—and that was all it took.

On a topic like artificial intelligence, however complex, at least I had a wealth of previously printed material to serve as a launchpad. What if your subject is new or esoteric, and not much has been written about it? If you're plotting a science-fiction novel, for example, you may be tackling a field so far out on the leading edge that it has no obvious leaders.

No matter how esoteric the subject, there's probably an association relating to it. As soon as you get more than two people doing or thinking about something, it seems, they'll get a logo, a newsletter, and an official organization. Try looking up your topic in *The Encyclopedia of Associations* (Gale Research), found in any major library. Google, again, is another valuable resource for tracking down even the most obscure organizations. Call or write to the associations you find listed; chances are good that they have a spokesperson or can send you a copy of their newsletter (or it may be online), which will contain a wealth of leads.

Another trove of esoteric experts is the university system, which harbors experts on almost every subject imaginable and some you'd never imagine. Peterson's guides to colleges and universities are a quick way to find schools with the right academic departments, from Islamic Studies (Hampshire College or the University of Michigan, for example) to sports medicine (Boston University, Indiana State). Most schools have their own Web sites now, too; you can try your favorite search engine or take a stab with www.(schoolname).edu.

University public-relations staff are eager to place their experts in print—think of them as your paid expert-arrangers (they won't mind, honest!). You should try to build a relationship with the PR folks at the colleges and universities in your area, including sending them copies of stories in which you've cited their faculty, so they'll know you're for real. Be sure to get a copy of area schools' media guides—handy, free brochures listing faculty experts by topic.

Wrangle media guides from any major university with specialists in areas you frequently cover. With the phone, fax, and computer, geography doesn't need to be a barrier. In fact, you can tap a database of experts from universities around the country via ProfNet, now part of the PR NewsWire service, online at www.profnet.com.

You can also buy books listing experts, such as *The Yearbook of Experts, Authorities & Spokespersons* (Broadcast Interview Source), which also has a Web presence at www.expertclick.com. While these experts may be more interested in pushing themselves than in answering your questions, they can at least give your quest a jump-start.

Once you find one expert, after all, you can tap that person for other names. A leading mycologist is likely to be an expert not only on mushrooms, but on who's who in mushroom research. I always make one of my last interview questions some variation on, "Can you suggest anyone else that I ought to talk to about this subject?" On the artificial-intelligence story, for instance, my university expert gave me the name and even the phone number of a leading corporate researcher across town. Tap their expertise—and then tap their Rolodexes!

Your Most Important Tools

Now you've got a strategy, you've hunted down eager experts, and you're ready to charge, armed to the teeth with . . . a pen and a notebook? Yes, even in these days of high-tech weaponry, the writer's most effective research and interviewing tools remain the humble pen and low-tech notebook. But bear with me: It's not as simple as it sounds. There are tricks to efficient note taking, tricks only slightly less sophisticated than a guided missile or a $600 toilet seat.

Early in my career as a writer, I learned the hard way (notebooks scattered all over the room, and is that quote I want in the notebook on the chair or in the pile of photocopies atop the aquarium?) to take all the notes for one story in a single notebook, clearly labeled on the front. If your fact gathering requires more pages, only then should you go to a second volume ("Rick Bayless Profile B"). Number the pages consecutively, from one, to whatever it takes.

Your notebook isn't just for notes from interviews. Take the time to copy the salient points from any secondary sources into your notebook, rather than relying on marked-up photocopies or dog-ears in books. Not only does this save you from an unsightly and unworkable sprawl of information once you sit down to write, it actually aids the writing process in two ways. First, it forces you to begin distilling the data for your story; you will always have more facts than you can fit in. Second, taking notes from secondary sources places that selected information more firmly in your mind, where your subconscious can begin shaping it into original prose. Later, when you need a piece to fit the puzzle of your unfolding story, it will be in the back of your mind, as well as in your notebook, ready to pop into place. A photocopier, by contrast, copies information only to another dead piece of paper, not into the lively confines of your creative brain.

Copying material into your notebook not only helps you remember the salient facts, but also why this information is important to your story. If you must copy it down, rather than simply slapping a book or article on the photocopier, you're forced to think about the reasons these facts are useful—how these notes advance the angle of your story. It might sound as though taking the time to copy research notes into your notebook is a waste of time, especially when high-tech alternatives like the photocopier are available. But, in fact, the time you invest at this stage will save far more time later, deeper in the writing process, when you must bring order out of a chaotic mass of information. That is the very heart of writing, and the sooner you begin this work, the better.

Whether copying from the printed page or taking notes from interviews, you will, however, need a way of writing quickly. Some writers learn short-hand for this purpose; others develop their own personal shorthand of codes and abbreviations for common words. My notes would be undecipherable to anyone else—and not just from my legacy of years of "U" for "Unsatisfactory" grade-school penmanship. I write "w/" for "with" and "&" for "and," of course, but other codes are quirkier: "cp" means "computer" and "x" (as in 4×9=36) stands for "time." You'll develop your own system as you go along.

You can create other codes for an individual story, never to be used that way again. In the notebook for my horse-breeding story, for example, "thb" is short for "thoroughbred" and "h" means "horse"—though in a story about, say, a stage magician it might stand for "hypnosis." When profiling someone, it's surely not necessary to write the subject's full name every time it occurs in your notes: "Rick Bayless" could be just "RB" or "B." The same holds for a corporation—"M" for "Microsoft" or "E" for "Enron."

Here are some actual examples from my horse-breeding story notebook, with translations:

> *"ltd prtnerships—own pt int in sevl h rather than full in 1"*
>
> ("Limited partnerships means owning a part interest in several horses rather than a full interest in a single horse.")

> *"Gen Risk—1 of fw Ky Derby filly winners"*
>
> ("Genuine Risk was one of the few Kentucky Derby filly winners")

> *"most dram grwth as res of entr of Arab byers fr Gulf States fnnl huge amts cash 2 biz now most signif thb owners"*
>
> ("The most dramatic growth came as a result of the entry of Arab buyers from the Gulf States, who funneled huge amounts of cash into the business. They are now the most significant thoroughbred owners.")

You get the idea. An important point to note, however, is that I *can* still decipher my notes (though, given the scrawl of my handwriting, probably no one else could). The speediest shorthand system in the world won't help you if you get home and can't read what you wrote.

We'll talk more about note taking in a later chapter as it applies in particular to interviews. But first we'd better consider the steps for gathering notes in the first place: How do you start filling up that notebook?

Exercises

1. Select a magazine you'd like to write for and analyze one of the articles. Highlight, with a marker or colored pen, those portions of the article that carry information or quotes attributed to someone. Make a list of the people quoted and write alongside each how you think the source was located.

2. "Fact-check" an article from your favorite magazine or a chapter from a book, as though you were a researcher double-checking the information before publication. For those facts you can't confirm from public sources, write down what you'd need to do (e.g. telephone an interview subject) to check these facts.

3. Using a media guide or information on the university's Web site, make a list of at least five experts from your nearest college or university's faculty who might be used as primary sources for a story.

4. For each of the experts in number three, list at least one story idea (such as an article, or a fictional piece drawing on the person's area of expertise) that could be developed after interviewing this expert.

5. Using the sources and starting points in this chapter, identify at least one expert you could contact for information to help you write each of these stories:

    a. a mystery novel in which the victim is poisoned by the chemicals found in art supplies
    b. an article about the possibility of life on other planets
    c. an article offering coping advice to the recently widowed
    d. a romance novel set in 18th-century Scotland
    e. a book for grandmothers who are raising their grandchildren
    f. a science-fiction story about time travel via black holes
    g. an article debunking astrology
    h. one of your own current writing projects

CHAPTER 7

SPEEDY RESEARCH, THE OLD-FASHIONED WAY

Few parts of the writing process can be more time-consuming than research—gathering the raw material, from disparate and unpredictable sources, that goes into making a rich and credible story. For example, spy novelist Alan Furst, whose stories are set in Europe between 1933 and 1945, pores over books by journalists from that period, personal memoirs, autobiographies, novels written during those years, and political, intelligence, and military histories to get both details and the flavor of the times. He also buys old books and maps. Furst adds, "I once bought, while living in Paris, the photo archive of a French stock house that served the newspapers of Paris during the Occupation, all the prints marked as cleared by German censorship."

Short of moving to Paris or wherever you're writing about, how can you find the time and resources to get the facts and "color" you need to make your own writing come to life? These days, of course, the Internet can help you research across the globe without leaving your desk—more about that in the next chapter. But, as amazing as the Internet has become, it still doesn't have everything you need. Sometimes, like Furst, you'll have to rely on "old-fashioned" resources, such as books, periodicals, journals, and libraries.

To make the most of such traditional sources in a minimum amount of time, you need to develop what I call "research radar." The writer's lot, you see, is that you're never really "off duty"—you're always researching. That's the bad news. The good news, though, is that by constantly keeping your research radar on, you can find the information you need—and facts you didn't even know you needed—in the most efficient way, without having to bury yourself in the library for long stretches at a time. It's as though you have a radarscope in the back of your brain that blips whenever you come across something that might help in your research quest. It's not that you're constantly fretting about your research needs; when something on your targeted topic appears, however, you pounce.

This research radar works—better, in fact—even if you have more than one writing project in progress at a time. Say you have an assignment for a piece on special products for left-handers, a science-fiction short story in the works that involves radio astronomy, and a tentative idea on the boom in superhero movies. Idly flipping through a magazine, ostensibly relaxing, you might spot an ad for a lefties' mail-order house, the name of a scientist at the Very Large Array radio telescope who's made some discovery way out there, and a celebrity update mentioning some star who's just signed to do *Superman Marries Wonder Woman.* Grab some scissors and start clipping.

Setting Your Brain to "Scan"

Let's look at some of the ways your research radar might sweep in information while you're doing something else. The daily newspaper is an obvious place to start. At various times, I've subscribed to as many as five daily newspapers: two competing local papers, *USA Today*, *The New York Times'* national edition, and the *Wall Street Journal*. Now, I could hardly read every word in four or five newspapers and get any writing done, much less have time to fritter away eating or sleeping. But I am a highly efficient scanner. That's one of the great things about newspapers: They're built for scanning, with those helpful tags called "headlines" to facilitate decisions about whether articles merit your further attention.

Scanning is ideal for the writer's research-radar mode. Just as you might stop and study a story on your favorite team or a *USA Today* item about your old home town, you need to train yourself to pause when your scanning hits a topic you're researching. It's like programming a mental alarm: If you're researching an article on unusual pets, bells should sound when your retinas reach an item on Vanna White's pet snapping turtle.

Recently, for example, I had three assignments in progress: a couple on online subjects, plus a travel piece tied to shopping destinations. From a week's newspapers I might clip:

- a news brief about a competitor of the online database I'm reviewing
- mentions of several Internet sites (one from *Advertising Age*, for example), relevant to my other online piece, about marketing resources online
- one of *USA Today*'s ubiquitous charts with a statistic for my travel and

shopping article ("We're taking our families along on trips more often . . .")

- a real prize—a whole article about an unusual store that's become a tourist destination in itself.

Or I might, in other weeks, find nothing. But either way, I won't miss much that's of potential relevance to my research.

The bits and pieces—single facts, statistics, solo examples—are more common than whole articles that exactly match what I'm researching. That's why my scanning has to be finely tuned, to go beyond the obvious and see connections to my current work in the pile of newspapers. For my online marketing research, I scanned not just for stories strictly about "marketing information online," but for anything about marketing, anything about online or the Internet, even anything more broadly about business, innovation, and information technology. If an article got caught in that wide net of possibilities, I'd scan it more closely to see if there were some useful nugget buried within.

Other parts of the newspaper are simply regular stops, because they touch on topics I frequently write about. So *USA Today*'s Home Tech page routinely gets scissored, for example, as does the Science Times section inside the Tuesday *New York Times*. Once you learn a newspaper's "architecture," you'll be able to zip to those pages that most often make fodder for your scissors.

But it's not just reading the daily paper that can turn into research "work." Magazines, of course, are equally full of facts and leads. I typically read—well, scan—both *Newsweek* and *Time* magazines, plus *Entertainment Weekly*, for the same broad range of research prospects I get in newspapers. The "front-of-the-book" briefs sections in all the weeklies make good clipping for trends that you might be tracking or statistics to support a point you're making.

Specialty magazines are more likely to have whole articles of use to your research, so you should keep up with any niche publications in your own areas of specialization. If you've decided your novel's detective will be an archaeologist, for example, start subscribing to *Archaeology* magazine. A few issues of *Sky & Telescope* might help that science-fiction saga. If you don't want to clip these magazines because you want to keep them, mark the pages with Tape Flags instead. These little tabs, clear on one half and brightly colored on the other, work like baby Post-It Notes—and you can write on them to remind yourself why you flagged this particular page.

Don't forget to scan the ads, too, particularly in specialty magazines. Magazine ads can help you research new and unusual products, find companies (and hence sources) in your topic area, and snare phone numbers and addresses. The ads in a travel magazine might have more specifics on a destination you're researching than any of the articles; ads in computer magazines often tell about new products before the stories do.

Even watching television can be "work" for a writer—though this one's even harder to explain to your spouse than lounging around reading a magazine. ("Honest, honey, I'm only watching 'Baywatch' reruns to research that article about lifesaving techniques . . .")

The other challenge is capturing research nuggets as they zip past on the tube. You can't just "clip" something from television. Even if you had your VCR primed at all times, you rarely realize a television bite might be useful until after it's almost over. So, compulsive as this may sound, I try to keep a little pad and pen next to my TV-watching chair. It's hard to capture more than a lone fact, name or notion from television, even if you are prepared. So I don't depend on television for in-depth research, just leads to learn more—the name of an innovative company in a field I'm following, a locale that might fit a travel roundup. From there, I head for more standard references to develop the details. If not for that television tidbit, however, I'd never have known to look in the first place.

Radio can work the same way, especially if you're a National Public Radio fan like me. If you do most of your radio listening in the car, though, you may find it even tougher to take notes—at least without endangering other drivers while you scribble instead of watching the road. Fortunately, NPR archives most of its content on its Web site (www.npr.org), so you can listen to that useful piece again once you get home.

Hitting the Books at the Library

At some point, of course, your research mission will begin to require your full attention, to fill in the gaps from your "radar" work. The fastest way to do this kind of "old-fashioned" research is to rely on your own collection of reference books. If you have to run to the library every time you need a smidgeon of information, you'll put more mileage on your car than on your keyboard. Every writer needs a basic reference library, the contents of which will vary according to your areas of specialization and interest. In addition to almanacs, a dictionary, encyclopedias, a thesaurus, *Bartlett's Familiar Quotations*, and other general works, my shelves include specialized books on computers, movies, travel, and other topics that I've often covered. The point here isn't to prescribe particular books for your home library—we'll mention some specific titles later—but to suggest that fast fact gathering begins at home.

For most stories, however, you'll eventually need to go to a library. Note that I said "*a* library," not "*the* library"—for indeed, there are many different kinds of libraries to choose from. In most large cities, you'll find neighborhood public libraries, a main public library, a college or university library, and often various specialty libraries. It's important for your research efficiency that you pick the right library for your story's needs.

Among public libraries, your neighborhood branch is clearly the best bet if you just need a simple fact or two, readily found in basic reference works. But generally, you should head straight for the main branch, where you'll find a full line of reference books, periodicals, and the databases and indexes needed to tap them quickly.

For anything technical, or if your local public library isn't large, you may want to go right to the nearest college or university library. Call ahead: Most will let you use their reference collection and periodicals even if you're not a student or faculty member; a few academic libraries have special arrangements under which the public can even check out books (sometimes you have to be a donor to the school, which is a tax-deductible investment worth considering). Large universities typically boast specialized libraries—in art, business, engineering, law, or other areas of emphasis—in addition to their main collection; don't overlook these. The Association of College and Research Libraries of the American Library Association, 50 East Huron Street, Chicago, Illinois 60611, telephone (800) 545-2433, ext. 2523, www.ala.org/acrl/, can help you identify academic libraries near you that specialize in your subject.

The next step would be to try one of the wide variety of specialty libraries dedicated to almost every subject. These include historical societies, museum libraries, newspaper libraries (call ahead, as public access is usually limited), and even corporate libraries (where you may have to explain your purpose to the librarian in order to wheedle your way in). The Special Libraries Association, 1700 Eighteenth Street, Northwest, Washington, DC 20009, telephone (202) 234-4700, www.sla.org, is a good place to start tracking down these resources.

Another useful guide to libraries, which can probably be found in your own public library, is the *American Library Directory*, which catalogs more than 30,000 U.S. and Canadian libraries. Online, you can try LibDex (www.li

bdex.com), an easy-to-use index to 18,000 libraries worldwide, library homepages, and Web-based library catalogs. Be sure to consult the library's online catalog before you go, to make sure it actually has what you need and to find related resources you didn't know existed.

Once you find the right library, it's important to use it right. You should cultivate a good relationship with the librarians, particularly the reference librarians. But don't expect them to read your mind—you have to learn to ask the right questions to elicit the answers you need. For example, suppose you're trying to track down the Thoroughbred Owners and Breeders Association. You might ask, "Do you have a phone book for Lexington, Kentucky?" Unless your library has an unusually good phone book collection, however, the answer will probably be *no*—and then you'll be at a dead end. But if you focus your question more exactly—"I need to find the address of the Thoroughbred Owners and Breeders Association"—the librarian could turn to a general reference such as *The Encyclopedia of Associations* and come up with an answer. (For single-shot questions like this, don't forget your library's "Ready Reference" telephone line, if it has one. Why trek down there if a phone call can get the answer for you?)

In general, though librarians can be immensely helpful in pointing you in the right direction, answering ready-reference-type queries, or cracking tough research nuts, it's fastest to do most of your research yourself. You know exactly what you're looking for, what angle the information must plug into. By doing it yourself, you'll avoid getting too much information or having to sort through lots of stuff that's not quite right. Again, here's a case where spending some time up front saves time in the long run.

But don't wade right into the stacks and start grabbing anything that looks useful. By tackling the available research materials roughly in order of increasing complexity and specialization, you'll be able to learn about your subject in such a way that each new bit of knowledge builds upon what came before; you won't stumble over unfamiliar concepts apart from a context in which they can be made useful to you. Every project will be different, but here's a rough outline of the order in which you might tap various resources:

1. Encyclopedias, almanacs, and other general reference works for a lay audience
2. Periodicals for a general audience
3. General-interest books about the particular field

4. Specialized reference books
5. Specialized periodicals
6. Technical books in the field.

For example, research for your thriller with a mathematician hero (and good luck with selling that one!) might start by reading the encyclopedia entries under "Mathematics" for an overall survey of the subject. Next, you might get a snapshot of current concerns in the field from magazine articles. Then you could check out a couple of books about mathematics written for laypersons, such as *Innumeracy* or *Journey Through Genius*. That might be enough, and if so, you should certainly quit right there—don't over-research. If not, however, only then (once you'll understand something of what you read) should you go on to mathematics-specific reference books, scholarly journals, and books written for mathematicians.

Even within this rough order, you should try to tap similar, potentially overlapping resources in succession. Read all the articles you find on teaching mathematics one after another, for instance, before moving on to the articles about business and industrial applications of math. That way, the material will be fresh in your mind and you'll be less likely to waste time writing down duplicate information. You'll also be more likely to gain a quick, coherent understanding of a sub-topic—and to be able to gauge whether or not you need to go a level deeper in your research.

As you take notes, be sure to write down your sources and what library you found them in. After all, you know what they say about even the best-laid plans: You might have to make a second trip to the stacks, so leave the equivalent of a trail of breadcrumbs.

Mastering the Catalog

So far, we've mostly stuck to the books in the library with an "R" for "reference" on their spines. For many research projects, that's as deep as you'll need to go into the shelves. Sometimes, though, the fastest way to get the facts you need is to wade into the library catalog—again, don't forget that you can do most of this catalog exploration online at home—and check out a (small) pile of books on your subject. For example, my horse-breeding story required an overview of the subject, rather than just a collection of specific facts. The specifics I would get from my interviews; what I needed was the broad familiarity, the sense of trends and historical background that could only be gotten from in-depth reading.

That's a good rule of thumb, in fact, for judging whether to concentrate on reference books, or regular books: If you need facts, go to the reference shelf. If you need a feel for a subject (in addition, of course, to whatever specific facts might wind up in your notebook), head for the library catalog.

Suppose that you're working on a historical blockbuster set in Mozart's Vienna. To find the population of Vienna in the latter half of the eighteenth century, pictures of what people wore, or what they called their money (pounds? ducats? moolah?), rely on reference books. But to immerse yourself in the times, to get a sense of how the people lived, you'll need a book or two (not twenty, or you'll never get your own book written!) from the 900 section of the general stacks.

If that "900" reference threw you, then you also need a quick refresher course in how to use the library beyond the reference desk. And, yes, there are faster, more efficient ways to find what you need in the stacks.

The "900" comes from the Dewey Decimal System, which you probably learned in grade school:

000s = **General Works**
100s = **Philosophy**
200s = **Religion**
300s = **Social Sciences**
400s = **Language**
500s = **Natural Sciences**
600s = **Useful Arts**
700s = **Fine Arts**
800s = **Literature**
900s = **History and Biography**

You can get a more in-depth primer on the good ol' Dewey system online at www.oclc.org/dewey/.

Many libraries, however, have switched to the less-familiar, Library of Congress classification scheme:

A = **General Works**
B = **Philosophy, Psychology, Religion**
C = **Auxiliary Sciences of History**
      (archaeology, for example)
D = **History: General and Old World**
E, F = **History: America**

G = Geography, Anthropology, Recreation

H = Social Sciences

K = Law

L = Education

M = Music

N = Fine Arts

P = Language and Literature

Q = Science

R = Medicine

S = Agriculture

T = Technology

U = Military Science

V = Naval Science

Z = Bibliography, Library Science.

See www.loc.gov/catdir/cpso/lcco/lcco.html for more on the Library of Congress system.

It's useful to know these broad classification schemes, but unless you're prepared to memorize the zillions of sub-categories (let's see, is "PN" French literature or Russian literature?), your best bet is to start with your own library's catalog. These catalogs generally let you search for books by author, title, and subject; some online versions also support key words and other handy tools. Suppose you don't know the specific book you're looking for— as is frequently the case when doing research for writing. You can search by subject, of course, but that may yield more titles than you can readily make sense out of. Research expert William L. Rivers, author of the excellent *Finding Facts*, suggests deciding what the title of the perfect book you need would be—*if* someone had written it. Then look up the title you've invented; in a large library, Rivers says, you'll hit the jackpot about half the time.

Another trick I use is to search by subject, or by the one appropriate title that I *do* know, to find the specific code—either Dewey Decimal or Library of Congress—for the section of the stacks that generally has the books I need. Then I go there and browse almost as I would in a bookstore. (Again, some online catalogs will also let you do this digitally, stepping back and clicking forward in sequence.) It's often much faster to figure out from the actual book whether it's useful than by deciphering the catalog entry; this also saves me from having to write down a long list of book titles, and numbers for specific books that may already be checked out anyway. There in the stacks,

I can tell at a glance or a quick flip what books are clearly too old and out-of-date, too scholarly, or not detailed enough. Librarians would probably shudder at this method, but it works. It's also a strong reason to shun those prison-like libraries where they don't let you back into the actual stacks, but make you fill out little slips of paper for every book you want to see.

You can even use online bookstores, such as Amazon.com (www.amazon.com) and Barnes and Noble (www.bn.com), with their in-depth descriptions and reviews, to find the books you need. These sites often include actual, digitized pages from the books; pay particular attention to contents pages and indexes, if so. Then, once you've compiled a list of likely titles, consult your library's online catalog to see if you can check them out for free.

Once you've found books that might be useful, how many should you check out? There's probably a good reason that God gave us only two arms and the ability to carry no more than the weight of a sack of potatoes or two. But even if you've been pumping iron and can cart home a whole shelf load of books, control yourself. Remember that eventually you'll have to quit researching and start writing, and that this is a story, not a PhD thesis. I've seldom checked out more than a half-dozen books for even a complex magazine article—and then I *scanned* the books, rather than reading them cover to cover! Go much beyond ten books, unless you're tackling a book-length project, and you're crossing the line into research as an excuse not to do the hard work of writing.

Exercises

1. Interview the reference librarian at your local library. What's the most unusual question he has had? The most common? What advice can she share about making use of the reference collection?

2. Using the online catalog for your local library, or that of the Library of Congress (catalog.loc.gov), identify at least one book you could check out that would help you write each of the stories from the exercises in the previous chapter:

   a. a mystery novel in which the victim is poisoned by the chemicals found in art supplies
   b. an article about the possibility of life on other planets
   c. an article offering coping advice to the recently widowed

d. a romance novel set in 18th-century Scotland

e. a book for grandmothers who are raising their grandchildren

f. a science-fiction story about time travel via black holes

g. an article debunking astrology

h. one of your own current writing projects

3. Now try finding one book for each of the stories listed in number two, using your favorite online bookstore, rather than the library catalog.

4. Pick one of the books you identified in number two, and see if you can "browse" adjacent books using the catalog, as described in this chapter. Use this technique to find at least two other potentially useful titles.

CHAPTER 8

WORKING THE WEB

The other day, after finding some obscure fact on the Internet in less time than it took me to get a second cup of morning coffee, I marveled aloud to my daughter, "What did we ever do before the Web?" She could truthfully answer, "I don't know, Dad," because she doesn't—the Web became a full-fledged phenomenon about the time she was old enough to start handling a keyboard.

But for writers who are, like me, a tad longer in the tooth, the Internet has indeed wrought a revolution in the way we work. Assignments come and go by e-mail. Our work might not even appear on a printed piece of paper, instead helping to fill the insatiable maw of the World Wide Web.

It's in the realm of research, however, that the Internet has made those of us who remember the Olden Days feel like old-timers from the horse-and-buggy era: "Well, you young whippersnapper, I remember when I had to walk five miles in a blizzard to the library just to look up the GNP of Madagascar . . ." Libraries? Reference books? There are days when I forget they exist. Though, of course, such "old-fashioned" research remains the gold standard for writers, I confess that writing the previous chapter was agony: Schlepping to the library to look things up seems so inconvenient nowadays. Can't we just use the Web? (In fact, when it came time to double-check the titles in the last chapter, that's exactly what I did. Most major libraries have their catalogs online, including the mammoth Library of Congress at www.loc.gov.)

The sheer ubiquity and sweeping scope of the Web, though, present a thoroughly modern set of challenges for writers. No more trekking through a blinding snowstorm for a single fact; rather, today's problem is finding the facts you need amid a blizzard of information that's all only a few mouse clicks away. With the explosion of information technologies in recent years, the writer's ability to find facts fast has increased exponentially. These days the challenge isn't so much finding what you need to know as separating it from everything that you *don't* need to know.

What once would have taken hours or days, trips to the library, and tedious waits for interlibrary loans now can be done in minutes. Even if you don't live near a major research library, the Internet brings a virtual library to your fingertips. But unless you also have the skills of a librarian, it's just as easy to get lost in that virtual library. The Internet may deliver the information to your desktop, but you still have to be a savvy researcher. When you're searching the Web, ten thousand hits can prove as much of a dead end as zero.

Matching Your Mission

To get results instead of headaches from your Web research, the first step is to think about what kind of information you're after. Are you looking for one or two stubborn facts to fill in the blanks in a story that's otherwise mostly written? Do you need just an oddball bit of data—such as the GNP of Madagascar—to lend authenticity to a chapter of your novel? Or are you at the very beginning of the writing process, teasing out leads to resources and potential interviews? Are you still trying to decide, say, whether a novel set in Madagascar is right for your thriller idea? Either way, your online research strategy needs to fit your mission—one size definitely does not fit all.

If you're just using the Web for quick answers, it's the digital equivalent of a ready-reference bookshelf, or a tireless reference librarian. The trick is to find the right "book"—in this case, Web page—that can rapidly and reliably deliver the nugget of data you need.

For example, not long ago I was writing about the history of robots—a timeline, essentially—for *ID* magazine. I had several items that I knew I wanted to include, but I lacked a key piece of information—such as the date, which is pretty much essential for a chronology. Remember the movie *Metropolis* with its gleaming female robot? So did I, but I didn't remember the year it was made, and without that fact I couldn't put it in my timeline.

Quickly filling in such factual gaps, in part, depends on developing a repertoire of reliable Web sites on topics you often cover. For movies, for instance, I depend on The Internet Movie Database site (www.imdb.com), a treasure trove of all things cinematic. Type "Metropolis" in the IMDB search box, hit "Go" and the answer appears: 1927. You'll discover your own favorite specialized sites from recommendations in related magazines and, to be honest, trial and error, and luck.

Other facts that you need fast don't have ready-made reference sites (or if they do, you don't know about them yet). So you'll need to turn to your arsenal of favorite, all-purpose tools: The two I rely on most regularly are Encyclopaedia Britannica Online (www.britannica.com) and the Google search engine (www.google.com).

The first is a no-brainer. With the world's most renowned encyclopedia at your fingertips, many of your quick-info worries are over. The annual subscription fee is peanuts compared to shelling out for a whole set of hardback encyclopedias. Besides searching its own content, Britannica does a Web search, so you can find answers that aren't even in the encyclopedia. When I needed to find another date for my robot timeline—remember the robot in "The Jetsons" television series?—the Britannica site actually proved to be the speediest solution (if least likely, given the print original's some-what stuffy reputation). Though "The Jetsons" weren't in the encyclopedia proper, the site's Web search promptly found one of its recommended sites—an in-depth "Jetsons" fan page—with a complete series chronology (the show first aired in 1962).

Once you're out on the wild Web and researching beyond trusted re-sources, however, you do need to take what you find with a grain of salt. While the author of that "Jetsons" page obviously knew way more than is healthy to know about any one television series, and could surely be trusted for such a basic date about his object of obsession, not all the "facts" you'll find are true. If you're not sure about the source, try to raise your confidence level in your findings by searching for the same facts in several different sources. I could have searched any of my favorite search engines—besides Google, I regularly use HotBot (www.hotbot.com) and AltaVista (www.altavista.com)—for "Jetsons 1962," which would have found an *Entertainment Weekly* list of great moments in science fiction, confirming that date.

(The *Entertainment Weekly* list was a long one, however. To save scrolling down pages trying to eyeball your search term, use your browser's built-in "Find" function, typically under the "Edit" menu. In Internet Explorer for Windows, you can call it up quickly with ctrl-F. Just type in the word you're after and this feature will find it on the current Web page.)

Web searches also work wonderfully for getting famous but only partly remembered quotes just right, or checking who said them. What city was Gertrude Stein referring to when she said, "There's no there there"? Search-ing for "There's no there there" and "Gertrude Stein" instantly returns the answer: Oakland.

Solving a Problem Like "Maria"

Sometimes the fact that's leaving an ugly hole in your article proves trickier to find. That robot from *Metropolis*, for example—what was its name? The Britannica article on *Metropolis* director Fritz Lang fails to mention that detail.

For puzzles like that I usually turn to Google, a deceptively simple-looking search engine that relies, in part, on an unusual strategy to separate the wheat from the chaff of the Web: It ranks sites by how often they are linked to by other sites. So, while Google is not directly employing human intelligence in selecting its sites (as does another of my favorites, the classic Yahoo! at www.yahoo.com), it does add a human factor second-hand. Google is also lightning fast, and you don't need to master complicated search phraseology to get the results you need. Just type in a bunch of words—"Metropolis robot Fritz Lang" (adding the director's name to weed out sites merely about metropolises). It's no wonder that "to google" has begun to enter the language as a verb. (I'll bet you've already tried "googling" yourself to test your Web renown, haven't you?)

Google is also my first choice for finding any "official" site that I can't quite guess the URL for. What's the Web address for the National Archives? You might not guess it's www.archives.gov, but Google can find it in a flash. Looking for Dodge cars? Google knows it's www.4adodge.com. (You can even try the "I'm Feeling Lucky" button, which takes you straight to the site Google thinks is your best bet.)

Two other points are worth noting about Google: The "Similar pages" option on the results page lets you get more of the same once you've found one site that's in the right ballpark. And the "Cached" feature takes you to the page as it was when Google found it—with your search terms conveniently highlighted—even if it's subsequently changed or the site has since gone to dot-com heaven. A nifty little time-travel trick.

But sometimes even Google runs up against a toughie. That *Metropolis* robot question, for instance, proved oddly elusive. Google found me a bunch of sites about the movie, but unless I wanted to learn a lot more about 1920s German Expressionist cinema than I had time for, I needed a shortcut. All the sites mentioned "robot"—it's central to the movie's story—but none had the name.

Finally, I found a page that referred specifically to the lead robot as the "robotrix." Close, but not quite enough. So I tried another handy search trick: Search again, including your close-but-no-cigar information to narrow it down. Sure enough, "Metropolis robotrix" found four sites on Google's first results page with the long-sought name: Maria.

Finding Your Magnet

But what if your research needs are more wide-ranging, more fundamental? Just as the Web can be a handy substitute for a reference shelf, so too can it make it easy for you to delve into the world's largest "library," following leads among the digital "stacks" to flesh out a query into an article, to find experts for interviewing, to create credibility for your novel, and to do most or all of the secondary research that used to require mastery of the Dewey Decimal System. (Should that be "Dewey" or "Dewy"? I checked with Google, of course.)

If you're near the start of crafting a book or article rather than in the final, fill-in-the-blanks stage, you need a more methodical approach than what we just looked at for finding fast facts. You'll want to cast a wider net. You'll still face the challenge of sorting the wheat from the vast amount of chaff on the Web, but here it pays to expand your harvest a bit.

To answer my simple robotic date quandary, I used a rifle approach—targeting my Web research as narrowly as possible. But to get started on the whole topic in the first place, I adopted more of a shotgun strategy. I started with my favorite search engine, Google, and typed in the broadest query I could think of: "robots history." Google does a good job of prioritizing results, so some of the links on the very first page I got were worth following. But with 131,000 total results, I quickly figured out that I'd cast my net *too* wide.

That's one of the joys of the Web—there's no penalty for mistakes. If you try something and it doesn't work, no Web librarian is going to come yell at you. Simply keep experimenting, narrowing, and expanding your search, until you get results that are just right. (Another plus of Google is that each result includes that "Similar pages" link, so you can use any on-target hits, even from an otherwise much too wide search, to further focus your search.)

The most effective searches often spring from imitation. Since what I was writing was essentially a timeline or chronology of robots, after my 131,000-hit first try, I thought, "What the heck? What I'm really looking for is somebody else's timeline to get me started and give me ideas." Sure enough, searching Google for "robots history timeline" turned up three timelines of robotic history on the very first page of results.

You'll often be amazed at how easy it is, if you ask the question right, to find exactly what you're looking for on the Web. Not just single facts, but whole Web sites on the most diverse and obscure subjects are just waiting for you to ferret them out. (For another project I needed a crash course on, of all things, that distinctively Southern treat, GooGoo Clusters candy. I found a page full of sites devoted to all things GooGoo, including an official site at www.googoo.com with a complete history of the candy. Who'd have thought it?)

You can also think of Web research to help jump-start a story as tossing a magnet into a pile of scraps; everything iron will stick to the magnet when you retrieve it. The trick, of course, is picking the right "magnet." Again, think in terms of imitation. If you can find or think of one good example of what you're after, you can use it as a "magnet" to find others. With my robots article, the obvious thought was Frankenstein's monster. Though not technically a robot, Frankenstein's monster had both the cultural and historical associations I was after. I could guess that if I found sites that mentioned both "Frankenstein" and "robots," they'd be likely to help get me started. It worked! Try typing "Frankenstein robots" into your favorite search engine and see if you couldn't start, er, assembling an interesting story from the first few pages of results.

Once you find a few leads online, you can also use the Web to follow them up. For another story, on Scandinavia, my search for starting points turned up a random mention that the year 2000 was the thousandth anniversary of Leif Eriksson's landing in America. Sensing a nugget I might turn into a lead, I did more Web searching with terms such as "Leif Erickson Viking anniversary." In a few minutes, I'd found a Smithsonian site about an exhibition on the Vikings and the official Canadian site about the area in what's now Newfoundland where they landed, plus a calendar of commemorative events. That was enough to build my lead around.

Expert Opinions

Sometimes what you need to rev up your research are experts. If only you could find a few people to interview on your topic, your story would really take off. Here, too, the Web can come to the rescue.

First, try the sites that specialize in matching writers with people who know what they're talking about. We've already mentioned some of these in chapter six: ProfNet (www.profnet.com) is probably the best-known such site. The brainchild of some university PR folks, and now a service of PR

Newswire, ProfNet lets you search a database of more than four thousand academic experts. Or you can post a query, and college and university PR officers will respond by e-mail with their best fit for your needs.

You can also go fishing for experts at:

- Expert Source (www.businesswire.com/expertsource)
- FACSnet (www.facsnet.org/sources/newssources)
- Experts.com (www.experts.com)
- MediaResource (www.mediaresource.org)
- Bznet USA (www.gehrung.com/biznet/biznet.html)

Amazingly, all these resources are free—you can have others do your legwork, digging up people for you to interview, and it doesn't cost you a dime. Of course, they're all trying to get their stories out and their clients' names in print, but if you go into it with your eyes wide open there's no reason not to take advantage of these services.

Sometimes, though, you'll have a story that doesn't lend itself to ready-made experts or PR assistance. You can still use the Web to find sources—it just takes a little more digging.

Your best bet for finding experts in a more general Web search is often to turn to what you might think of as "expert" directory sites—sites, like Yahoo! (www.yahoo.com), that have some human intelligence behind them. When you're trolling for experts, you're more likely to want official sites rather than fan pages and enthusiasts' creations. If you're writing a novel in which, say, solar power plays a role, you'll want to look for experts at the American Solar Energy Society (found at Yahoo! under Science> Energy> Solar Power, along with more than a hundred similar resources) before you tap Bob's Amazing Home Solar Energy Kit Web Showcase and Lemonade Stand. Remember, Yahoo! is not a true search engine; it's really a directory, assembled by hands-on humans rather than Web "spiders," so it's a good bet for mainstream, official, professional sites.

If you strike out at Yahoo!, you can still use it to find what might be called mini-Yahoo!s—other directory sites for specialized interests, where you can search for more obscure expertise. For example, when I wrote a feature for *Family Tree Magazine* on how to get started researching your Southern ancestors, I started at Cyndi's List (www.cyndislist.com), which functions for genealogy much as Yahoo! does for the Web as a whole. There I found sites that specialize in the South—from the Center for Southern Culture to the individual state pages at USGenWeb (www.usgenweb.com), a national genealogy volunteer project—and then scoured those for contacts. In that case, I followed up my finds by simply e-mailing a request for tips and advice that I could quote in my article; other times, you'll need to follow up by phone or in person.

You can also find sources simply by following writers who've gone before you. If you're trying to find someone you can, say, interview about robots, search the archives of magazine and newspaper articles online. If you find Professor Victor Frankenstein of Transylvania Polytechnic Institute interviewed in *The New York Times* about his work in robotics, it's a safe bet he'd be happy to chat with you, too.

Even with the worldwide reach of the Web, of course, you'll still have to make the occasional trip to a non-virtual library, pick up the phone and call sources, and even sometimes see your subjects in person. The Web can't solve all your research problems, but it can cut out the most time-wasting parts of the process and let you initially explore a topic much more widely.

Computer Smarts

The other downside of the Web's excess of riches—besides the needle-in-a-haystack challenge of trying to find the right facts fast—is that you can easily become a victim of your own success. It's so easy to find information online that you can quickly drown in a sea of results. You wind up spending all your time wading through your notes, picking over your printouts, and decoding your downloads, instead of writing.

One cure for Web-induced information overload is to learn a few computer tricks—sort of a "hair of the dog" approach, you might say. We've already seen one such shortcut: When faced with a long Web page you've clicked on after a search, find your keyword using the "Find" command in your Web browser. Here are a few other technical tips that can make your Web research more efficient and leave you with notes that are easier to write from:

- To save your findings from a bunch of different Web sites without winding up with research notes that look like a ransom demand, discover the "Paste Special" command. Select a chunk from a Web page, "Copy" it, then go under the "Edit" menu in Microsoft Word (either PC or Mac) and pick "Paste Special." Choose "Unformatted Text" from the options and even the most crazy-quilt Web text will be added to your document in plain-vanilla type. I use this so often that I've created a macro for it and assigned a keyboard shortcut: You just need to select "Record New Macro" under

"Macros" on the "Tools" menu, do the "Paste Special" routine while Word "watches" you, and then save your series of actions. Assign an unused keyboard command to your macro—on the PC, I use Alt-V, similar to the Ctrl-V for ordinary pasting—and you can now paste plain-vanilla copy with just a keystroke. (If you're using Word 2002 on a PC, there's a bug that keeps this from working as it should. You'll need to edit the resulting macro to read "Selection.PasteSpecial DataType:=wdPasteText, Link:=False" to make it work right.)

• If you're printing your results, don't just hit "Print." Aside from the cost in dead trees of all the paper you'll waste, you'll later have a hard time finding the information you really wanted. Instead, select only the section of a Web page that contains the info you want, then pick "Print" from the "File" menu and click the "Print Selection" button in the resulting dialog box. (If your browser doesn't support "Print Selection," for gosh sakes upgrade. In the meantime, copy the selection you want, use the "Paste Special" trick in Word or paste into a plain text editing utility, and print.)

• Make sure your browser's "Print" options are set to print the Web page address—the URL—as a header or footer on every page you print out. Otherwise, you'll wind up with a sheaf of printouts and no idea where they came from, either for attribution or for going back to check something. You can set this as your default using "Page Setup" under the "File" menu in most browsers.

• Find a Web page with lots of links you need to reproduce in your writing, or that you want to save for clicking through later? Or just have a particularly successful Google search? There are two easy ways to preserve those links, one digital and one on paper. For a digital, clickable copy, go under "File" and save the page right on your computer, either as HTML or (if you want a copy with images and all) as a Web archive. Then you can open it up later from your hard drive, whether or not you're online. For a paper copy complete with links, check the box in your browser's "Print" dialog box (under the "Options" tab) that says "Print table of links at end." You'll get a regular printout, followed by all the URLs; otherwise your printout would just show the links as underlined words, with no clue to where they're linked.

• Similarly, you'll often come upon a Web page full of goodies—or have an unusually fruitful search—that you want to explore, link by link, without losing the page or having to hit the "Back" button over and over. The solution is simply to open the link in a new window: Right-click on it if you're a PC user, or hold down the Control key while clicking on a Mac, and select "Open target in new window" (or similar verbiage, depending on your software). Then explore to your heart's content—and just click the second window closed when you're done. Your original window full of links will still be there, underneath; no backing up needed.

• Can't remember what Web page you found that fact on? Take advantage of your browser's archive of recently visited Web sites—in Internet Explorer, it's the "History" folder. You can browse this list or, in more recent versions, search the History files much like any other collection of Web pages. If you've got an ongoing project and plenty of hard-drive space, set your History folder (under "Tools/Options") to keep pages for a time period long enough to cover all your research on that topic. (Of course, it will also preserve all of the recipe and shopping pages you visit, so beware if you're surfing at work.)

• Can't find a fact even though you've saved it—somewhere—on your hard drive? Both the "Find" (also called "Search") command in Windows and "Find File" (a.k.a. "Sherlock") on the Macintosh can hunt for files, not only by file name, but also by content. Type in a keyword associated with that elusive info and you can quickly gather all the files containing that word; then you can use your word-processor's "Find" command to track it down within each suspect file.

If all this seems like a lot of hassle and technical gobbledygook for a gizmo that's supposed to be *your* servant, not the other way around, well, maybe it is. But it's worth learning a few tricks to get the most out of this marvelous creation that brings a world of information right to your desktop. It's still a heckuva lot better than walking five miles—or was it fifteen?—in a snowstorm to the library.

Exercises

1. Search for your own name using at least two different search engines, such as Google (www.google.com) or AltaVista (www.altavista.com), and compare the results.

2. Use the Web to find the Gross National Product of Madagascar. Keep searching to find the most up-to-date figure you can. What site(s) gave you the best answer?

3. Suppose you're writing a novel set in Scotland and you need some basic dates in Scottish history as a framework. Use your favorite search engine and the techniques from this chapter to find a timeline of Scottish history on the Web.

4. Use the categories in Yahoo! (under "Directory") to find at least one Scottish organization or archive that might be helpful in researching the story in number three.

5. Use the "history" function of your browser to go back and find again a page you used in exercise three. Practice using "Find" on the Web page to find a key word or phrase. Now copy the paragraph containing that phrase and paste it into a word-processing document without any distracting formatting ("Paste Special" if you use Word).

CHAPTER 9
MAXIMIZING YOUR INTERVIEWS

As solitary as the craft of writing can be, an essential element of most good stories is talking to people before you sit down at the keyboard. For nonfiction, that's probably obvious: If you're writing a profile of a famous scientist, an interview with your subject will be the heart of your preparation. Even if you're writing about a *what* rather than a *who*, you'll likely need to enliven your prose with quotes; at a minimum, you need to consult some experts to fully research your topic.

Fiction writers might be tempted to skip this chapter, thinking that your stories come out of your head and, after all, you can simply make up all the quotes you need. Think again: The most successful fiction writers spend hours interviewing experts, insiders, and others who can ground them in their subject and lend their make-believe an aura of verisimilitude. Consider best-selling thriller novelist Greg Iles, for example. For his World War II blockbuster *Black Cross*, Iles interviewed and consulted more than two-dozen people, including five doctors, two electrical engineers, five language specialists, and others from California to Scotland. If he hadn't known how to efficiently get what he needed out of those people, the novel might never have been written, or would have failed to plunge readers into its scenes as a page-turner must.

So you need to interview people—but how do you find them? We've already talked about identifying experts for your research. Most experts can be reached the same way you found them in the first place: through a PR department at a particular organization, or via some association. Others can be found by checking *Who's Who in America* or any of the dozens of specialized Who's Who editions. *The Address Book: How to Reach Anyone Who's Anyone* by Michael Levine is another handy resource for doing just what its title describes. And you'll be amazed at how many phone numbers, addresses, and e-mail addresses, even of prominent individuals, you can retrieve via online phone books, such as Switchboard (www.switchboard.com), or just by using your favorite search engine. You can also use Web tools in tandem: Try Google to figure out where a possible interviewee lives, then get contact info with Web white pages. Often, if you can find out where someone lives, you can easily get a phone number—even if it means calling all three people by that name and asking, "Is this Jane Doe, the biochemist?" Dust jackets of books are great resources for finding out where authors live. I once tracked down half-a-dozen science fiction writers for a story on future technology that way, with nothing more to go on than blurbs like "William Gibson lives in Portland, Oregon."

I keep emphasizing phone numbers here because almost every successful interview starts with a phone call or at least an e-mail. Never just drop in on somebody; always make an appointment. Even if you're planning only a phone interview, you may want to use the first call to introduce yourself and set up a mutually convenient time to call back.

Phone, E-mail, or In Person?

When *can* you get by with just a phone interview—with what John Brady, in his classic *The Craft of Interviewing*, calls "the McDonald's of journalism"? Use the telephone interview for round-up stories, when you need a little bit from a lot of sources (like my horse-breeding and science-fiction articles). Use it to gather background information and supporting quotes and anecdotes for a profile: Call the subject's friends, relatives, and archenemies, but go see the subject in person. Use the phone to gather specific, individual bits of information to fill out a story. But keep in mind that, as Brady notes, you must be even *better* prepared for a telephone interview than for an in-person encounter, because no winning smile or small talk can cover your gaffes over the phone.

E-mail "interviews" are even more impersonal, but you can get away with using e-mail for short pieces, some round-ups, and stories where you just need facts, not "color." These days, it's tempting to do everything by e-mail. If you need the human touch, though—and most stories do—resist the temptation to take the easy, e-mail route.

Nonetheless, the telephone is almost always, by definition, faster than traveling to an in-person interview. So plan your in-person interviews carefully and sparingly, opt for subjects nearby before those several hours or days away, and try to package your interviews to minimize travel time. If you need to talk to three people in Manhattan, try to arrange to see at least two of them in a single excursion. (Of course, this saves money as well as time!)

Some stories by their nature demand that your eyes be on the scene; part of your research is going someplace and seeing or doing something. My horse-breeding story, because it was business-oriented and wide-ranging, could be done over the phone. By contrast, another assignment for the Federal Express magazine, about a historic art gallery in Gettysburg, demanded that I go there: I needed to see the art and the town, not just interview the owners.

Occasionally, merely traveling to an interview won't be enough; you'll have to physically pursue your subjects. With busy celebrities, you may want to avoid using the word "interview" at all, with its connotations of a long, static encounter. Try instead to arrange a "chat," or just to "talk" with a celebrity—even while he or she is doing something else. I've interviewed singers (Loretta Lynn, Gene Simmons of KISS) in their dressing rooms before a performance. John Brady got an interview with Jessica Mitford, author of *The American Way of Death*, for *Writer's Digest* by driving her to the airport. Often these stolen slices of time can expand without the subject consciously acquiescing: William Manchester's first interview with President Kennedy, according to Brady, was supposed to last just ten minutes, but stretched to more than three hours. Manchester got so much out of the president, he later said, because he'd done his homework. He'd prepared for the interview, so he was able to keep the conversation flowing—and JFK enjoyed it.

Another classic story of solid preparation is the time A.J. Liebling interviewed jockey Eddie Arcaro. Liebling's first question was, "How many holes longer do you keep your left stirrup than your right?" Clearly, the *New Yorker* reporter had done his background research and knew something about the racing game. "That started him talking easily," Liebling later recalled, "and after an hour during which I had put in about twelve words, he said, 'I can see you've been around riders a lot.'"

Compare those encounters with the opening question a reporter once asked naturalist John Burroughs, "By the way, Mr. Burroughs, just what do you do?"

Yes, here's yet another instance where an investment of time beforehand will save time—or prevent a total disaster—during the actual interview. As author Cornelius Ryan (*The Longest Day*) once put it, "Never interview anyone without knowing 60 percent of the answers." This may sound like a waste of time, but it's not. Rather, it's a strategic apportionment of time. Learn the basics in the library and online; then use your interview time to get the color and quotes that can only be gained by talking to someone. Think of my Rick Bayless interview: I went in already knowing the details of his career; what I needed from talking to him was the human factor that would put flesh on those bare facts.

When you prepare for an interview, you should scribble down a list of possible questions. You may not have to ask all of them, or you may not be able to ask everything; nor should you ask only those questions on your list if a more fruitful line of conversation develops. Write down your questions in a natural order, imagining how a conversation might run. At the same time, though, you should make sure that the questions most crucial to your angle are asked early on. What if your subject gets called away unexpectedly, or your interview takes longer than you've been allotted?

The unexpected does happen, and stories do take unanticipated turns. Both for that reason and for simple time efficiency, you shouldn't *over-prepare* for an interview any more than you should skimp on your pre-interview homework. You must strike a balance between impressing your subject as a sincere person who's thought about what questions to ask, and pretending to know as much as your subject does. Don't bluff or lead your subject into pat answers. John McPhee says he likes to cultivate an "air of density" and to seem "as blank as the notebook pages" when he interviews, so as not to limit his freedom to learn and to be surprised. If that seems contradictory to careful preparation, think of the rest of Liebling's experience with Eddie Arcaro: Once he won the jockey's confidence, Liebling knew enough to shut up and let Arcaro talk. Sometimes you have to know a lot in order to know when to say nothing.

To Tape or Not to Tape?

So you've got your subject, prepared your list of questions, and put fresh batteries in your tape recorder—you're ready to interview, right? Maybe not. Hold off a minute on that last point, and consider using those batteries for something really important, like the television remote control.

I'm getting into controversial territory here, I know. Opinions about whether interviewers should use tape recorders run as fierce as the debate over whether martinis should be shaken or stirred. I come down adamantly on the "agin it" side. Part of this is a legacy from my first cover assignment for *TWA Ambassador* magazine: an interview with Paul Erdman, who'd just hit the best-seller lists with a couple of thrillers based in the unlikely milieu of banking. I still remember the thrill of jetting out to the California wine country, sitting by Erdman's pool, and listening to him discourse into my tape recorder on the future of the world's economy. It's a good thing my memory of that encounter was so vivid, because when I got back to the office I found that my tape recorder, like the economy in one of Erdman's best-sellers, had crashed. After a few minutes of the splash-and-whirr of Erdman's pool skimmer, the tape was a blank. If my memory hadn't been in high gear—and if I hadn't also been taking some notes—my cover story would have been a blank as well.

But my prejudice against tape recorders isn't just a lingering suspicion about the cussedness of machines. Rather, it stems from a lesson I learned the hard way from my Erdman story: Only the most vivid and memorable quotes should wind up in your story, anyway. *Nobody* is so quotable that every word from his or her mouth must be recorded.

This lesson was reinforced, rather vigorously, during my three-year stint as a newspaper columnist. During this time, I was interviewing for and writing three feature stories a week. If I'd tried to keep up that pace while painstakingly transcribing taped interviews before writing each column, I'd have quickly turned into one of the oddballs I sometimes wrote about ("Burned-Out Ex-Columnist Listens to Tapes All Day While Giggling Maniacally").

If this sounds like laziness, it's not—just the opposite. As Pulitzer Prize-winner Tracy Kidder (*The Soul of a New Machine*) once said, "A tape recorder tends to make me lazy, so I might stop taking notes and miss a lot." Kidder believes that his note taking is actually *more* accurate than the results of tape-recording. The machine, he insists, fails to catch the subtleties of an interview. In recording *what* people say, it misses *how* they say it: the gestures, the facial expressions, the relationship of speaker to setting.

As you scribble, you should concentrate on capturing the "true" voice of your subjects, so that later, when you turn your compressed notes into a story, it's like adding water to dehydrated food (only tastier). If you can capture the voice and personality of your subject, your story will be much more "true" than if you transcribe every word accurately but miss the person behind the words.

Moreover, just as taking notes from your secondary sources forces you to distill the material, taking notes in an interview makes you edit while listening. You'll soon learn to scribble down only what's essential while politely nodding and mumbling "uh-huh" as your subject rambles on. Don't worry: You'll still have four times as much raw material as you can or should use in an article. "If you fall behind," journalist Max Gunther once advised, "the reason probably is that you are trying to take down the subject's words too fully." Only about 10 percent of the words uttered in an average interview, Gunther guessed, are genuinely meaningful.

It's this boiling-down effect that is so important to both efficient interviewing and, ultimately, writing not only faster but better. Obviously, it's a time waster to sit and transcribe taped interviews. But the greatest time-saver in taking notes is the way it forces you to focus on what's important in the interview: *Will you use this quote? Is this information what you're really after?* If the answer is *no*, then don't write it down so you won't have to deal with it again later!

This is time saved and focus strengthened in the writing process itself, in the decision-making and selecting that is the hardest, most time-consuming part of writing. Taking notes on the fly demands that you think about your story as it is unfolding in the interview. You begin to shape and select your material in the back of your mind, even as most of your brain is formulating the next question. And that's a highly effective synergy. The ongoing editing of your material begins to affect the direction of your questioning. You know what gaps must be filled with answers or anecdotes, what areas have been covered and needn't be queried again. As you gain experience, the story (or parts of it, in longer assignments) will begin to write itself in your head during the interview: *Here's the opening. Here's a perfect transition from this subject to that. Here's a quote that coincides perfectly with that previous phone interview with the subject's college roommate.*

Of course, to successfully rely on your notebook rather than a tape recorder requires highly adept and efficient note taking. You'll need to know shorthand or develop your own system of notetaking shortcuts, as we discussed in chapter six. (In England, by the way, it's almost unheard-of for a journalist not to know shorthand.) You'll need, ultimately, to be able to decipher—to decompress, if you will—your own notes. Don't be like humorist Robert Benchley, who once wrote a piece on the impossibility of decoding his own notes—presumably because he couldn't understand his notes for the piece he'd originally intended to write!

But beyond those basics, there are a few note-taking tricks you can adopt to ease the process of not just writing down an interview as it happens but editing it as you go. I single out good material, the stuff I know will fit the story I've envisioned, even as I'm interviewing: Immediately after scribbling down something particularly useful, I'll draw a rough slash, or line, beside it in my notebook. That's my signal, when I'm reviewing my notes and organizing my story, to pay particular attention to this section of scribbling. I'll also put crude brackets—[ ]—around material that represents my own observations, either about what the subject is saying or about his surroundings. While the subject is babbling on about something less than germane to my story, I'll use the time not only to catch up with my note taking but to write down the colorful details that help bring the story alive: trinkets on the person's desk, little signs on her wall, how she's dressed, characteristic actions like tenting one's fingers or leaning back in one's chair, habits of voice, even the view out her window. All these things I set off by brackets, so I know instantly that this isn't direct quotation; no need, then, to put quotation marks around everything else I take down.

This sort of material, incidentally, can be as crucial to your story as the quotes you gather. Part of the trick of really effective in-person interviewing is to capture this kind of telling, specific detail, even while getting what you need directly from the source's mouth. "*Show* us, don't tell us," an editor will often admonish—and such notes become an important part of the "showing." When interviewing someone for novel research, too, you never know what salient detail might find its way into your book: The funny sculpture on the real-life mathematician's desk might be just the visual clue to your fictional mathematician's character that readers need. If you're going to go to the time and trouble of a face-to-face interview, after all, you might as well make the most of it; otherwise you should stay home and use the phone.

Now, if you're *still* daunted by the prospect of entering an interview without the security blanket of a tape recorder, let me just add a few words about the ultimate in interviewing-without-a-net: relying on memory alone. Truman Capote, fearful that even the presence of a simple notebook would prove off-putting to his subjects for *In Cold Blood*, practiced memorizing an interview by having a friend talk to him. He'd tape the conversation, for checking purposes, and then write up the interview strictly from memory. When the write-up matched the tape with 97 percent accuracy, Capote figured he was ready to go to work on *In Cold Blood*.

While I'm a long way from a Capote in either writing ability or memory skills, I know from experience that it is indeed possible for a writer to fly solo, without even a notebook. When *TWA Ambassador* sent me out to a California chess tournament to interview chess champion and jack-of-all-games Walter Browne, I found myself hounding the great gamesman for interview time. Every moment, it seemed, he was either actually playing chess or preparing for his next match. I finally got the time I needed by going to dinner with him—but the restaurant Browne picked was too dark to take notes, even if I'd been able to wield a pencil along with my knife and fork. So we talked—more of a dinner conversation than a formal interview, the casual atmosphere seeming to put him more at ease. And then, after I bade Browne good night, I raced back to my tiny motel room. Frantically, I wrote down all I could recall of the evening's several hours of revealing conversation. Much to my amazement, I remembered almost everything of importance (just as I had, with a few more notes, reconstructed my Erdman interview).

The point is not to urge you to throw your notebook in the trash heap with your tape recorder, but to underscore the point: Yes, you can get what you really need with notebook alone. Yes, you will remember what is truly important for your story, with or without a notebook. And it's only the most memorable material that belongs in your writing, anyway. If you couldn't remember it (with a little help from your notes), it's probably not good enough or central enough to put in the story.

The Interview as First Date

Now you're really ready—but how do you get people to say interesting things to fill up that notebook? It's hardly making the most of your interviews, after all, if most of the answers that you scribble down are "Yes," "No," and "I dunno."

The art of the interview has been likened to a seduction. To succeed, it's often suggested, an interviewer must worm inside a subject's defenses—the ultimate goal being, of course, to lure the subject into saying something he shouldn't, into making some startling or embarrassing revelation. If the interview is on television rather than for print, the ideal seems to be to reduce the subject to tears. That's a dandy approach if you're Woodward, Bernstein, or Mike Wallace. But most of the interviews you'll encounter as a writer are more like a first date.

In interviewing ordinary folks—interview virgins, if you'll pardon the expression—your goal is to establish a rapport, not to crack their defenses and get them to confess something. You're aiming for an easy, comfortable time—yes, a lot like a first date. (If you aim for more on a first date, well, let's just say you're never going to date my daughter if I have anything to say about it.)

Even most of the interviews you'll do with subjects who've been interviewed before—whether they're corporate spokespeople, university professors, book-touring authors, or television stars—ought to have much the same goal. Sure, you might get that corporate veep to let slip that the new Acme Exobike decapitated lab rats in testing and isn't actually safe for humans. Or you could squeeze the truth about her awful childhood and abusive stepfather out of that television soap star. But it's not likely. Instead, it's more likely that your efforts to play investigative reporter will prove ham-handed enough to make your subject clam up or cut the conversation short.

Initially, this "first date" approach might seem directly counter to our goal of speedy and efficient research. Depending on how accustomed your subject is to being interviewed, you might need to make small talk before getting down to business. Accept an offer of coffee or iced tea. Pet his dog. Reveal a little about yourself—if you have kids and they have kids, great—and be yourself.

Don't be too quick to pull out your notebook and start writing things down; if your subject spills a particularly colorful quote during this getting-to-know-you time, etch it in your memory and scribble it down later, when the interview lags. (Here's another reason for my prejudice against using tape recorders: Hauling out some gadget is yet another warning sign that the subject is now Being Interviewed, and puts the subject on guard just when you're trying to get conversational.)

But starting out with small talk doesn't mean that you're unprepared for the interview or willing to merely let it meander. You'll have a list of questions prepared—though it's better not to make your subject too aware of that list. Gradually, as the conversation warms up, start weaving your questions into the talk. Keep your tone casual—no need to suddenly signal that The Interview Is Starting Now. If you go into the interview knowing exactly what you need to come out of it with, you'll be better able to slide your questions into the conversation and know when you can wrap up.

Throughout such an interview, gentle steering works better than insistent probing. Keep nudging the conversation toward the answers you need to write your article: "How'd you get started inventing stuff, anyway?" and not "What proof do you have that this gizmo of yours really works, that it isn't just another high-tech rip-off?" Ask open-ended questions, not ones inviting "yes" or "no" answers. Get the conversation flowing, build trust and—who knows?—you might get your subject to reveal something, after all.

Interviews with subjects who are prepared, who are on a public relations mission, can be harder to turn into such fruitful conversation—but that's all the more reason to stick with the "first date" approach. When a corporate spokesperson or hawker of some product comes to the interview with a headful of canned answers, you need to turn the encounter into a conversation rather than a recitation. Trying to make the interview an interrogation instead seldom works, despite what you may have seen on "60 Minutes."

Corporate spokespeople and others "doing interviews" typically have a message they want to get out. The better-prepared ones have a tightly focused message—no more than three key ideas, which they aim to repeat three times—and will relentlessly turn the interview to communicating that message.

But is that so bad for you as an interviewer? After all, you're trying to capture and communicate a focused story that readers will care about. If your subject is prepared with a clear message and colorful anecdotes to illustrate that message, you'll have a much more productive session—and ultimately a better story—than if you're interviewing a rambling subject who can't express his ideas with examples meaningful to ordinary readers.

So, to an extent, you should cooperate with well-schooled subjects. And if they're not yet "pros" at getting their message out, help them! Draw out those anecdotes. Ask questions that invite them to make their central points (you'll need these points for your story, after all). If that just-right quote was actually scripted for your subject, well, at least you've got a great quote for your piece.

While cooperating to create an efficient, productive interview for you both, remember to keep it conversational. If you go along when your subject is "on message" and play to his preparation, he'll grow more comfortable and be less adversarial. Like a first date, success in such an interview depends on both parties loosening up a bit.

Once you've turned the interview from a performance into a conversation, you can try to flesh out the pre-programmed message by eliciting fresher, more personal answers. You can even stretch the boundaries of that message by gently tugging in unexpected directions. Ultimately, you can build on the rapport with your subject by asking (in a nonconfrontational way, as you might pose an aside to a friend) surprising questions. If you've been interviewing an oil-company executive who's been tirelessly "on message" about her firm's superior environmental record, for example, you might get around to asking, "What decisions have you had to make that have kept you awake nights?" or "Back when you were in college, was this what you imagined yourself doing for a living?" You might actually get an unscripted answer, especially if the exec hasn't already been put on guard by your previous questions.

Cracking the Toughest Cookies

Surprise can also be effective with the toughest interviewees—the ones who've been interviewed a zillion times before and who, unlike the well-prepped executives and other PR-driven subjects, really don't have a message. Indeed, they'd just as soon not be talking to you.

For instance, I like to tell about interviewing Gene Simmons of the rock-band KISS, backstage before the band played the local auditorium. He was in full regalia, spiked boots up on the dressing room counter, and barely tolerating my presence. Finally I asked him, "What does your mother think about what you do for a living?" It turned out Simmons had bought his mother a nice new house with his KISS earnings, so she thought his career choice was just fine. That question opened him up—and gave me my story's lead.

Then there was the big television star, in between hit series, who came home to the little college he'd graduated from—where, local lore had it, he'd spent more time on fraternity hijinks than in class. I was a writer still young and green enough to be awed at the thought of meeting in the flesh someone I'd seen on the screen. But when the big television star showed up for our interview—late—he wasn't alone. His old college buddies were with him, and it soon became apparent that they'd started the homecoming party hours ago. The big television star sat down at the head of the conference table, whipped out a bottle of whiskey that had already suffered some serious sipping, took a swig, and slid the bottle down the table to his pals.

This was, I realized, going to be a tough interview. At least the big television star offered me a drink, too. Given how the distracted, interrupted, and ultimately abbreviated interview was going to turn out, maybe I should have taken him up on it. At best, tough interviews can be frustrating. At worst, they can be downright frightening. (At least the big television star wasn't inspired to demonstrate his old college wrestling moves on me.)

But a tough interview doesn't have to mean tough luck on your story. With some street smarts and savvy preparation, you can get what you came for out of almost any interview, no matter how tough.

Did I get a story out of my whiskey-swigging big television star, even though talking to me was obviously the furthest thing from his mind? You bet I did (though after he read it, if he read it, he might have wished he *had* tried a few wrestling holds on me).

Tough interviews come in all shapes and sizes. Let's start with those interviews where the answers you elicit run along the lines of "yeah" and "I dunno"—where a long conversation barely yields enough to make you flip a page in your notebook. If you know you're going to be interviewing a likely tough subject of this sort—a child, say, or a taciturn old farmer, or (heaven help you!) a teenager—plan ahead for the extra time you may need to get beyond answers of one syllable. Keep in mind our "first date" approach to establish a rapport.

Try to get away from that awkward sitting-across-from-each-other setting that may make your subject feel like she's being interrogated. Ask for a tour of your interviewee's home or workplace. Seek out something he's proud of, something he's eager to show off—and to talk about. When I used to interview a lot of rural folks who weren't used to talking with reporters, I liked to get them up and out of the house. Walk me around the farm, I'd suggest. Show me how you make maple syrup, I'd ask. Inevitably, getting out and about into territory—and subject matter—they felt comfortable with loosened them up and led their talk into quotes I could use.

For really hard cases, John Gunther once suggested, "One thing I have found out is that almost any person will talk freely—such is human frailty—if you will ask him the measure of his own accomplishment." Ace inquisitor Barbara Walters once revealed to *The New York Times* her five "foolproof questions for the over-interviewed":

1. If you were recuperating in a hospital, who would you want in the bed next to you, excluding relatives?
2. What was your first job?
3. When was the last time you cried?
4. Who was the first person you ever loved?
5. What has given you the most pleasure in the last year?

Note that "If you were a tree, what kind of tree would you be?" is not on the list. (Walters insists she asked that celebrated "twee" question only once.)

The other cure for an interviewee who doesn't much want to talk is a strong dose of preventive medicine. Nothing can turn an interview into a tough one faster than showing your ignorance of the subject. After all, lack of preparation says to your interviewee that this interview isn't really important to you—so why should it be to him?

If the interview's bound to be tough because you have to ask some tough questions—and no amount of preparation can sugarcoat that—at least don't start by blazing away with both barrels. Work to establish a rapport, just as you would with any interview where you have the time to do so. Ask some basic, matter-of-fact questions first. Try to put your subject at ease as much as possible. Part of this strategy is as much practical as it is psychological. A very tough question, after all, may be the last question you'll get to ask—your interviewee may take such offense, or react so angrily, that he'll stalk out of the room instead of answering (or have you thrown out). So ask some of the other questions that you need answers to before broaching one that could end the interview!

Not even the most uncooperative subject necessarily has to keep you from writing your story. Remember, after all, that I went ahead and wrote up my tough interview with the big television star. If your editor allows it, you can even use the circumstances of your tough interview to help sketch your subject for the reader. I painted the scene of the television star drinking with his buddies—not to get back at him for a lousy interview, but to give readers some insight into this guy. He'd shown me that, despite his stardom and success, he hadn't come all that far from the hijinks-happy frat boy who'd gone to college in our little town. That interview scene, coupled with anecdotes from locals who'd known him when, was every bit as effective in characterizing the television star as a stack of pithy quotes from him would have been.

In an extreme case, you don't even have to succeed in interviewing your subject at all to write a story. Gay Talese once "profiled" crooner Frank Sinatra for *Esquire* magazine in an article describing Talese's ultimately unsuccessful quest to interview the Chairman of the Board. Since Sinatra's health was part of the singer's excuse for dodging Talese, the article came to be headlined, "Frank Sinatra Has a Cold." And it's hard to imagine that the article could have been any more readable or revealing if Talese had actually gotten his truly tough interview.

Keeping 'Em Talking

Once you do get your interview rolling and your interviewee talking, how do you keep it going—and in the right direction?

"The object," author John Gunther once observed of interviewing, "is to get the interviewee relaxed, to make him really *talk* instead of just answering questions." Keep that in mind as your interviews unfold. It's important, not just in the obvious sense that you want to get as much out of a free-talking subject as quickly as possible, but in the broader implications of an effective interview for your writing. Good quotes and colorful facts make writing easy. Yes and no answers, grunts, and evasions make for agony at the keyboard.

Practice is the best teacher of productive interviewing technique, but there are some simple tricks that can immediately make your interviews flow better. As I've already suggested, it's best to start on a friendly note and seek to establish empathy with your subject. Follow his or her lead—a little small talk at this stage is not necessarily a waste of time. Besides, you can use the small-talk time to take notes on your subject's surroundings, appearance, and mannerisms. Not only in the beginning but throughout the interview, you should avoid questions that invite yes-or-no answers. You're looking for telling quotes, after all—not monosyllables. And don't waste time on questions that merely confirm what you already know from your research: "So, you graduated from Harvard in 1957?" On the other hand, don't lob questions that really have no answers, or that are so broad they generate useless generalities: "How do you feel about the world these days?" or "How do you feel about being a songwriter?" To get results, you've got to strike a happy medium between the too-specific and the blandly general.

The aim is to get momentum going, to establish a natural conversational rhythm. As Robert Louis Stevenson once put it, "You start a question, and it's like starting a stone. You sit quietly on the top of a hill, and away the stone goes, starting others."

Once the interview gets rolling, except for an occasional question to keep it going or steer it in the right direction, the most efficient thing you can do is shut up and listen. Never get so caught up in the conversation, so overly empathic or argumentative, that you wind up talking as much as your subject. Never, even more seriously, get so full of yourself that you forget who's the interviewer and who's the interviewee. Talk about wasting time! "The worst thing an interviewer can do is talk a lot himself," Liebling advised. "Just listen to reporters in a barroom. You can tell the ones who go out and impress their powerful personalities on their subject and then come back and make up what they think he would have said if he had had a chance to say anything."

So probably the best thing you can contribute to the dialogue in an interview is: "Uh-huh." When your subject is pouring his heart out, say "uh-huh." When your subject is spilling her guts, say "uh-huh." It's the interviewer's universal solvent, guaranteed to keep the interview going without taking it over yourself. If "uh-huh" gets too repetitious, you can really go wild and try "Yes" or "I see." John Brady calls this principle "the sympathetic noise." Not only is the sympathetic noise useful in stalling for time while you scribble the truly interesting response to your previous question, Brady says, it's also a highly effective follow-up "question."

A variant on the sympathetic noise is simply to feed back to the subject what he or she has just said. This can serve the interests of clarity, in making certain that you understand what you're hearing; it can also, by reinforcing and slightly rephrasing the subject's words, spark the next round of good stuff. Such a follow-up, Brady advises, "can unleash a torrent of anecdotes and naked quotes."

Of course, maximizing an interview sometimes requires that you do more than merely keep your subject talking; even in the most productive exchange, you'll occasionally need to steer the talk toward the lines of your story. Certainly, for example, you should pursue the details of a topic if your subject seems to be skimming the surface—but not at the expense of the conversational flow of the interview. "If you make a man stop to explain everything," Liebling advised, "he will soon quit on you, like a horse that you alternately spur and curb." Better, generally, to gently turn the talk back to subjects still vague or unclear to you: "Getting back for a moment to what you said about . . ."

Be firmer, though, when your interviewee veers completely off the track. If you're researching a chapter in your crime novel about a high-rise hotel, it's all well and good to get the manager chatting about what mints his staff puts on the pillows each night—but what you really need is info about hotel security. Don't hesitate to take the talk back to your area of interest, as quickly as possible. If you let your subject wander too far and too long astray, it may be hard to guide him back without seeming rude: "Enough about your little dog Checkers, already, Mr. Nixon. What about this scandal?"

Knowing When to Quit

In several examples so far, I've mentioned a detail or anecdote that made an ideal opening; other times in interviews, you'll be lucky enough to chance upon a bit that makes a perfect closer, a dynamite "hook" for your story, or a sort of epiphany, summing up your subject in a way no fancy words of yours could do. Or maybe your subject relates an experience that, lightly fictionalized, becomes the turning point of your novel. Usually, such gems are anecdotes, and a skilled writer/interviewer can recognize them the moment they are uttered.

If this "magic anecdote" doesn't appear of its own accord, early on in an interview, it's easy to get frustrated and try to force it. There's no magic formula, alas, for eliciting the truly telling stuff. All you can do is be alert— don't miss it!—from the very start of the interview to the last words out of your subject's mouth, even after you've flipped your notebook closed.

The trickiest revelations come at the end, after the interview is apparently concluded. By this point, your subject may well be at his or her least guarded; you will have had your maximum opportunity to establish empathy. The nuggets dropped here, as you conversationally collect your coat and amble toward the door, epitomize the importance of squeezing the most out of every instant of time with your subject. In researching a story I wrote about a woman who's proselytizing for homes built out of straw bales (yes, I used the three little pigs and the first pig's house made of straw in my lead), I was all packed up and heading out the door when, almost as an afterthought, my subject gave me the quote that I hung my ending on:

> So, no, even though straw bale houses may seem at first glance just like thick-walled versions of conventional homes, they are different. They even feel different, often with more rounded walls and lumpier surfaces. The thick straw bale walls keep exterior noises out and interior noises in (one family Catherine knows built a straw bale rehearsal room for their bass-playing son). Inside a straw bale house—well, the word "cozy" keeps coming up. "It feels like an embrace," says Catherine.
>
> Huff and puff all you like—these straw houses are for keeps.

But I never would have gotten that little quote if I hadn't kept my ears open and my mind churning as I headed for the door—and if I hadn't whipped open my notebook again the second I was politely out of sight. I've taken some of my best notes after the interview is over and I'm on my way home. It's like the "spirit of the back stair"—you always come up with the perfect line just as you're slipping down the back stairway. The writer's advantage is that, for you, the conversation doesn't have to end as long as you can open your notebook again. So keep alert during every second you're with your subject, even as you're heading out the door—and be prepared to take some more notes the instant you're alone.

The opposite extreme is the interview that never seems to end because your subject won't shut up, or you're too reluctant—*Have I got enough yet? Or should we go on for another ten hours?*—to bring it to a close. How do you know when to *stop* interviewing, when you've got a magic hatful of anecdotes and it's time to go home to your keyboard? The question may sound frivolous, but it's linked to a lot of time wasting. People *like* to talk about themselves; once you get somebody rolling, he or she might happily bend your ear until all your notebook pages, front and back both, are full—and you're scribbling on napkins. Or, if you're doing many interviews for a single project, there's always that temptation (or feeling of inadequacy): *Maybe I need just one more.* Yet another interview can also be a way of putting off your real writing.

The ideal, of course, is to know in advance exactly what you want from each interview—as I've already prescribed—and to sit down to write as soon as you've got it all. Life isn't always that tidy, unfortunately, so you'll have to develop an intuitive feel for when your notebook is full. John McPhee says that his rule of thumb is that when he starts hearing the same information a third time, he knows he's done interviewing. Without the resources of the *New Yorker* behind you, you might want to stop one iteration earlier. If you feel like you've heard it all before, it's time to get on with your story.

The same goes for individual interviews. When you've covered everything you needed, or you start to hear the same answers over again, it's time to wrap it up. William Manchester once said he figured that he'd gotten all he could out of an interview if he'd elicited ten good anecdotes. Or, if you've clearly outstayed your welcome—say, a previously friendly subject starts to clip his answers and look at his watch—ask your most crucial remaining questions and make a graceful exit. "One last question," you might say, as a signal that: (a) you need to wrap up this marathon and get on with your life, or (b) this ordeal is almost over, if the subject will humor you just a smidge longer. "I don't want to take up too much of your time . . ." is another of my favorite getting-ready-to-exit lines. (Which, admittedly, leaves me open to the reply, "No, no, I've got plenty of time. Have I told you yet about my cat's hernia operation back in '54 . . . ?") Manchester said he used to like to wrap things up with, "Is there anything you think is important which I haven't asked?" If the reply is negative, you can hardly be judged rude for leaving, right?

Close your notebook—but not your ears—and head slowly for the door. Make any last-minute notations as the door swings shut behind you, then head for home. Put on a fresh pot of coffee. It's time to get down to writing, faster and better.

Exercises

1. Write a short profile of yourself that combines quotes (you can make these up—after all, you're the subject!) and exposition to create a sense of what you're like as a person.

2. Watch an interview on one of the popular television "news magazines" or morning news programs. Critique the performance of the interviewer: How well does he or she ask questions that get to the heart of the subject rather than merely elicit canned responses?

3. Interview a friend, a family member, or someone else you have reasonably easy access to, such as your boss, a local small business owner, your minister, etc. Write a short (e.g. five hundred words) profile based on your interview. Use a combination of quotes, paraphrasing, and description to capture not just the substance of the interview, but some aspect of the subject's personality as well.

4. Tape an interview from a television "news magazine." As you watch the tape, try taking notes of the most important things the subject says. Now go back and compare your notes to the tape: How well did you do in capturing the essence of the interview? How accurate was your note taking?

5. With another taped television interview, try watching the tape without taking any notes. Now write down or type out as much as you remember of what the subject said. Again, compare your notes from memory to the tape and see how you did.

CHAPTER 10

GOODBYE, WRITER'S BLOCK!

Why did you decide to become a writer? Was it the glamour of book signings, selling your movie rights, and hobnobbing with other literati? Or was your motivation more internal—a burning desire to share your unique vision with the world? Whatever motivated you to become a writer rather than, say, a plumber or an aerospace engineer, it was probably not the appeal of sitting alone for hours on end, struggling to put one word after the next. As Gene Fowler memorably put it, "Writing is easy. All you do is stare at a blank sheet of paper until drops of blood form on your head."

So it's no wonder that we invent endless ways to put off the actual work of writing. We've even invented something called "writer's block" to justify and explain our procrastination about doing what is, after all, our job. Oddly, you don't hear plumbers complaining about "plumber's block" (or, if you do, they mean something gross in your pipes). Aerospace engineers don't wring their hands and flail their protractors (do they still use protractors?) over some mysterious inability to, well, aero-spatially engineer.

But we're *writers*—we're special. What's really special about us is an amazing ability to invent excuses—writers are good at inventing things, remember—to stay away from the real work of authorship. We'll do anything rather than write: *Honey, the lawn needs mowing—I think I'd better do it before I tackle that next chapter. In fact, gosh, the neighbors' yard needs mowing, too. What do you know? The median strip over on the freeway is looking a little shaggy, now that I think of it . . .* Many of the time-wasters I've already talked about in previous chapters—over-researching, endless interviewing—are essentially excuses to avoid real writing. You could probably speed up your writing production significantly without reading another sentence in this book if only you could master the willpower to make yourself simply sit down and *write*.

Wait, come back! It's not as easy as it sounds, this willpower stuff. We humans are weak creatures; otherwise there'd be no market for chocolate or nacho corn chips. The best tactic for building up your willingness to write is not relying on some neo-Nietzschean willpower exercise (like quitting cigarettes, only much harder), but rather removing some of the fear and loathing that accompanies staring at the blank page and trying to make one word follow the next. In short, don't try to go *through* your writer's block; instead, undermine, and ultimately dismantle it.

For here's the plain truth: Except perhaps for a few truly psychologically disturbed cases, there's no such thing as writer's block. There are only disorganized writers—writers who don't know where their next sentence is going. If you don't know where your writing is going—if, like Columbus' sailors, for all you know the next instant may take you off the edge of the world—it's no wonder you're fearful of writing. In that case, writer's block is only a logical defense mechanism. It may even be your mind's quite rational effort to save you from yourself, to keep you from writing until you know what the heck you're doing.

This chapter will show you how to conquer writer's block, once and for all, one brick at a time.

Working Hard or Hardly Working?

It probably seems impossibly contrary for me to follow that stirring speech by proclaiming that your first step in dismantling writer's block, once all your research and interviews are done, is to do nothing. But that's the way the mind works best, and if you're going to write faster and better, you need to learn to go with, not against, your own brain.

Whether they know it consciously or not, most great writers work this way. Ernest Hemingway, for example, used to sharpen twenty pencils each day before he could settle down to write. Sharpening pencils wasn't the point; what mattered most, I suspect, was the routine that allowed Hemingway's unconscious to get a head start on his conscious writing. Similarly, Thomas Wolfe had to wander the streets all night before he could work, sleepier but wiser, the next morning. Thornton Wilder took long walks to prepare for writing.

Even when I was under the gun as a newspaper columnist, I tried to schedule my interviews far enough in advance of my deadlines to allow a few days' rumination on what I'd heard. Your unconscious is a marvelous organizer and problem solver, even when (especially when) you're not aware it's at work. While you're sharpening pencils or ambling on a long walk, taking a shower or mowing the lawn, your unconscious will be sorting the pieces that must fall into place and make a story for you. Rushing the process will only slow you down in the long run.

This is the work, as Kenneth Atchity notes in *A Writer's Time*, that only time can do. "Percolation," he calls it—and you know what they say about a watched pot. Put your story away, even if only for an afternoon, in a pile, a file drawer, or just the back of your mind. "Start things down the track," Atchity advises, "and let time's engineering do most of the work."

Your percolating or gestation period may vary from task to task, or as you gain greater experience (and your mind begins to recognize the patterns a story might fit). Certainly, it varies from writer to writer: Georges Simenon, the prolific French mystery writer, took just two days to be ready to write the next of his four hundred novels; William Faulkner required six months.

Soon, however, you will find yourself feeling as James Thurber did. "I never quite know when I'm not writing," Thurber once said, half in complaint. "Sometimes my wife comes up to me at a dinner party and says, 'Dammit, Thurber, stop writing.' She usually catches me in the middle of a paragraph. Or my daughter will look up from the dinner table and ask, 'Is he sick?' 'No,' my wife says. 'He's writing.'" Thurber wrote mostly in his head because his eyes were too poor for staring at the page; you'll find that letting your head lay the foundation before you start writing will keep you, too, from having to stare at an empty page.

Pulling Together the Pieces

This "head work," as opposed to paperwork, is so important because it begins the organizing, the shaping, and molding of your mass of material. Your subconscious is expert at spotting patterns, at connecting the dots. Once your material is organized—first in your head and then on paper or floppy disk—the rest is just carpentry. The real art lies in developing the blueprint; the writing is mere craft.

Consider Michelangelo, who was once asked whether carving his statue of David was difficult. Carving the *David* wasn't the hard part, the great sculptor is said to have replied. The great challenge was finding the block of marble that contained the *David* within it. Once that was accomplished, he simply carved away everything that wasn't the *David.*

How do you begin to find the masterpiece that's hidden within your own material? Start with the notions of structure and focus that we explored in chapter three. Try thinking of your writing challenge in big chunks: opening, statement of theme, development of theme, conclusion. Or: conflict, complications, climax, resolution. Then break down the largest chunk, such as the development of your theme or the various complications your protagonist will face, into subpoints. To take a simple example, if you're writing an article about the secrets of smart car shopping, are there four key things your readers should do? Six? Eight? Write them down. If you're profiling an artist, are there five crucial turning points in her career, events that stick out above the rest of her life the way fence posts poke up above a picket fence? List them. What are the five, or seven, or ten biggest hurdles your fictional hero must face en route to retrieving the stolen computer disk—the ways in which things will go from bad to worse until your hero's ultimate triumph? Scribble them on a piece of paper.

Each of these subpoints will naturally attract a grouping of supporting information, scenes, exposition, and examples, as the poles of a magnet gather iron filings. Or, thinking of fences again, the details of your story will string out between the fence posts like the boards of the fence. The most important thing is to figure out what the "fence posts" are and where they go; that way, if you're interrupted, or if the story's too long to write in one sitting, you must make it only to the next fence post to get back on track. And you only need to worry about one section of "fence" at a time, knowing that the rest are waiting for you when you're ready.

Write down simple labels for each of your chunks of story: "evaluating the engine," "her first gallery exhibit," or "the bad guys blow up his car," for example. You might use something as simple as a yellow legal pad, leaving several blank lines between each label where sub-subpoints can go later. (You can indent these secondary and tertiary points a bit to make their place in the hierarchy obvious at a glance.) For longer works, each chapter might get its own page on the pad.

When you have a rough plan of action—let's not even call it an "outline," lest the "O-word" scare away those who were scarred by I-A-1-a-style outlining back in fifth grade—match your series of small chunks to your notes, research, ideas about characters and plot twists. What do you want to make sure to include from your notes under "evaluating the engine"? Where are those great quotes about your subject's first exhibit? You wanted to include a minor villain based on your first boss—should it be the bad guy who blows up the car or the one who breaks your hero's finger? Scribble enough on your pad—perhaps noting page numbers from your notebook—to remind you of what's supposed to go where in the actual writing. Neatness doesn't count; the point is to make your work bite-sized enough that you can swallow a whole section in a single writing stint.

The "O" Word

You realize what you're doing, don't you? Even though we've carefully avoided calling this process "outlining," in effect, you're building a basic outline. It may not have all the bells and whistles that Microsoft Word's Outlining toolbar can generate for you, and it might not pass muster with Mrs. Griswold, your fifth-grade teacher, but it's an outline all the same. Pretty doesn't matter here; making your actual writing work easier does. For the writer looking to beat writer's block, the most useful exercise boils down to simply putting down on paper what you're going to do before you do it.

Writers may run screaming from the idea, haunted by unhappy grade-school memories, or disdain outlining as inimical to letting their creative juices flow. But if you've been following along so far, you'll see that the hard truth is inescapable: Writing faster and better depends on finding your focus and then harnessing all the material necessary toward that end. To wrest order out of the chaos of your notebooks and ideas scribbled on Post-It Notes, you must have a plan—a map that gets your story (and the reader) from start to finish. And, whether it's a high-tech creation on a computer, complete with Harvard labels and a detailed hierarchy of fonts and indentations, or our humble scrawl on a yellow legal pad, the outline is the cartographic key to successful, stress-free writing.

Listen to Pulitzer Prize-winner Jon Franklin: "I don't care what you've heard, or what your literature teacher said, *or even what the writers themselves said.* Every writer of any merit at all during the last five hundred years of English history outlined virtually everything he wrote."

But what if you just can't work that way? Franklin is still more blunt in defining a professed inability to outline. "In telling yourself you can't outline, what you're *really* saying is that you can't think your story through," he says in *Writing for Story,* "and if that's actually the case—which I seriously doubt—then you'd better give up your writing ambitions before you become successful enough for people to discover that you don't know what you're talking about."

Of course, if you've stuck with me this far, then you know it's not as difficult as it seems to think your story through. And the thinking, not the outlining, is the hardest part.

Whenever I preach the gospel of outlining, I like to use the example of John McPhee, the *New Yorker* writer—not because his approach is the only way, or even the best way, but because McPhee's methodical method shows so clearly the connection between focusing your story, and the mechanics of outlining. Because McPhee, though a nonfiction writer, crafts pieces that read like short stories or novels, with scenes, dialogue, and characters who spring to life, his approach can be equally enlightening for fiction as well as nonfiction writers.

Not surprisingly, McPhee credits an English teacher, Mrs. Olive McKee, for inspiring his approach to outlining. He defines his outlines as "logical," a term Mrs. McKee would no doubt approve of. Yet McPhee's outlines for his deftly crafted, intricately structured nonfiction tales are no schoolbook I-II-III, A-B-C creation. As William L. Howarth describes the process in his introduction to *The John McPhee Reader*, McPhee begins by typing up his notes. The typed notes go into a binder. McPhee then works his way through the binder, coding each segment of notes with the topic under which it falls: "Voyageurs" or "Loons," or acronyms such as "GLAT." The topics also go onto index cards, one topic per card.

"After assembling a stack," Howarth explains, "he fans them out and begins to play a sort of writer's solitaire, studying the possibilities of order. Decisions don't come easily; a story has many potential sequences, and each chain produces a calculus of desired and undesired effects. . . ."

When the shuffling of the index cards finally results in a satisfactory structure, McPhee thumbtacks them to a bulletin board. He then photocopies his notes and scissors apart one copy in order to sort the segments of notes, by topic, into file folders. Each folder corresponds to an index card on the bulletin board.

One folder at a time, McPhee writes his way through this "outline." A steel dart on the bulletin board marks his progress through the topics on the index cards.

"Structural order is not just a means of self-discipline for McPhee the writer," Howarth adds. "It is the main ingredient in his work that attracts his reader. Order establishes where the writer and reader are going and when they will arrive at a final destination."

Methodical as his technique may seem, its very mechanical nature forces McPhee to confront the structural challenges of his story—*before* the first draft gets written, not after his story has driven itself off an organizational cliff. The method is mechanical, yes, but the mechanics disguise great artistry: In shuffling his simple index cards, McPhee is like a maestro bringing music out of the multiple voices of the orchestra, or like a sculptor finding the beauty that lies hidden within the stone.

Making It Work for You

If you're now running out to buy index cards, file folders, and a steel dart, great—you've found the religion of outlining. Your own outlining process doesn't have to be the same as McPhee's, however, or even as complex or orderly. The secret isn't in the cards, folders, and dart but in the organizational thinking an outline forces you to do.

My own approach to outlining was admittedly inspired by McPhee's, but since most of my stories are less daunting than his book-length projects, I scaled his process back a bit. (I also honed this technique as a newspaper feature columnist, which didn't give me much time for photocopying and scissoring.) I don't do anything much fancier than the legal-pad process we walked through a few pages back. As I mentioned in chapter one, for an article-length project, I start by scratching out my main points, in rough order; these are more or less the equivalent of McPhee's index-card topics. By and large, these points come from my head rather than from my notes. They are subject to change, reordering, addition, and deletion. But I figure that if I can't remember a key point without referring to my notes, the point probably won't be memorable to the reader, either.

At this stage I concentrate on the broad motions of the article: where I'll start, how I'll hook my readers, what I need to get done between there and the ending. Relying on my head rather than my notes lets me concentrate on the focus and angle I've chosen without being tempted by colorful but irrelevant detours from my notebook. Beginning with a pretty skeletal outline keeps my attention on the map from here to there, not the roadside attractions.

Once I've grappled with my basic structural challenges (the legal-pad equivalent of McPhee's index-card shuffling), in a sense my hardest work is done. The rest is filling in the blanks, matching my notes to my outline, and fine-tuning. Next, I number the pages of my notebook and go through each page to find material that supports each of the points in my outline. Whenever I find a quote, fact, or detail that I'll probably want to use, I highlight it in my notebook and note the page number in my outline. I may also add subpoints to my outline to reflect the details from my notebook. The order of these subpoints, too, is important, and so the outline evolves as it is fleshed out. Here I may even decide which quotes, for example, to use in what order—as indicated by the little page numbers on my legal pad.

After I've worked my way through my notes, I'll quickly review the beefed-up outline to make sure that everything still fits where it is and that the logical flow makes sense. I may move subpoints or whole chunks of outline and attached page notations. The point of outlining isn't to fix your organizational scheme in concrete: Rather, it is to force you to confront exactly these structural questions.

The resulting stew of scribbles may look like chaos, but to the writer who has worked it through, this outline is just the opposite: a finely tuned blueprint from which to write. Map in hand, I know where I'm starting, where I'm going, and how to get there. Paradoxically liberated by this act of rounding up my thoughts, I am free to concentrate on getting there in style.

Making Connections

All right, you say, but how does it really work? Let's look at a real-life example of how a simple story comes together. It's an example of how successful writing is really the business of making connections. Whether you're writing an article or a book, a short story or a novel, you're taking an agglomeration of information and ideas and artfully putting them together into a cohesive whole—like a child turning an unruly pile of Legos into a colorful plastic spaceship or a blocky schoolhouse. The pieces, of course, should belong together—like the interlocking legs of two Lego blocks—or else you've got a work that ultimately won't hold together for readers. But their connections may not be obvious until you gather them all together and begin assembling your story.

On the most sweeping level, making connections in your writing means deciding on your angle, your theme, your "take" on the subject at hand. Many different stories could be written about your chosen topic, just as a child can make many different objects from the same pile of toy blocks: Which one will you create?

So, for example, not long ago I was writing a story about a Florida resort for an in-flight magazine. This was a routine travel story, though the resort itself was certainly extraordinary. But to turn my pile of notes into an a cohesive whole, I had to begin making connections.

I needed an angle, for starters. What overall point did I want to make about this resort? What would be the unifying thread I would use to connect my material? "Here's a Florida resort" is not a story, because it lacks an angle. I tried to think about what makes this resort unusual: It's on an island, which is sort of interesting, at least among U.S. mainland resorts. It has the Atlantic on one side and a marsh wilderness area, not far from the Okefenokee Swamp, on the other—okay, that's promising.

I looked through my notes. I reread them, highlighting points I wanted to make (and that I'd somehow need to connect) in my article; these page numbers would later end up as annotations in my crude outline. Most of what I thought was interesting about this resort—and hence that readers might find interesting—somehow had to do with nature, how it had been built to make a minimal impact on its unusual setting between ocean and marsh. Seven of the resort's golf-course holes hug the Atlantic, more than any other resort in the nation. The courses are irrigated with recycled water. Lights on the pathways are shielded and dim, so as not to disturb nesting sea turtles.

I was beginning to make connections—like (to switch toy metaphors) putting together the pieces of a jigsaw puzzle. All these pieces with bits of blue—they make a sky. And these green ones make the lawn in the picture on the puzzle box. I was figuring out what picture I wanted to make: Here's a resort that manages to please both vacationers and Mother Nature.

Once you've found your angle, the rest of your story should come together pretty quickly. If your angle doesn't suggest an opening and at least one possible way of organizing your writing—making connections—from there, think again: You may not have the right angle on the story you're tackling.

In the case of my travel story, once I'd decided to connect my collection of facts with the theme of how this resort makes the most of its natural surroundings, ideas for an opening started popping into my head. I asked myself: What, of all the things I saw and experienced at this resort, best epitomized the harmony with nature and the remarkable setting? The answer was easy, because it was my closest brush with nature there (other than getting desperately seasick while deep-sea fishing): Horseback riding on the beach. It also connected the marsh and beach, since our ride began in the forest between the two.

On my outline, this became a few scribbles—just enough to jog my memory of what I wanted to include, what I wanted to accomplish:

Horseback riding
Ocean hammock—200 yrs.+ (Span. moss, live oak, egrets)
Beach—sandpipers, 13 mi.
Location—S-most Atlantic barrier isl., NE-most Fla.

In the actual writing, I turned this handful of points, and my experiences, into a brief second-person narrative. I worked to plunge readers into the picture while also quickly establishing my locale and sneaking in a few key facts noted in my outline (the trees are as old as two hundred years, the beach extends thirteen miles, the island is the southernmost of the Atlantic barrier islands, on the northeast coast of Florida). Even when trying to set a scene, as I did here, it's important to pack your prose with information; readers aren't looking for mere pretty words and pointless description. In fiction, too, everything you communicate must make a difference in your story, and a connection with the larger whole. If you show a gun on the wall in the first act, Chekhov advised, it must be fired by the end of the play; your outline is the perfect place to plan where to show that gun.

When I fleshed out my outline points, my opening paragraphs became:

> You duck a low-hanging branch, barely visible in the light filtered through the "ocean hammock" forest of trees as much as two hundred years old, and clutch your saddle's pommel more tightly. The horse picks its way through the sandy soil, which is criss-crossed with fallen branches. Spanish moss drapes from the live oaks, making the path like parting curtains. Off in the dappled shade an egret wades for its supper in a marshy pond—you long to look harder, but you have a horse to hang onto.
>
> Then, suddenly, your horse surges up a sandy slope and the forest gives way to sky, an undulating expanse of ocean and a swath of white sand. Sandpipers, scooting along the tide line, scatter in surprise. To your left and right, beach extends as far as you can see—a shimmering sampling of the thirteen miles of beach on Amelia Island, southernmost of the Atlantic barrier islands, a scenic fingerling at the northeastern corner of Florida.

What made me settle on this opening was what it allowed me to do next. By putting readers on the beach and setting them in motion towards the actual resort, I could quickly describe how the man-made parts of the picture fit smoothly with nature. In my outline, the next section looked like this:

3 golf courses
hotel seems almost natural—249 oceanvw rms, villas, 1,350 acre

Which I turned into:

> You barely notice when the forest on your left gives way to the
> more manicured green of golf holes—three world-class courses,
> artfully tucked between beach and marshlands. . . . Even the
> hotel, with its 249 ocean-view rooms, and the villas filling out
> this 1,350-acre resort and residential community, seem almost
> natural phenomena. And that, of course, is the whole idea.

Then I was ready to begin delving into the details of the resort's eco-friendly
development, followed by more specifics on how the golf courses were crafted
to meld with their surroundings. Next, it was easy to segue to the resort's
extensive program of nature activities ("Nature is also part of the fun here . . ."),
and quotes from the staff naturalist. Each of these was a point in my outline,
with a page number indicating where in my notes I'd find the facts or pithy
quote I wanted to include here. So far, the story almost wrote itself—because
it was easy to make connections between my facts.

But almost every story or section of a book also has its share of information that must be imparted but that may not connect as neatly to your
theme. I couldn't leave out the resort's new shops and spa, for example,
though those points less obviously linked to my nature-loving angle. Fortunately, if readers have stuck with you this far—perhaps half or two-thirds
of the way through your story—you can now get away with less elegant
connections.

So I just played my transition off my nature theme:

10 shops, new spa—sm to spring naturally

Which became:

> Even the resort's newest developments—ten upscale shops and
> a spa, new in 2001—seem to have sprung up naturally among
> the magnolias and Spanish moss. . . .

And then I plowed ahead with the facts I knew readers would also want to
know.

At the end, however, I was careful to return to my opening image, to tie
all my connecting threads together. I took off from a brief section about

the options for buying property within the resort area, using that to plant the notion of wanting to stay for more than just a vacation. My outline took it from there, winding back to my horseback-riding opening:

beach back into forest
wish you were beachcomber

Which became my final paragraph:

> As your horse navigates the steep sandy hill from the beach back into the sheltering forest, the sandpipers resume their foraging, and the whisper of the ocean at your back begins to fade, you really can't blame anyone who's been to Amelia Island for wanting to call it home. And you begin to wonder: What kind of a living can you make as a beachcomber, anyway?

Getting From Here to There

Making connections made my resort story easy to organize, open, and end, and ultimately easy to write. Transitions, of course, were a snap, because I'd already done most of the hard thinking about getting from topic A to topic B—which is absolutely crucial to speeding up your actual writing. Your outline should give you links from one thought or topic to the next. Sometimes these can be obvious and direct—like the link between the resort's eco-friendly golf courses and its other nature-centric activities. Or they can be subtle, almost sneaky—like the transition between the resort's nature activities and its more commercial ones, which "seem to have sprung up naturally among the magnolias and Spanish moss."

Transitions can be physical, visual, or simply verbal. But, however you accomplish them, if you know before you start writing that you can get from here to there (and how you'll do it), you can hit the keyboard without fear that you'll write a section and then not know how to begin the next one. As an editor, I check for transitions to make certain the reader is carried smoothly along from the lead to the close; as a writer, you'll find your work goes much faster if you, like your ultimate audience, are swept along in logical, seamless sequence.

So try to make each specific item under the general headings link somehow not only to the overall topic but also to the item before and the item after. You can use the principle of similarity: If I'm talking about waterfowl along the beach, it's easy to jump to a section about the seashells also found on that same beach. For greater logical leaps, you can also use the trick of contrast—those handy paragraphs that often begin with "But. . . ." Similarly, you can "bounce" from topic A to topic B, as I did when I needed to introduce information about the resort's fishing options. How could I get readers from the beach to out on fishing boats? Simple: "When nature doesn't come to you on Amelia Island, you can always cast for it . . ."

Or how to connect the swimming pools to the resort's elegant restaurants, since I could hardly leave out something as important to the resort experience as eating? Well, the pool does have a small place to eat, so . . . I combined the similarity and contrast techniques to make the connection:

2 heated pools
poolside grill→*restaurants*

Yes, that arrow was in my outline; I knew I'd be making that connection. Once I'd thought of that solution, I didn't want to forget it! Notice how, in turning these notes into sentences, I also reinforced the connection to my larger theme of a resort in harmony with nature:

> Order something cool and wet from the poolside Beach Club Grill, lie back and ponder how nice it was for nature—and nature-sensitive developers—to provide all this for your vacation.
>
> Poolside is hardly the only dining option, of course. . . .

You don't have to have every transition nailed down to the last comma before you're ready to write, but your outline should provide a basic guide to getting there from here. As long as the items in your outline flow smoothly, you can approach the actual writing with confidence that the transitions will work. For one thing, it's a lot easier to write transitions between topics in logical sequence than it is to craft labored, awkward links between subjects that don't really belong together!

Think about how your own stories connect: What binds your key points together and interlocks them like puzzle pieces? What opening epitomizes that connection and can launch you logically into at least the first half of what you must communicate? How might your ending finally sew it all up? Your answers are what shape the stories only you can write. The connections you make will weave your vision of some part of our world for readers.

Will it be a spaceship or a schoolhouse? Without you, it's just a pile of blocks.

Making It Up as You Go Along

But what if you're making up all those building blocks? Do you really need an outline to write successful fiction? Opinions on outlining in fiction appear to be as fiercely divided as, say, those who love cilantro and those who think it tastes like soap, or those who love baseball's designated hitter rule and those who think it's the work of Satan. Science fiction writer Octavia Butler (*The Parable of the Sower*), for example, makes the classic argument against outlining in fiction: "If I outline a story, I feel I've already written it. It loses immediacy for me," she told an ABC-TV Web site interviewer.

On the other hand, Jeffery Deaver (*The Bone Collector*) says that outlining is essential to creating the kind of novels he writes—"a well-structured story that delivers emotional punches at appropriate times." He told Authors on the Web, "Doing this involves carefully guiding the main story, the subplots and the back stories relating to all of them and to a resolution with, ideally, several twists at the end. Although many writers can produce a book like this by simply sitting down and writing without an outline, I can't."

Others who come down on the anti-outline side include Robert B. Parker, who says he has no idea what will happen when he sits down to write one of his Spenser detective novels, and Lisa Scottoline, author of the Bennie Rosato legal capers. Scottoline argues that not outlining keeps her story flowing smoothly, as she goes along from page to page simply asking, "What would happen next?"

Among authors who do outline, Jonathan Kellerman, author of the Alex Delaware novels, echoes Deaver's reasoning that he's "not smart enough to keep it all in [his] head." Outlining is also a vaccine against writer's block, says Kellerman. But he admits that once he actually starts writing a novel, he seldom looks at his outline—and the final product often varies widely from it.

Perhaps most tellingly, romance novelist Barbara Delinsky, author of *Flirting with Pete* and other titles, says she wrote her first few books without outlining. But, as she describes it on her author Web site (www.barbaradelinsky.com), after fifteen novels knocked out without an outline, she then decided to tackle something more ambitious: a five-hundred-page book instead of two hundred pages. Though she did a bit more planning for this novel, she struggled with it until a new agent suggested, "the more time I spent in preparation, the better the finished product would be." So Delinsky outlined her next book, *A Woman Betrayed*—and, she says, it became "a stronger, better-written book and more copies of it were printed and sold than of any of my earlier novels." Now she prepares for all her books with an outline under a dozen pages long, which she supplements with character sketches.

Though these successful fiction authors seem to be coming down solidly on two quite different sides of a very sharp fence, I think that when you listen closely to them, most novelists are actually saying the same thing about the need to prepare to write. The differences come down to the writer's psychology: Some feel more comfortable having everything planned from page 1 to page 455; others crave the spontaneity of making some of it up as they write. Even among the anti-outlining crowd, few really claim that they sit down at the keyboard without having given any thought whatsoever to what they'll write. The outline advocates admit that some people might be able to keep all those balls in the air and write without an outline—just not them.

So Octavia Butler, who says she doesn't outline, goes on to say, "I need to know when I begin something about the main character. I need to know the end of the story. And I need to know the title, which kind of keeps me on the straight and narrow; the title reminds me where I'm headed. If I write without knowing the end, it's like deciding a journey and not knowing your destination; you could be going anywhere and nowhere. If I write without knowing my character very well, my character is liable to sound like anybody or nobody." That doesn't sound all that different from the approach of outliner Barbara Delinsky, does it?

Even Stephen King, who seems to say in his how-to memoir *On Writing* that he never outlines, does tell the story of the "Eureka!" moment in which the story of *The Stand*, which he'd been struggling with, finally crystallized for him. In "a frenzy of excitement," he wrote a page or two of notes to capture the story as he now envisioned it, then spent the next few days turning it over in his mind to make sure it really worked as he hoped. Not a formal outline, certainly, but neither did King simply launch into this multi-hundred-page opus without some sort of plan.

That's all you need, really—some sort of plan. How detailed and how formal a plan you need is up to you, and depends on your psychological makeup and your skill set as a writer. Even in nonfiction, as I've grown in experience, I find I can bang out shorter, uncomplicated pieces without my treasured yellow legal pad. But it's not that I'm striking out without a plan; rather, I've done this enough that I can make and keep the plan in my head.

If you're a beginning writer, I'd suggest that you err on the side of over-planning rather than striking out with what may turn out to be an inadequate map for your writing journey. As you grow in confidence and the ability to keep your story straight in your head rather than on paper, your outlines can become more sparse, more bare bones. For now, to write faster and better— no matter what you're writing—try doing more "homework" before you sit down at the keyboard. And if you think you're suffering from writer's block, remember that Mrs. Griswold had the cure for that way back in fifth grade.

Eight Tips for Outlining Success

Assuming that I've convinced you to give at least some sort of outlining a try, here are some quick tips to keep in mind as you start making the "maps" for your stories:

1. Your outline should grow directly from the focus of your story— whether that comes in turn from an editor's assignment, your query, or sheer inner inspiration.
2. Resist the temptation to skip outlining in order to "save time." It's precisely the process of outlining, however crudely, that will save you that precious time.
3. Use your outline to compress and distill your story, packing it with information and events. "Dense" stories turn out to be much faster to write than fluffy ones with the information and action far between, since you don't have to make up so much on the fly.
4. Employ comparison and contrast to impart "movement" to your narrative and to smooth your transitions. If your story's pace zips right along, so will the writing of it.
5. Don't be afraid to jettison material, even notes carefully marked in your outline, if they don't fit into the actual writing of your story.
6. Particularly if space or time is precious, use your outline to winnow your notes; don't write for the trash can.
7. Don't worry at this stage about where your paragraphs will begin and end; that will work itself out in the actual writing.
8. Outline even your detours and asides, to make sure you have a route back to your main narrative.

Got it? Good, because—at last—we're ready to start putting one word after another. But don't worry about "staring at a blank sheet of paper until drops of blood form on your head." As you'll see, all our preparation is about to pay off.

Exercises

1. Pick a short story or article you admire and outline it. Your outline should fit on one side of a legal pad.

2. Analyze the transitions of the piece in number one. Draw arrows between logical connections. Circle any spots where transitions are weak or strained.

3. Write the key points from your current writing project (or a chapter from a book-length project) on something you can reshuffle easily, such as index cards or pieces of paper.

4. Experiment with various ways of ordering the key points from number three. Reshuffle your story until you find an order and an organizational strategy.

5. Use your reshuffled key points to create an initial outline for your current writing project.

CHAPTER 11

STARTING YOUR STORY

As long as there have been writers, there has been agony over how to start writing. Plato supposedly rewrote the first sentence of his *The Republic* fifty times. Authors of all stripes have tried everything to get their creative juices flowing, confronting the blank page from almost every imaginable vantage point: Hemingway, Lewis Carroll, and Virginia Woolf all wrote standing up. Truman Capote, Robert Louis Stevenson, and Mark Twain tried it lying down. Willa Cather read a passage from the Bible, more for prose style than for divine inspiration. Edgar Allan Poe sat his Siamese cat on his shoulder before starting a new poem.

Starting, that's the hardest, slowest part. Breathes there a writer who actually *enjoys* writing that first sentence, the opener, the lead? (Or "lede," as some newspapering types spell it, thinking perhaps a trick of orthography will make the problem go away.) As Peter De Vries (*The Tunnel of Love*) once put it, "I love being a writer. What I can't stand is the paperwork."

Why all the agony? Why not just start writing?

If you really had to ask those questions, you're obviously a non-writer—an accountant in disguise, maybe—who's somehow sneaked all the way to chapter eleven. The opening, after all, is not merely the beginning. Write it wrong, and it can also be the *end* for turned-off editors and readers. As editor Brian Vachon has said, "If that first and most important paragraph does not slap and sparkle like the sun in water, then we editors can't bother unduly with the rest." Or listen to nonfiction guru William Zinsser: "The most important sentence in any article is the first one. If it doesn't induce the reader to proceed to the second sentence, your article is dead. And if the second sentence doesn't induce him to continue to the third sentence, it's equally dead."

With so much riding on the opening, such a weight bearing down on a few frail sentences, you'd do better to wonder how anything ever gets written.

Aliens and Tailfins

As if that's not enough pressure, I'm about to add some more: Your opening lines should point the way for you to write the rest of your story. The hard work of crafting your opening should be like climbing to the top of roller-coaster track: From here on there will be ups and downs, but there's nowhere else to go but forward. Just hang on and enjoy the ride.

Before this latest load piled on the humble opening makes you decide to give up writing and take up something sane, like Hollywood stunt work, let me quickly add: Don't panic. If you've come this far along the path to writing faster and better, you'll find that writing openings is suddenly much less awful—and much quicker—than it used to be.

The reason for this is the same reason that your openings will now function like loading the gun to fire off your entire story: By now, you really and truly understand what your story is about. You've focused on the idea and the angle, and religiously kept that focus through research and interviewing. You've outlined your story from start (gee, your opening is already in the works, isn't it?) to finish.

What this means is your opening is no longer like some alien organism, grafted onto the body of your story from afar in order to grab readers' attention. Forget the artificial, unnatural, souped-up opener. You know the sort I mean: Gimmick openings, juiced-up openings, falsely mysterious openings—writers, in their desperation to get the darned thing started, have tried about everything that can be done with a pile of words and some punctuation. You've seen openings like these (maybe you've even written some):

The false surprise:

Bob Durant was battling an alien invasion. Like a scene straight out of "The War of the Worlds," the aliens were everywhere—in offices, in stores, even in our homes.

But these aliens weren't from Mars. As an officer with the Border Patrol, Bob was after illegal aliens, undocumented workers who . . .

The unwelcome second person:

You are dead. Sixty seconds ago, you were alive, driving your car, heading home from a party. You'd had a little too much to drink.

The evening started out like any other evening . . .

The Andy Rooney wannabe:

Did you ever wonder how much helium is stored in the U.S. Helium Reserve system? And did you ever wonder how come all that helium doesn't just float off into space?

Answers to those questions and many more can be found in the offices of the American Helium Council . . .

Aside from being simply awful openings, these made-up examples, and their real-life kin commit a structural sin: They are all tacked-on gimmicks, the writing equivalents of the humongous tailfins that sprouted on American cars in the fifties. Did the tailfins make the cars drive better or more smoothly? Did they have anything at all to do with transportation? Nope—they existed solely to catch your eye. From a transportation standpoint, the tailfins might as well have been attached to rocks.

You know by now that we're not looking for openings like tailfins. The opening doesn't stand apart from the whole, a pretty bauble that serves only to entice the unwary reader; rather, it is essential to the whole, the beginning of a journey that you and the reader are taking together.

Starting in the Middle

I'm not saying that your openings can or should be dull. Just the opposite: By starting your stories with your best, most telling material, you'll write openings that are compelling without resorting to gimmicks or trickery.

Look at the Greeks, who knew a good lead when they saw one. Remember when we talked about beginning *in medias res*? By starting the story in the middle, in the very heart of the action, and then filling in the reader on what has gone before, Greek authors from Homer to Sophocles succeeded in encapsulating their stories in their openings. They took their best stuff and led with it, confident that the audience, once hooked, would hang on for the ride. If Homer had started with, say, Odysseus's childhood or his wooing and wedding of Penelope, we might never have stayed with the story until the action got good.

Starting *in medias res* is also faster for the writer. You get to write the easiest, most dramatic material first. Lead with the part of the story that almost tells itself; the rest will follow, and fast.

Your outline can help here. The outline of a story that starts *in medias res* is pretty basic, but mighty useful. Much condensed, it's always going to follow this fundamental pattern:

Open at a dramatic high point, pre-climax

Exposition on opening scene

"Hook" or other pivotal paragraph

Flashback: How we got to this point

Catch up to the main flow of the narrative at the point of the lead

Continue to climax and conclusion

Once you develop a sense of what moment—not too early, not too late—to lead with, this becomes an almost foolproof scheme for a story. I've used it for tales of everything from science to romance, animal husbandry to art. For example, I once set out to do a yarn on "turtle tapping"—guys who hunt snapping turtles by tapping for them in the mud with long metal poles. (Go figure.) I could have started with my protagonist setting out for the creek, gathering his gear; I could even have led with how he learned this arcane practice. But I knew the fastest way in and through the story was to start with the turtle tapping itself:

Turtles love mud. At the first snap of fall, they burrow into the ooze and sleep like the dead, safe as babes—they think—in the dank, gooey, lightless cradle of a creek bank. Turtle paradise.

Wayne Olson probes the mud with a steel pole as tall as he is and slender as a finger, flaked with rust. He pecks out a pattern as precisely as a maestro with a baton, orchestrating a symphony in the muck: *Pocketa-squish. Pocketa-squish.*

Thunk.

The sound of pole striking turtle—a hollow, anybody-home? kind of sound—stands out like a bass-drum beat in a tinkly piano concerto, once you know what to listen for. . . .

By starting with the "thunk" of finding a turtle, not only was I able to get the story quickly under way and hook the reader, I was also able to convey a lot of information fast, here and in the subsequent paragraphs. I set the scene, started the explanation of what was going on, and introduced my main character. The opening itself was easy to write, because I had solid, colorful material to weave into it; then, with that much territory already covered, I was able to approach the rest of the tale with much less trepidation. I soon backtracked to the background leading up to this actual tapping of a turtle, then (flashback complete and main thread rejoined) I zipped forward to the conclusion, which had Olson eating his catch (of course!).

The classic use of *in medias res* in fiction (besides Homer, that is) is of course in mystery novels, where it's often most effective to begin with a body and then explain how it got there and got dead. No wonder Lawrence Block, author of *A Stab in the Dark, Hit Man*, and a zillion other mysteries and thrillers, advises, "Don't begin at the beginning." But even today this technique is hardly reserved for "page-turners" where it's obviously imperative to start off with a bang. Salman Rushdie's *The Ground Beneath Her Feet*, for example, begins with the disappearance of American expatriate singer Vina Apsara; from there, Rushdie then unspools the lives of Apsara and two men in India who love her and the events that led up to her disappearance.

Whether you begin your story truly in the middle or just identify a bang-up spot early in your chronology to launch a conventional narrative, the important thing to remember is the principle of starting from strength. Open with good, solid stuff that you can build the rest of your story on, not a jerry-built lead that's going to topple under the weight of subsequent paragraphs.

It's probably worth noting, by the way, that this approach also leads to better storytelling. Just ask the Greeks.

Focusing Your Opening

Let's look at several different solutions for creating an opening that springs from your focus. The simplest approach, of course, not so different from starting *in medias res* but without those chronological complications, is to wade right into the heart of your story. Two or three warm-up sentences and then *bam!* your focus is front and center.

That's the approach I took for an assignment for *Logic*, a magazine for Control Data Corp. Here's how the editor summarized my focus in the published article's subhead: "Faced with a predicted shortage of technical brainpower, corporations team up with educators to train the engineers of tomorrow." That meant my article had to accomplish four things:

1. Establish the problem (predicted shortage of technical brainpower)
2. Establish the needs of corporations

3. Establish the needs of colleges and universities
4. Show how those needs have led to corporations teaming up with educators, and how these partnerships have addressed the problem in number one

A tall order, especially since the editor wanted me to spend the bulk of my word allotment on the specific examples in number four. So I decided to lead with number one:

> "What do you want to be when you grow up?" Ask any classroom of children that eternal question and the answers will range from "firefighter" to "astronaut" to "cowhand." How many want to be *engineers?* Not a hand will go up. Engineering is hard, complicated and difficult to define with a drama that matches dousing fires or riding the range.
>
> In the United States, companies are realizing . . .

And I was already into point two. As I detailed points two and three, examples and statistics would substantiate my lead's broad assertion, but I'd at least gotten the problem on the table and started down the road toward solutions.

Notice, though, that I still sugarcoated the opening. I started with children, a familiar situation, and easy rapport with readers. Not until the third sentence did I mention the hard, complicated and undramatic subject of engineering. You don't need "tailfins," but neither do you want to run the reader down with the first sentence:

> Nobody wants to be an engineer. . . .

"Neither do I," thinks the reader, turning the page.

Still, however true to my focus, was this the best possible way for me to start the story? Let's just say it was my best choice given the material I had. If I'd had a real-life anecdote that dramatized the problem, that might have been a more vivid start:

> Ten years ago, Professor Charles Smith's Introduction to Engineering class was held in an auditorium seating 200 students. Smith needed a microphone to be heard over the rustle of note-taking. Late-arriving students had to perch on the stairs.
>
> This semester, however, Smith is holding Introduction to Engi-

neering in his office. All three future engineers can fit comfortably around his kitchen-sized conference table . . .

Another attractive option would have been to depict a scene that exemplified the solution to the problem in action:

The freshmen shoulder their book bags, flirt and jostle in the hallways just like any other group of college students. But these young engineering students aren't heading to a conventional classroom behind ivied walls. Their classroom is the roaring, clanking heart of a General Motors assembly line . . .

The important thing to note in these options, like the lead I actually used, is that all spring from the story's focus. They dramatize or otherwise try to intrigue the reader with one of my central points. (After all, it's hard enough to communicate three or four key points, without wasting the lead on making a point not crucial to your story!) All are integral to the thrust of the article—they all do some of the work that my words had to complete. Not a tailfin in the bunch.

Building From a Collision

Think about what makes a good story, whether fact or fiction. The essence of many good stories is conflict: two forces, two ideas, two trends in opposition or contrast. If the real focus of your story is some sort of collision, that ought to be reflected in your opening. And by starting your story with two opposing notions, of course, you make it easy to organize and write the rest.

In my actual lead for *Logic*, the contrast is between kids' traditional ideas about careers and the demanding yet in-demand field of engineering. My made-up "Professor Smith" opening contrasts the popularity of the class a decade ago with today; the scene of students at GM plays stereotypical ideas about college life against the image of a factory.

Because conflict and contrast lie at the heart of so many stories, and because they make for instant reader interest, they are ideal for structuring openings. Conflict and contrast in the lead put the action out front: *Hey, readers, we're butting heads here! Ideas in collision, read all about it!* (Much more interesting and reader-grabbing than harmony, the status quo, or when all is as expected.)

The ultimate example of opening with a collision of opposites, of course, has to be Charles Dickens's memorable beginning of *A Tale of Two Cities*:

> It was the best of times, it was the worst of times, it was the age
> of wisdom, it was the age of foolishness, it was the epoch of
> belief, it was the epoch of incredulity, it was the season of Light,
> it was the season of Darkness . . .

Even if you don't aspire to quite such rhetorical heights, conflict and contrast can help start your story with a bang. For example, when writing about people, real or fictional, it's the surprising juxtapositions within a character that makes that person interesting—worth writing about, in short. If your hero is a sterling goody-two-shoes in every respect, he's a yawner. Who wants to read about someone with no flaws? As author Dorothy Allison puts it, "If all of your characters are good girls who go to church on Sunday morning, what can happen?" She remembers growing up reading about such boring goody-two-shoes as the Bobbsey twins. "All those stories about the ragged but clean poor were so saccharine they made my teeth hurt," Allison says. "I prefer people who are good solid Christian people—who *shoplift*."

If that's your character, don't make readers drone through four or five chapters of clean living before discovering the surprise that makes this person interesting! Grab us with your compelling contrast right from the start:

> On the way home from church, where she'd listened to a stirring
> sermon on sin and then served lemonade for the Ladies Auxil-
> iary, Bertha Finch stopped by Wal-Mart and tucked a cut-glass
> pitcher under her ample dress. Breezing out of the store with
> her shoplifted treasure close to her bosom, smiling cheerily at
> old Mr. Watkins, the greeter, gave Bertha almost as much of a
> thrill as this morning's sermon. The pitcher would be lovely for
> pouring lemonade next Sunday, Bertha thought . . .

Similarly, if you uncover some surprise or insight about a profile subject, don't hide it—make it the focus of your story and the seed for your lead. For example, I once set out to do a story on the head of the local IRS office, timed to tax day, April 15. What I found out, however, was that the IRS boss was perhaps the only guy in town who *wasn't* scrambling over taxes on April 15. I harnessed that contrast—the relaxed tax-man on the busiest tax day—to start my story:

> Today, tax day, is a day like any other day for Bob Huss, tax
> man. While his fellow citizens ponder a midnight deadline, the
> arcane numerology of tax forms and the prospect of Leaven-

worth, Huss goes about the business of the Internal Revenue Service. Just another working day. . . .

This theme of confounding expectations, set up in my opening, continued through the story. You'd expect a guy who audits your taxes to look scary, right? But Huss proved as ordinary and mild-mannered as they come. And so on. I'd expected April 15 to represent the unleashing of an audit monster; instead, I found an ordinary guy with a job to do.

Along the same lines, when I went to profile sports tycoon John W. Galbreath, I (and my readers) expected a Donald Trump of the horsey set. What I found instead was a man who could have been anybody's grandpa. So I led with this contrast:

> John W. Galbreath has sold thirty thousand homes and changed skylines all over America. His baseball teams have won three World Series. He is the only horse owner to win both the Kentucky Derby (twice) and the English Derby. . . . [His houseguests] include former president Gerald Ford and Queen Elizabeth II.
>
> Yet Galbreath insists he's nothing special. "Just an ol' country boy. Just one of the gang."

To make the lead click, I loaded the first paragraph with as many examples of Galbreath's extraordinary success as I could pack in. That set up the "punch line" of the second paragraph: "Just an ol' country boy." Even if readers respond with disbelief ("Yeah, right."), at least the opening elicits a response. And then readers have to read on to see if their response was right.

Surprising leads can even (surprisingly) feed into your endings. Ayn Rand fans can probably quote the startling opening of her novel *The Fountainhead* from memory:

> Howard Roark laughed.
>
> He stood naked at the edge of a cliff. The lake lay far below him . . .

Now, immediately the reader wants to know why this guy is outside, naked, and what the heck he has to laugh about. Or is he just crazy? Once we learn (on page two) that this naked guy is a recently expelled architecture student, we're even more curious: What would you have to do to get kicked out of *architecture* school? We're hooked, and the story zips along for nearly seven hundred pages from there.

But, 695 pages later, we come back to the undaunted figure of our hero, still poised by a large body of water: "Then there was only the ocean and the sky and the figure of Howard Roark."

Setting the Pace

Because your opening sets up and launches into all of what's to come, it's also crucial to the rhythm of your writing. Your opening lines set the pace; whatever comes next either follows this initial rhythm or plays off against it. Your lead starts your story fast or slow, jerky or smooth, thoughtful or theatrical.

At the most basic level, rhythm rules the ebb and flow of your opening: how it builds to a punch line, how it rolls forward into the body of your story. A staccato rhythm can act as an attention-getting gun burst at the very start, or as a contrast once you've got some momentum going, but one burst after another (say, a series of short sentences) can create an off-putting, beat-'em-over-the-head effect. Similarly, a series of long, languid sentences in the opening must build to some sort of release, lest the reader grow weary and wander away while your sentences wander.

Look at the almost musical ebb and flow of words with which Mark Twain begins *Huckleberry Finn*:

> You don't know about me without you have read a book by the name of *The Adventures of Tom Sawyer*; but that ain't no matter. That book was made by Mr. Mark Twain, and he told the truth, mainly. There was things which he stretched, but mainly he told the truth. That is nothing. I never seen anybody but lied one time or another, without it was Aunt Polly, or the widow, or maybe Mary. Aunt Polly—Tom's Aunt Polly, she is—and Mary, and the Widow Douglas is all told about in that book, which is mostly a true book, with some stretchers, as I said before.

Try counting the words in each of Twain's sentences and you'll see how he builds to an effect, like a punch line ("That is nothing."), then rolls away: 25, 14, 12, 3, 21, 33. The opening unfolds with the ease of talk, but within each longer sentence are little staccato bursts that serve almost as extra punctuation: "mainly," "Tom's Aunt Polly, she is," "as I said before."

In your own writing, aim for openings that combine long and short rhythms to create a pleasing effect that also, not so incidentally, mirrors the content. Here's how I started a *Travel & Leisure* story on the Black Hills of South

Dakota—note the medium-length start, two longish rambles, and a following burst, accentuated by making it a separate, one-sentence paragraph:

> Legend has it that Paul Bunyan created the Black Hills as a burial cairn for his great blue ox, Babe. But those of a more scientific cast of mind will insist that the rough peaks of the nation's oldest mountains were made 70 million years ago, when subterranean pressure lifted a 50-mile-wide chunk of what is now South Dakota and Wyoming above the surrounding flatlands. Eons of creation have worn away the resulting dome into a crazy-quilt of granite needles, canyons studded with vivid agate, plateaus glistening with mica and rose quartz.
>
> That's what the scientists will tell you.

Not to sound like a broken record, but you can hardly miss the role of conflict and contrast in this lead. And of course the dichotomy I set up at the start—the scientific, geologic Black Hills versus the mythic place—ran throughout the story.

This is the broader role of rhythm in your opening: To underscore the themes that will play out all the way to the conclusion. The larger rhythm of my Black Hills article was a counterpoint between these disparate ways of viewing the place. So, having given the scientific viewpoint its initial due, I continued with the Native American point of view:

> The Indians say the Black Hills are a sacred place, though not because any giant white man's ox is buried there. . . .

Back and forth the story went, following the rhythm inaugurated in the opening. At the end, in four bursts again accentuated by paragraphing, I brought the drumbeat of the beginning to its natural conclusion:

> Some say a myth is buried in these hills. The Indians say spirits dwell in the heights. They say this is a sacred place.
>
> Perhaps they are right.

This is an ending, not a beginning, so it might seem I've strayed from this chapter's topic. But my point is that the opening can't be separated in your structure from the body of the story, or even from the end. The opening can't be a tailfin add-on. It must draw readers into your focus, spark off the conflict and contrast of your angle, and begin the rhythm that will beat behind your story to the final word.

Setting the Scene

Particularly when writing fiction, your opening section often needs to firmly locate readers in the *where* of your story. The temptation, of course, is to go on and on about your setting with paragraphs of static, descriptive detail. Victorian novelists could get away with this, perhaps, but their readers lived lives untroubled by such distractions as MTV, the Internet, cell phones, and telemarketers. In the twenty-first century, you have to set your scene while getting on with the action. A lovely, descriptive passage won't cut it for your opening; you have to also clue readers into why they should care about this place. Ideally, say, while liltingly painting the moors on which your novel will unfold, your first paragraph will also have someone murdered in an especially grisly way.

Even your descriptions must be active rather than passive, to start your story rolling. Don't write, "There were birds in the trees"—instead, put those birds and even the trees in motion (oh, and be specific—what kind of birds? trees?): "Sparrows flickered among the aspens, rattling the leaves . . ."

See how Ernest Hemingway sets his scene in the opening of *A Farewell to Arms*:

> In the late summer of that year we lived in a house in a village that looked across the river and the plain to the mountains. In the bed of the river there were pebbles and boulders, dry and white in the sun, and the water was clear and swiftly moving and blue in the channels. Troops went by the house and down the road and the dust they raised powdered the leaves of the trees.

Never mind that we'd want to rewrite "there were pebbles and boulders" to be more active—concentrate on that third sentence, where Hemingway interrupts this idyllic scene with the sudden interjection of troops. Here's menace, danger, not merely a pretty setting. And he intertwines the troops and the scenery with vivid, active detail: "the dust they raised powdered the leaves of the trees."

Can you see, too, how Hemingway's opening springs from the focus of his story? Throughout *A Farewell to Arms*, he juxtaposes images of life and death, of nature and war—why wait until, say, chapter three to get started?

Ideally, in your stories, you should aim to start not merely with a scene but with what we might call a *telling* scene. That is, look for a scene that exemplifies the point of your piece. Here's a simple example—not exactly up to Hemingway standards—from a story I wrote about a local arts project:

> Maybe it's the slanting yellow light, like a giant stick of butter jutting through the open doorway of the old theater, illuminating the dance of dust motes, that lets Dru Ruebush see possibilities instead of problems here.
>
> To you or me, the El Sol Theatre—a pueblo-art deco fantasia on the outside, smack in the heart of downtown Silver City's Bullard Street—looks like a wreck inside. Bags of trash cover the stage. Jagged holes have been torn in the ceiling, as though the Hulk recently passed through. Oh, and did we mention why the sun streaming through the door looks so dramatic? No lights. No electricity—it's been ripped out right at the box.
>
> But Dru Ruebush, the proud new owner of the El Sol with his wife, Gina, looks deep into the shadows, up the slope of tattered, mustard-colored seats, past the grime that thickens the aisles, and sees the home of America's next great regional theater.

Here are our old friends conflict and contrast again. I wanted to paint as grim a picture as possible of the theater's current, run-down state to contrast with my subject's grandiose dream. But look at how much information I managed to pack into these three paragraphs, even while waxing poetic about the mess: who, where, what's it look like, what are some of the problems (no electricity). Sure, the telling scene can be your chance to get colorful in your writing, a place to unsheathe those turns of phrase you've been longing to use. But it must *grab* readers, not merely mesmerize them with its poetry, and haul them along into the meat of your story.

Speaking Metaphorically

Another popular technique in fiction, which can also be applied to nonfiction, is opening with what we might call the "telling metaphor." Now, cooking up a metaphorical scheme for your story is a hazardous undertaking. But, done properly, it can add a depth and finesse to your writing that makes it more than just the sum of your words. If you're going to go this route, it's almost an absolute that you start it at the story's beginning.

You don't have to have a complex symbolic scheme, the stuff of future dissertations, in mind to begin with a telling metaphor. Sometimes a metaphorical approach simply works in the same way that a good anecdote or vivid scene does—encapsulating your theme and getting things going with a bang. The great A.J. Liebling, for example, started a lengthy *New Yorker* profile of the Longs of Louisiana political infamy like this:

> Southern political personalities, like sweet corn, travel badly. They lose flavor with every hundred yards away from the patch. By the time they reach New York, they are like Golden Bantam that has been trucked up from Texas—stale and unprofitable. The consumer forgets that the corn tastes different where it grows. That, I suppose, is why for 25 years I underrated Huey Pierce Long. . . .

That notion of "traveling badly," like "sweet corn," (I know, it's actually a simile rather than a metaphor) launched Liebling into his thesis: "the corn tastes different where it grows." For New Yorkers, baffled by the enduring appeal of the Long dynasty, Liebling proposed to go down "where it grows" and see why the "corn" tasted so sweet to Louisiana voters.

Your "telling metaphor" can also arise out of the material itself—a piece of the story is thrust into the opening, where it's made to stand for the whole. I started a story on an exhibition of Grant Wood paintings this way, by letting one lesser-known painting act as a metaphor for the artist's entire life:

> In "Death on the Ridge Road," Grant Wood poised a low-slung sedan near the top of a hill. The sedan, in the left lane, has just passed a pokey Ford. But a blood-red truck looms in the storm clouds atop the hill, about to deliver tragedy.
>
> That painting might have been a map of Grant Wood's career. When the Iowa artist painted it in 1935, Wood was zooming toward the top of the artistic world, fueled by the phenomenal success of his "American Gothic."

Two paragraphs further on, I completed the metaphor: "Seven years later, Grant Wood was dead, his reputation a wreck." (Note the "wreck" allusion to the impending crash of the painting.)

At the story's end I subtly reintroduced my opening metaphor. (Frequently, you'll find your lead metaphors also solve the tricky problem of how to end the tale.) I concluded with Wood's actual death:

On his deathbed, Grant Wood told his friend and fellow region-alist artist, Thomas Hart Benton, that when he got well he was going to change his name. He would move where no one knew him. He would start all over again in a new style, take a different route. But it was too late.

Another example of how a metaphor can give you not only a lead but an ending, and in the process add a thematic unity to your work, is one of my favorite stories from my newspaper days. It was also one of the hardest to write: an on-deadline report of the funeral of a young man in a tiny northeast Iowa town who was one of the few casualties of the Grenada invasion. Obviously, this was a tragedy. But how could I make it more than just a stock, war-victim story—how could I make it uniquely about this particular young man? As in the Grant Wood story, I used a small piece of knowledge about the subject to epitomize the whole:

> Harpers Ferry, Iowa—The morning opened leaden and low, wind whispering of cold rain.
>
> Lousy weather for baseball, Rusty Robinson might have said.
>
> Pvt. Russell L. Robinson, 22, was an outfielder, a son of Harpers Ferry and a gung-ho Army Ranger. Last week, on the sunny Caribbean island of Grenada, somebody pitched him one he couldn't handle . . .

Here, really, I combined an opening scene with an opening metaphor, contrasting the metaphor with the reality. Notice how quickly, however, I segued from the metaphorical to the hard facts. The story went on: "A few hours after he parachuted in with U.S. invasion forces on Oct. 25, a rocket struck his jeep."

After the details of the funeral, my metaphor provided a framework in which to pour the final facts. I closed the story on a note reminiscent of how I'd begun:

> As the mourners drifted away, the last rifle report seemed still to echo in the wounded air, like the crack of a bat driving one deep to the outfield wall, very deep indeed.

In a sense, one of the most famous leads of literature—the opening of Herman Melville's *Moby Dick*—falls into this same "telling metaphor" category. After his well-known "Call me Ishmael" first line, Melville soon launched into the imagery of death and funerals:

> . . . Whenever I find myself growing grim about the mouth; whenever it is a damp, drizzly November in my soul; whenever I find myself involuntarily pausing before coffin warehouses, and bringing up the rear of every funeral I meet . . . then, I account it high time to get to sea as soon as I can.

In the end, of course, Ishmael watches Ahab go down with his ship, and the sea and the image of death come together in a final metaphorical flourish: ". . . then all collapsed, and the great shroud of the sea rolled on as it rolled five thousand years ago."

As Melville certainly knew, the telling metaphor can give your story a thematic structure at the same time that it lifts your work to a more thoughtful plane. And it almost always sets you up for at least one possible ending. But be careful! Not for nothing did the *New Yorker* for years run groaning little clips headed "Block That Metaphor!" A lead metaphor mixed or run amok, or overly labored, can turn a good story into ludicrous dreck.

Clearing Your Throat

Once you're ready to write those all-important opening lines, for gosh sakes' write them. That is, don't waste your time and the readers' time with a lot of what I call "throat clearing" before really starting your story.

Writers who top off their stories with unnecessary, introductory fluff remind me of nervous public speakers, clearing their throats to stall for time. Instead of getting to the point and grabbing the audience's attention, a "throat-clearing" writer hems and haws, circling the real point of the story like a small plane trying to find a safe place to land on rocky ground. By the time such a writer gets done clearing his throat and is ready to begin, his readers may have wandered off in search of an author who'll get to the point.

Ironically, many throat-clearers put off the real start of their stories because they mistakenly believe that's what real writerly writers are supposed to do. Jump right into it? Isn't that rather, well, cheap and sensational? Aren't you supposed to engage the readers' intellect a bit, set the stage as it were, before launching into the meat of the matter? *No! Who cares? Get to the point!* By the time you finish clearing your throat, today's impatient readers will have turned on the television, tuned into the Internet, and dropped out of reading your story.

The disease of authorial throat-clearing generally comes in three strains. You may find yourself susceptible to one or more—or all three, which can be readily diagnosed by the snoozing readers lying all around your writing.

First and most common is simply not knowing how best to start your story or book. You hem and haw in the opening because you don't *have* a real opening, or at least you haven't identified it yet.

We've already prescribed the cure here: focus and structure. What's your story or book really about? If you can't answer in twenty-five words or less, the odds are you don't have a point or don't know what it is. Go back to the first few chapters of this book and reread them. Go ahead, we'll wait.

Okay, got your idea in focus? If you still can't get started, your problem is structural. For a chronological narrative, you may be trying to cover too much (opening your account with the Big Bang, for example). Don't fall into that James Michener trap of beginning at the dawn of creation—he opens *Hawaii* with "Millions upon millions of years ago . . ."—or even just a few years before your action really starts. Or you may need to find an appropriately pivotal event to start with, flashing back in time from there. For a non-chronological piece—a roundup, trend story, or an essay, for example—you just need to find the opening that most effectively grabs readers and epitomizes the point you're trying to make (your focus).

We've already talked about structure, too, so let's concentrate on the two pitfalls peculiar to the throat-clearing writer. In both instances, you may successfully have identified a powerful place to start your story—but then you deliberately choose not to begin there. Instead, you bury the real opening and make readers put up with your *ahem-ahem* before getting to the good stuff.

A popular variant of this throat-clearing problem is the Why I Decided to Write This section. Book authors seem particularly susceptible to the Why I Decided to Write This virus, perhaps because they mistakenly believe that in the spacious confines of a multi-hundred-page book they have the luxury of lolling about, explaining the story behind the story. Take another look at the crowded bookshelves competing for your readers' attention and dollars: There's no time, not a sentence, to waste!

The other hard truth you have to accept is this: Nobody cares why you decided to write this book. Readers bought it to experience what the title, book jacket, and back-cover copy promised them, which is probably not something like: "Discover the thrilling story behind the story of how the author gathered the courage to sit down at her computer keyboard and compose sentence after sentence . . ."

Yet in workshops and retreats I see writer after writer droning on in the opening chapter about how their books came to be, what inspired them to write, what they hope readers will take away from all their hard work. There may be a fascinating book buried under that self-reflection, but only the most dogged readers are going to discover it.

I know how painful this is. You desperately want the world to know how you've struggled for your art and to understand your hopes and dreams for your book. Okay, write your deeply personal account of Why I Decided to Write This, if you must. Print it out and share it with your family and friends. Then delete it from your manuscript and get on with the actual writing. Get to the point, which is not Why I Decided to Write This but rather whatever the This is.

The other throat-clearing trap writers fall into comes from without instead of from within—from, I guess, seeing too many B movies and a few A movies like *Forrest Gump* that actually manage to pull off the Framing Device. Life may be like a box of chocolates, but most readers get impatient when they never know what they're going to get from your writing. So resist the arty temptation to start your story or book with some scenic, set piece that takes place long after your real action. Instead, get to the point.

The Framing Device isn't the same as what I advised earlier—opening at a pivotal point and then flashing back to show how we got there. Instead of grabbing the reader, the Framing Device opens with your subject in a cozy moment of reflection—on a park bench like Forrest Gump, or on the front porch in a rocker, reminiscing. Only after a few paragraphs or pages of needless throat clearing ("Ah, yes, I remember it as though it were yesterday . . .") does the real story start. At the end, of course, we return to the park bench or the rocker to complete the Framing Device.

But if you have a good story to tell, you probably don't need the Framing Device. It only postpones the actual opening that you should have started with instead. For example, at a recent retreat I worked with one writer who was writing a biography of a remarkable woman pioneer. He had a dynamite opening anecdote about the woman and her husband flying a small plane in the Caribbean, their fuel beginning to run low. When they radio the remote island airstrip for landing clearance, the only answer is static. This frightening situation sets off a roller coaster of events that winds up with the plane nose-down in Fidel Castro's petunia patch!

I'll bet you want to read his story just from that snippet, right? But that thrilling flight was relegated to second place in the manuscript, after a Framing Device of the woman, now aged, rocking and remembering (and, in a rare, double throat-clearing, explaining Why I Decided to Tell My Story). Readers turned off by this initial throat clearing would miss a heckuva yarn.

I convinced the writer (I hope!) to dispense with the Framing Device and put us right into that endangered airplane, aimed at Castro's posies, from the very first sentence.

If you catch yourself needlessly framing your own material, hit the delete key. Get to the point! Open with a bang, not a whimper or an *ahem*.

And if you've found the right opening bang, one that springs from the focus of your story and sets the pace for what's to come, pretty soon neither you nor your eventual readers will know where your opening ends and the body of your story begins. Both structurally and rhythmically, your opening lines should carry you and your readers into the next paragraph, and the next, and so on. Before you know it, you'll be writing your first draft.

Exercises

1. Pick an article or short story and count the length of sentences in the first two or three paragraphs. How well is the author varying sentence rhythm? Try rewriting the opening paragraphs with a more effective rhythm.

2. Think of a favorite anecdote that's happened to you or someone you know. Try telling it using the tools of description and detail to flesh it out and paint a scene.

3. Write a new lead for an article from your favorite magazine or a new opening for a favorite work of fiction, using one of the strategies in this chapter, such as starting in the middle; starting with an anecdote; starting with a scene; building from a collision or surprise.

4. Write your own opening for the current writing project you've outlined.

5. Switch around the chronology in the piece you've outlined. What happens to the impact of the story if it starts earlier in the actual chronology (say at the very beginning) or even later than "in the middle of things"?

CHAPTER 12

WRITING A FIRST DRAFT THAT'S ALMOST YOUR FINAL DRAFT

Too many writers simply can't write a solid first draft straight through. It's agony to them, a psychological and sometimes physical war they keep losing. Their first drafts are a chaotic mess of starts and stops, backtracking and second-guessing. Not until many time-wasting drafts later, with 90 percent of the hard-won first draft tossed out, do these writers begin to create a manuscript they can show anyone.

Such writers think they are being quite noble, of course—wrestling with the muse, looking writer's block straight in the eye hour after hour. They think this kind of inefficient stewing is the essence, the bitter heart and soul of the writer's art. They may never finish anything, but by golly, they sure do suffer like writers! They've got the bleary eyes, caffeine stains, and pencil nubs to prove it.

If that sounds all too familiar, by now I trust you've begun to realize it doesn't have to be that way. You can be organized, efficient and systematic, and still be a good writer—in fact, you'll be a *better* writer.

You know by this point that moods and the muse have nothing to do with the real work of writing. "A professional can write even when he doesn't feel like it," is how literary agent Scott Meredith once put it. "An amateur can't—even when he *does*." Author Ray Bradbury was even more hard-nosed in his advice to struggling writers: "Start writing more. It'll get rid of all those moods you're having."

People who let their inner demons get the better of their writing, whose first drafts must be painfully squeezed out through the chinks in their psyches, don't have a *writing* problem. They have an organizational problem, a willpower problem, a self-discipline problem. "Writer's block," Norman Mailer once observed, "is a failure of the ego—it's a matter of not being in charge of your own mind."

If you've been following along, chapter by chapter, you've already come further than you may realize toward taking charge of your own writer's mind. You'll find that the next time you sit down to compose a first draft, it will be less of a struggle. Instead of trying to assemble a thousand-piece jigsaw puzzle, you'll be solving simple, finite problems, one step at a time. You're in charge, and your first drafts—the first of many *fewer* drafts—will show it.

Getting Into the Flow

You know that feeling when your brain seems to be working in overdrive, when the words spill out effortlessly onto the page? Hours speed by, the pages pile up, and the next thing you know it's 4 A.M. and you can't believe how much work you've done. The heck with "no pain, no gain"—this was so painless, yet productive, you can hardly believe it was you doing the work.

Psychologists who study creativity call this mental process "flow." It's a sense of being vividly alive, plugged in, and productive. The creative work—whether it's writing a novel, crafting a sculpture, or cooking up a new recipe—just seems to happen, to *flow*.

Most of the groundwork we've already laid has been designed in part to help you achieve a sense of "flow" in your writing, virtually on command. We've blasted all the roadblocks between you and sitting down to write your heart out. Achieving this "flow" in your writing sessions is, in turn, the key to writing faster and better—really *writing*, the putting-one-word-after-another part of the task. As the words come flowing, as all your preparatory labors come into play exactly as planned, you'll write faster than you ever thought possible.

To reach that point of "flow" when you write, it's important not to rush the process. This isn't like a mystery novel where you can skip ahead and read the ending. The *process* is how you put the stuff into your head so it will be there when you need it. Nothing makes it harder for the words to flow effortlessly than if you have to stop in mid-stream to figure out where you're going, or what luggage you should have packed.

The process is a way of building what Kenneth Atchity calls "creative pressure." In effect, you've been putting off that first draft as long as possible—doing worthwhile work in the meantime, of course. You've been putting it off until you can hardly stand it anymore, until you're just itching to get to that keyboard and let off some of that creative steam.

Writers who get frustrated over their first drafts are writers who try to short-circuit the process. Every time they begin to build up a head of creativity, they unleash it by blowing off partial drafts, pieces of leads, or fragments of dialogue. A couple of pages of that and they're spent.

You should never sit down to write a first draft until you've gone through the whole process, until you know what you're about to write, and you can almost read it off the backs of your eyeballs. Build that creative pressure till the bursting point. "When your mind wants to come up with something to write," Atchity observes in *A Writer's Time*, "it draws from storehouses of ideas and images. You can't pry an idea from a flat piece of paper."

The worst thing about trying to write without building up creative pressure is that when you fail—and you will—you'll be teaching yourself an unfortunate and inaccurate lesson: *You can't write. Writing is painful and frustrating and slow.*

Those are lies. You *can* write. Writing is joyful and liberating and fast.

If you think you spot a contradiction in all this, me trying to pull a fast one, hang on. Whatever happened to "A professional can write even when he doesn't feel like it"? How can you write on demand and yet build creative pressure?

Don't forget the *process*. A professional, in my book, is a writer who goes about the mundane, step-by-step details of writing: focusing, researching, interviewing, organizing, and outlining, crafting an opening. If you go through that process for every writing project, when the time comes to punch out sentences you'll find the creative pressure is right there waiting for you. That ordinarily elusive sense of "flow" will be at your fingertips.

Summoning the muse? This is all about having the muse bound and padlocked and filed under "M" in your desk drawer. Open it up and say, "Get to work."

A Good Enough Draft

Once you're ready to unleash your pent-up "creative pressure," success in writing a first draft right from the start depends on striking a happy medium between writing well and writing perfectly. The former is well within reach on your first draft; the latter is impossible, of course, and trying to achieve perfection will only bog you down. Yes, you should write a "keeper" of a first draft, one that requires an absolute minimum of revision—and you'll be able to accomplish that, thanks to the process we've already gone through. But, no, you won't be able to write a first draft that's absolutely flawless. The secret is not to let that fact keep you from writing as good and as clean a draft as you can. Or, as is too often the case, to keep you from writing anything at all. Perfectionists typically can never get any work done, because to take even the first step requires bringing something from the ideal world of your imagination into the inevitably flawed world of reality.

Let's tackle first the problem of sloppy first drafts—the "it doesn't really matter, because this is only a first draft and I'll fix it later" syndrome. Of course it matters! Why waste time and creative energy writing something second-rate when, with a little more discipline and concentration, you can write 95 percent of your final draft on the first try? The "I'll fix it later" mindset fritters away your time in two ways: in useless first drafts and in endless rewriting. Rewriting and revising are the number-one time-wasters for most writers, often consuming more precious hours than the rest of the writing process put together. Far better and faster to make your first draft almost your final draft.

So avoid what Scott Meredith called "first draft-itis"—writing loosely and carelessly, figuring you'll get it right a couple drafts down the line. As Meredith noted in his *Writing to Sell*, this kind of thinking is a "progressive disease." Once you start viewing your first drafts as just a way station en route to the paper shredder, this becomes a self-fulfilling prophecy. Before long, you'll have to write double-digit drafts to produce acceptable copy.

Instead, Meredith advised, "Write each page of your first draft as tightly and carefully as if it had to be sent to the editor the moment it was pulled out of the typewriter." In fact, it's a good exercise to pretend that your first draft will be your *only* draft. What if you were a newspaper reporter, writing on deadline, with an editor panting to snatch your copy away by 5 P.M.? How well could you write? Probably better than you think.

After all, think of all the groundwork you've already done. You've focused your research and interviewing, selecting the best material even as you gathered it. You've solved your organizational and transition problems. You've found an opening that springs naturally out of your material and, in turn, tugs you into the heart of your story. The hard work is done!

And your first impulses, when writing, are often not only the freshest but the best. That adjective you had to look up in a thesaurus might be too labored, too contrived. Writing as people speak, telling your story as naturally as you can, is often the best "style" with which to capture readers.

"Style" can be a terrible distraction, anyway. You're better off not worrying, at least not consciously, about your style; rather, write your first draft as plainly and clearly as you can. Keep in mind the old anecdote about the cub reporter who, when his city editor was caught short-staffed, was sent off to cover the Johnstown flood. Flush with "style," the raw reporter cabled back five thousand stylish words almost utterly devoid of facts. Most of the story read like his lead: "God sits tonight in judgment at Johnstown . . ." Frustrated and fuming, the city editor wired back: "Forget the flood. Interview God." Forget style; tell your story.

If you keep that in mind, you'll also be less likely to burden your first draft with what Richard Lanham, in *Revising Prose*, calls "the lard factor": fat, unnourishing words and phrases that you'll eventually have to cut out anyway. Why write them if you're going to wind up cutting them?

Even at the sentence-construction level, certain telltale words are almost always "lard." Avoid such extra words as "very," "so to speak," "as it were," and "as a matter of fact" unless they clearly contribute to your meaning and message. (We'll just take them out in the chapter on revision, anyway.) Shun in particular the lazy "There is/are . . ." construction at the start of a sentence. And guard against passive voice. Make nouns and verbs do the work of your sentences, instead of spending precious minutes typing extra adjectives and adverbs. Excess verbiage wastes time in the writing and in the ultimate excising; backwards and wimpy sentences take time to write and then to rewrite. Get the basics of your writing right, and free of extraneous words, the first time!

Whenever you sense your draft beginning to veer into "lard," quickly consult your notes and your outline and concentrate instead on communicating the key points you've set out. Use that outline like a lodestone, to keep your story always on course.

About this point in my preaching, a significant number of you, scarred by misguided writing teachers or equally misbegotten notions of the writer's life, are probably wondering: But aren't you supposed to overwrite, the better to boil down later on? Isn't writing sort of like making a fancy sauce— you whip up too much, then cook and condense it until it's just right? The late Jerzy Kosinski, for example, once spent twenty-seven straight hours writing a nineteen-page chunk of his novel, *The Painted Bird*. Then he revised and revised, until those twenty-seven hours and nineteen pages were boiled down to a single, sterling page. Isn't that how it's supposed to work?

Only Kosinski's garbage can will ever know for sure whether he condensed the right page out of those nineteen, or whether perhaps the novel would have been better with the original draft intact. This much is certain, however: That way of working is a good way to starve. How many writers these days are so successful that they can afford that kind of indulgence? Not me, and I'll bet not you either.

I prefer the approach of John McPhee, who likens writing to the sport of curling, in which the greatest effort is expended sweeping the ice clean to advance each shot. Sweep the ice clean in the path of your words, and your first draft will glide effortlessly toward its goal.

Putting Perfectionism in Its Place

The other extreme from "first draft-itis" is a fussy perfectionism that keeps you from writing smoothly through your first draft, because you're forever stopping to polish each word, each phrase, like a fine jewel. Perfectionists hate to actually write anything in the first place, since the real words on the page can never be as perfect as they'd imagined. Once they do buckle down to write, it's agony: They spend more time rewriting than writing, more effort with the thesaurus than culling the best from their notes. The end result is usually precious, overwritten prose.

So, while you want to write as clean and final a first draft as you can, it's important not to swing over to the opposite extreme, and worry your words to death. Take each chunk of your story as it comes. Write it straight through, then move on. If you didn't use an idea, a piece of information, a quote, or a scene where your outline said you would, don't stop and try to work it in; maybe it didn't belong there in the first place. Circle it on your outline if you think you might need it later but don't know where, or pencil it in further down in the outline where it might now fit. As you zoom through your plan, turning it into reality, don't leave any sentences you're really unhappy with and don't write "lard"—but don't break your momentum by fussily revising, either. (This is particularly dangerous with today's word-processing magic, which makes tinkering with what you just wrote so painless and seductive.) Try for a first draft that's about an A-/B+.

If you still find yourself tending toward perfectionism—frequently backtracking to the point that it's slowing you down—you can try some self-discipline tricks. Once a sentence is written, don't even let yourself read over it. Just write the next sentence and tackle the next item in your outline. This approach will make perfectionists mighty nervous, so here's how you reassure yourself: At the beginning of each writing session, allow yourself to reread the pages you wrote the day before. Let yourself do some minor tinkering, just to get it out of your system. (But no wholesale rewriting and no more than two trips to the thesaurus!) Take out a comma here and there, change a "glad" to a "happy," and by all means cut out any lard words that slipped through your defenses. Then you're ready to write the next section, your self-confidence bolstered.

This approach has two advantages. First, it forces you to put off your polishing to a point in your workflow when it won't interrupt your momentum. Second, reading what you wrote the day before is a good way to get your head back into the story, to recapture yesterday's "flow."

Writing One Paragraph at a Time

I keep talking about "momentum" because it's every bit as important to effective writing as it is to a winning sports team or a political campaign. Both within a given work session and from one day to the next, you need to build and maintain a sense of forward progress that carries you through the rough spots. All the hard work you've already done—brainstorming, researching, interviewing, outlining—has served to build up this head of steam. Now you've got to ride it to the final paragraph.

How do you keep from getting derailed en route? Let's first talk about an individual writing session. Writing faster and better is all about building blocks, putting them one after another to make a story. In a day's writing session, your building blocks are as basic as words, phrases, sentences, and paragraphs. I've already talked about how to strike the right balance between sloppiness and fussiness in your word choices, phrase construction, and sentence structure. The key to putting these building blocks together in a way that creates momentum is that much-misunderstood element of English composition, the lowly paragraph.

For the efficient writer, the paragraph is the ideal unit with which to build a story. Words, phrases, and sentences are a means to the end of creating a solid paragraph. At the same time, the paragraph is not so large a unit that you can't write it in one burst. Moreover, the paragraph meshes nicely with the outline you used to plan your story, especially for shorter projects, where it's easy to see how one or two items in your outline will translate into a paragraph. And a paragraph is not too much to think about: You can juggle the main point and the three or four supporting points in your head, keeping them straight long enough to actually set them down in words.

Admittedly, what you learned in English class about the paragraph and what you'll see in published prose don't always match. Newspaper writers tend to write paragraphs that are no more than a sentence or two. That's more a function of page appearance than grammar or style: A newspaper, built for rapid scanning, must present a bite-sized look to the wary reader, whereas magazines, particularly those aimed at a more settled-in-the-easy-chair audience, such as the *Atlantic* and the *New Yorker*, can get away with bigger blocks of type. Newspapers generally have narrower columns, making those *Atlantic*-esque paragraphs stretch far down the page like gray skyscrapers. The result is what newspaper columnist and *New York Times Magazine* usage maven William Safire calls "hyperparagraphication" in newspaper prose: "like feeding a baby tiny spoonfuls of mashed banana, building an appetite between insertions of the spoon in the ready-to-squall mouth." You needn't go to that extreme, nor should you emulate such literary stylists as William Faulkner, on the other side of the spectrum, who've written paragraphs that ramble on for pages.

Perhaps surprisingly, many advisers on how to write better prose (William Zinsser and Herbert Read, for example) downplay the importance of the paragraph, advocating what might be called a laissez-faire approach. But Strunk and White, in *The Elements of Style*, weigh in definitively with, "Make the paragraph the unit of composition."

How can you strike a balance between building your story out of well-constructed paragraphs and keeping your readers from squalling? In the absence of the old rules, it helps to keep in mind several up-to-date, organizing principles that make for successful paragraphing—and thus smooth writing. The labels are mine; if your grandchildren read them a hundred years from now, set down in a schoolbook as strict rules, please forgive me.

First and most sweeping is what we might dub the *modified grammar-school approach*. That is, while your paragraphs need not be constructed in a strict topic-support-support hierarchy, it is still useful to think of each paragraph as making a point—just *one* point. When you've made it, pound that return key and move on. So, again, in moving from the outline of your story to a first draft, you might think of each point in your master plan as representing one paragraph in your draft. Each point might have one to three, perhaps even as many as five, connected details or examples in your notes.

If you're writing a travel article about Seattle, for instance, you might have a spot in your overall organizational scheme where you want to mention Seattle's proximity to the Washington State wine industry. The paragraph growing out of this point might be built like this:

Seattle as a place to sample Washington State wine industry
1. Chateau Ste. Michelle winery
2. Columbia Crest winery

Each specific winery might consume a sentence or two, with a few facts about its setting, tastings, and tours. The whole paragraph, with set-up sentence and specifics, might take four or five sentences—a manageable glob on most pages and one readily consumed by even fickle readers.

By forming your paragraphs this way, each becomes a semi-stand-alone unit of thought, easily manipulated as you write and rewrite. Consider our make-believe story on touring the Seattle area, where your paragraph on wineries might be woven into a discussion on things to see and do in the city's outer reaches. Suppose you decided instead that Seattle's winery connections would fit more smoothly into a larger section on the city as a mecca for gourmets? Pick up the paragraph and move it! Or maybe you conclude that your story's main focus ought to be on Seattle as a fun place for families, and wineries don't really fit after all. Delete that paragraph.

Paragraphs that follow the modified grammar-school approach work like Lego blocks. Even before they're completely written, you can easily try them out in other locations, test their fit with other paragraphs, and move them to make new connections. If you decide that the paragraph on your hero's wicked stepfather actually works better in chapter seven of your novel, instead of chapter two, it's simple to cut and paste. Our modified grammar-school paragraphs also serve as handy units for combining into larger, more complex, even Faulknerian structures—without having to worry whether each component part will hold up under the stress of composing the whole.

The modified grammar-school approach will keep you clear of the extremes of "hyperparagraphication". But once you start gathering elements together to form paragraphs, it's easy to tilt to the opposite extreme: Like a snowball rolling downhill, your paragraphs keep accreting until readers get buried in an avalanche of unbroken sentences. The cure for such mega-paragraphs comes from recognizing the natural pauses and logical breaks in your prose. These aren't mandatory paragraphing spots, but your readers will thank you if, when in doubt, you hit the return key. These mini-breaks also give you a handy spot to catch your own breath, as you're writing feverishly away, now wholly unhampered by writer's block. (Hey, even writers need to go to the bathroom now and then.)

Start with an extension of the grammar-school strategy—think of it as the *enumeration break*. Whenever you have a subsidiary point to make that will take more than a sentence or two to explain, make it a new paragraph. Whenever you have a list (six must-see attractions in downtown Seattle), consider whether each element in the list will occupy more than one sentence. If so, make each element its own paragraph.

You can envision the enumeration break resulting in paragraphs like this:

The first thing . . .
Second, . . .
A third factor . . .

And so on—though it's not necessary to actually number your points.

A related invitation to hit the return key is the *elaboration detour*. Think of it as akin to the enumeration break but with only one subpoint. Essentially, you're detouring from the main march of your argument or narrative to elaborate for the length of a paragraph on one aspect of the previous paragraph. Take, for example, the relationship between the two paragraphs above: one introducing the concept of the enumeration break, the other presenting a helpful way to think about it.

You might use this elaboration detour to separate a general paragraph (Seattle has many attractions for the gourmet) from a specific illustration of an element of that paragraph (for example, wineries). By setting off the example in its own paragraph, you give the reader a break and signal your small directional shift. This is a particularly useful device in writing fiction, where you often need to deliver some background information without either confusing readers or departing too far from the main action:

> . . . Susan slammed the door behind Greg with such force that the old musket hanging above the fireplace rattled in its mountings.
>
> [Elaboration detour ahead!] The musket had been passed down through her family for generations. Susan had learned to load and fire it when she was a girl, but that was long ago. . . .

Of course, such elaborative paragraphs must ultimately be germane to your story. We're not interested in Susan's family's musket just out of historical curiosity. Its presence had better reveal something about the family—or, ideally, Susan should use it to shoot that bastard Greg in the next chapter.

Detours that don't merely elaborate but take readers in an opposite direction definitely demand a new paragraph. This is the *on-the-other-hand switcheroo*. Here the brief breather of a new paragraph prepares the reader for an idea in contrast to what has gone before. The *on-the-other-hand switcheroo* works with opposing viewpoints, balancing opinions, and cautionary notes. Need to inject a bit of not-so-fast-folks? Seeking to interweave two or more differing perspectives on an issue? Presenting the pros and cons? A paragraph switcheroo warns the reader of your bend in the road.

To use the *on-the-other-hand switcheroo*, look for signs of contrasting thoughts such as:

> *But . . .*
> *. . . however . . .*
> *And yet . . .*
> *(As well as, of course:) On the other hand . . .*

But the breaks in your story don't have to be as dramatic as divergent opinions. (Note the switcheroo there that practically begged for a new paragraph?) You should keep your authorial ear tuned for any sort of interruption in the action that can serve as a basic *paragraph-able pause.*

Quotations are the most obvious example of a shift that calls for a new paragraph: With each new speaker, or alternation in speaker, hit the return key. Just as your speakers catch their breath between speeches, so too should you let your readers rest with the tiny space of a fresh paragraph.

Other opportunities for paragraph-able pauses abound. Switching your authorial camera between persons, even if they're not speaking, lets you switch paragraphs as well. In a story with a chronological aspect, you might seize on a shift in time to start a new paragraph: the next day, at 8 P.M., and so on. Even minor changes of place call for a change of paragraph: farther down the street, on the other side of the room.

You can take advantage of the small pause, the break in rhythm, created by a fresh paragraph to emphasize what follows—even when readers might not be expecting a break. This *emphatic paragraphing* works like the print equivalent of a dramatic pause in speaking: Whatever comes after gains import from the artificial break. It is set apart, put in the spotlight.

Typically, emphatic paragraphing is used to set off paragraphs of only a sentence or two. The power of a suddenly new paragraph quickly dissipates over the span of several sentences. A short burst of a paragraph, on the other hand, gains potency not only from its indentation but from the visual variety on the page.

The emphatic paragraph can be a single dramatic statement, a quote, or even a question, such as:

> Would anyone notice that the musket had been fired?

Whatever excuse you use for starting a new paragraph—grammar-school lessons be damned!—keeping your writing flowing will be considerably easier if you end the previous paragraph with some thought to making a transition to the next. Your major transitions should be taken care of in your outline, but it doesn't hurt to pass the baton to the next paragraph with a little extra oomph. For example, look back at how we introduced the idea of the musket in the first paragraph of our little fictional example, then built on it in the opening of the next paragraph.

Transitions, leading yourself (and readers) smoothly into the next paragraph, are crucial to maintaining your writing momentum. Ideally, you should never have to stop to ponder where the story is going, or how you'll get there. Let your momentum carry you. That's how you establish "flow." That's how you write a first draft faster than you ever thought possible.

Writing Today and Tomorrow

But wait a minute. That momentum might carry you through today—what about tomorrow? You know the feeling: How often have you had a really good day of writing, only to sit at the keyboard the next day and not be able to summon up a single usable word? Your writing "flow" has been dissipated among your daily chores, your day job, your family, paying bills, even reading the paper and falling asleep.

Short of writing yourself to death (not to mention divorce!), how can you keep your writing momentum from day to day? How can you pick up where you left off with the same creativity and enthusiasm? The secret, you might say, is to trick yourself.

"Wait till I get to a good stopping point." Sound familiar? You're right not to stop writing except at a good stopping point, but your definition of that point is probably backwards. Don't work until you've completed a paragraph, a thought, a section, or a chapter, and then stop. Instead, force yourself to break away in mid-thought, even in mid-sentence.

Talk about creative pressure! Interrupting yourself in mid-creation keeps that head of steam from dissipating. Instead of walking away from the keyboard with a smug sense of satisfaction at all you've accomplished, you end the work session with an itch. If your work was going well, the itch to pick it up again where you left off will put your writing momentum in high gear the minute you sit down to work again.

Stopping in mid-work, even mid-sentence, fuels your momentum in an even more basic way. If you broke for the day in the middle of a sentence, well, the odds are pretty good that you know how you were going to finish that sentence. So when you start work again the next day, you know you can at least finish the sentence you started. That leads into finishing the paragraph, the section, the chapter . . . Before you know it, you really have picked up where you left off.

As your words and sentences pile up, seek a steady pace rather than exhausting bursts. Once you realize that you can indeed quit for the day and then start up again, just like an assembly-line worker who knocks off at the four o'clock whistle and then tackles a new set of widgets tomorrow, you can pace yourself. Getting a first draft done, as we've already seen, comes down to mathematics: At one thousand words a day (of a first draft that's very nearly your final draft, remember), you can write a four-thousand-word magazine feature from Sunday through Wednesday. You can polish off a 75,000-word novel in two and a half months. Even a blockbuster won't take you much more than two seasons to write.

For first drafts, that thousand-words-a-day figure is a pretty good rule. You should be able to crank that out in your spare time. For serious, full-time writing, two thousand to three thousand words a day is a respectable—and achievable—pace. Unless you have a deadline breathing down your neck, there's little reason to push yourself much harder. The key to writing "faster," really, is writing steadily and efficiently. You'll be further ahead with your one thousand "keeper" words a day than the disorganized writer who churns out several thousand words in a creative frenzy, only to trash most of them in subsequent drafts.

What you've been aiming toward, with all your focusing and outlining, is putting our old friend the "Pareto Principle" to work for you. Remember that 20 percent of your efforts usually produce 80 percent of the value of your work. All of what goes before is designed to turn your first drafting into that concentrated 20 percent of highly productive work.

You'll find another, less-scientific principle also holds true in your first drafts. It's a Spanish saying: "Life is short, but wide." You'll be amazed at how much productive writing you can fit into what's really only a short slice of time—how wide your writing life can be, once you get it organized.

If the Story Fits . . .

Our mathematics of 1000 or so words a day only works, of course, if you can write more or less to fit. If you're writing a 90,000-word novel and you wind up with 150,000 words instead, not only have you wasted sixty-some days of writing time, but now you have to go back and spend still more time cutting. Unless you have a few best-sellers under your belt, don't even think of suggesting to your publisher, "Gosh, why don't we just add pages to the book?" Pages cost money, and publishers hate to spend money. And for heaven's sake, don't shuffle your overwriting burden off onto your editor—"Why don't you just cut the parts you don't like?" You won't like the result any more than the editor (cursing you all the while and vowing never to employ you again) likes the process of doing the job you should have done.

No, what you need to do is make your writing project fit the box it's supposed to—right from the start, with a minimum of wasted motion. That takes planning, discipline, and all the other virtues we've talked about. It can also take time. Paradoxical as it may sound, the old excuse from harried writers to editors miffed at overblown manuscripts contains a lot of truth: "I didn't have the time to write it short." It's harder to write short than it is to write long. If you have a mountain of material, it takes more work to wrestle it into a coherent two-thousand-word shape than it does to just toss everything in and write five thousand words.

This axiom becomes more painfully true as the lengths get briefer. Writing two thousand words can be tough; writing five hundred words from the same pile of possibilities can be agony. Brevity may be the soul of wit, but the demands of brevity can leave you at your wit's end. Doubt it? Try writing what's called "flash fiction"—ultra-short-short stories that must deliver something worth reading in just a few hundred words.

Even longer articles can present a writing-short challenge, as editors and readers demand that you pack more into each package. "Round-up" articles so popular with service magazines, for example—10 ways to better balance work and family, 52 great weekend getaways—can add up to a brutal arithmetic: If you have a 2,500-word limit and must write 10 chunks—tips, products, getaways, what have you—plus an introduction, that means your ten items must average less than 250 words apiece. Suddenly, what seemed a roomy word count becomes a stingy straitjacket.

Brevity also rules in cyberspace, where the "screen" has replaced the page as the unit of measure for a story's demand on readers. When I worked as executive producer for an online "magazine," the importance—and difficulty—of writing short was hammered home. A full-blown restaurant review meant 500 words. If you get only 500 words to capture a place's cuisine, ambiance, and service—while also reporting the basics of location, hours and such—you really need to make every word count.

That experience, though, taught me volumes about writing to fit—whether in a chunk for cyberspace or a book-length project made up of many such chunks. I also discovered that brevity has an upside—don't forget that "soul of wit" part. You're doing readers a service by writing as concisely as you're able. Copy that's been boiled down to its essence benefits from more disciplined selection of content, sharper word choices, leaner, and more vigorous prose.

Of course, there's a right way and a wrong way to write short. Let's, er, *briefly* look at the right way. Take my example of a restaurant capsule, which you might be asked to write as part of a travel article (maybe a "Where to Eat" sidebar or section), as one of many short elements that add up to a guidebook, or as one chunk of a roundup ("Cowboy Cuisine: A Dozen Places to Saddle Up Your Taste Buds"). Here the challenge is to quickly yet colorfully communicate the essence of a place—to answer, in precious few words, readers' basic question: Would I want to eat there?

You'd confront a similar challenge in trying to briefly describe a place—the restaurant where your hero and heroine have their first date, perhaps—in your novel. Readers won't sit still for a lengthy detour about the food, the ambiance, and the service, when the real point is the romance, not the restaurant. But you still want to paint enough of a picture—in a miserly number of words—to put readers into the scene.

The first thing you might be tempted to do to conserve words in your first draft is to skimp on details. But carefully chosen specifics can capture your subject more vibrantly and yet more efficiently than empty generalities. Consider these alternative lines from a mythical capsule on "Buffalo Charlie's" restaurant:

> The Wild West really comes alive for diners at Buffalo Charlie's, where Western decor is the rule and all sorts of colorful historic knick-knacks re-create the feel of a restaurant home on the range. Even the mâtre d' and waitstaff wear costumes that powerfully suggest cowboy days.

Plenty of breezy writing there, but not much information beyond "Buffalo Charlie's has a Wild West theme." A few details can convey the same information, in fewer words, while better bringing the place alive to readers:

> At Buffalo Charlie's, saddles dangle from the ceiling and a war-

bonnet crowns the kitchen doorway. The chap in chaps is the mâtre d'; the cowboy-hatted waitstaff pack pencils in their pistol belts.

The first, flabby option comes to forty-eight words; the second, rich with specifics, weighs in at a lean thirty-three, including a little padding for wordplay ("The chap in chaps is the mâtre d' " rather than "The mâtre d' sports chaps"). Note that the second version still doesn't try to cram in every detail about the place—we don't learn whether the mâtre d' also wears a cowboy hat, for example, or whether the men's room door says "Gents." But by giving a flavor of the place, it lets readers make educated guesses about what's left out. (If you're a diner who hates places where the men's room is marked "Gents," odds are you'd want to skip Buffalo Charlie's.)

To save space, empty modifiers and qualifying phrases have been left out on the lone prairie: "really," "is the rule," "all sorts of," "the feel of," "that powerfully suggest." But note how the second, shorter version instead employs active, vivid verbs—"dangle," "crowns," "pack." When words are at a premium, you need to make every one work hard, right from the start.

That slimmer version also takes more chances with the language—you won't find "cowboy-hatted" in the dictionary, for one. Sometimes brevity demands a punchier, more kinetic, telegraphic style that could cause language purists to shudder. While you might not want to write a four-thousand-word narrative in this breathless "capsule-ese," it's a good fit for the bright and breezy form of the brief. So go ahead, within reason, and coin phrases, verbify nouns, sling the English language like our imaginary Buffalo Charlie's would sling hash.

Is it more challenging—thus potentially more time-consuming, as the saying goes—to write short? Until you get in the habit, sure. But once you've practiced the tricks of crafting fat-free copy from the start, you may find it's a diet you want to stick to. We'll talk later about strategies for revising your stories to make them shorter, but I won't kid you: That's harder than writing to fit in the first place. The secret of writing to fit is to never put those extra words down on paper. Otherwise, they become your words, your offspring, and cutting them starts to feel uncomfortably like infanticide.

Keeping your story to the right length begins way back, of course, several chapters ago, with focusing your idea. Figure out what this story is really about and what it will take to get it done. A 1,500-word column does not require the same amount of legwork and facts as a three-part *New Yorker* saga. A short story does not require as much scene-setting or character development as a 500-page novel suitable for lugging to the beach.

Then you have to keep that focus in mind all the way through your research and interviewing. Resolutely forbid yourself to go off on tangents that will later tempt you to weave them into your writing. Edit as you go, marking material you're sure to use and discarding as early as possible anything that's outside your focus.

Your outline becomes your chief weapon against writing too much. Here's where you must be the most ruthless, leaving out anything that takes your story astray or that, deep down, you know there's no room for.

Finally, when you're writing that first draft, use your outline as a kind of ration book. If you're one-third through the outline, you'd better not be much over one-third your total word allotment. If you *are* over, the earlier you recognize it and start reining yourself in, the better. One of the advantages of composing on a computer is that most word-processing programs will count the words for you, at any point. Check this "gauge" frequently. Think of it as a sort of reverse gas gauge: If it's almost full and you still have a long way to go, start conserving fast!

On the bright side, checking the mounting tally of your words also gives you a terrific feeling of accomplishment. Yes, by golly, your first draft really is happening. It's adding up. You're almost there.

Exercises

1. Rewrite the opening you wrote in the last chapter's exercises, leaving out any "lard words."

2. Write the next page or two, coming immediately after your opening. As you write, don't let yourself go back and revise anything except typos.

3. Go through a published short story or article and reparagraph it. Can you make the story's subpoints hang together better and the prose flow more smoothly?

4. Take the anecdote you wrote in the last chapter and rewrite it to fit in no more than five hundred words.

5. Now rewrite your anecdote in no more than 250 words.

CHAPTER 13

WRITING FICTION FASTER AND BETTER

Although we've been discussing fiction as well as nonfiction all along, right about here I can tell that you fiction and screenplay writers need a little extra convincing. Maybe it's the whole "muse" thing. "Yeah, getting organized and all might work for articles, even nonfiction books," you're saying, "but I want to create Art. You can't rush Art. It must spring from the creative pools deep within." Or words to that effect.

Well, I might say something about your use of hackneyed metaphors ("creative pools"? Give me a break!), but since this is a book on writing faster and better I'll concentrate on, er, dispelling your misconceptions like dropping a stone into the still waters of a pond. Sorry. Bear with me, okay?

Of course you can write spontaneously, waiting for your creative springs to leak or whatever. Joan Didion, for instance, told a *Paris Review* interviewer that she dives into her fiction with no theme or plot in mind, only a vague character and "a technical sense of what I want to do." Her story line, such as it is, doesn't emerge until *after* her first draft is done; she'll mark uncertain spots "chapter to come" and simply skip over them. Or there's Joseph Heller, who missed the deadline for his novel *Catch-22* by half a decade. "When I started *Catch-22*," he once revealed, "I thought writing novels might be a useful way to kill time."

If you have time to kill, you should flip past this chapter and go do your nails or something. Most writers, particularly beginning and struggling ones, don't have the luxury of approaching their writing without any planning, or missing their deadlines by several years.

Take William Shakespeare, for example—a hard-working and hard-pressed author if ever there was one. His publishers, Heminges & Condell, marveled, "His mind and hand went together, and what he thought, he uttered with that easiness that we have scarce received a blot from him in his papers." A "write fast, write clean first drafts" guy, no doubt about it.

Or, on a less lofty plane of penning, consider Edgar Wallace, a British mystery writer (1875–1932) and sometime playwright. Wallace wrote his play *On the Spot* in just two and a half days, and not one word had to be altered in production.

Yes, fiction writers of all stripes can learn to write faster and better, too. In fact, if you've been paying attention all along, you already know the basics.

Finding a Process That Works for You

Like any writing, successful fiction demands that you develop a process, a way of writing that works for you—don't worry if it wouldn't work for anyone else. You may not be comfortable outlining your fiction on yellow legal pads, for example; maybe note cards work better for you, or notes on a computer, or "mind maps" scrawled on marker boards. You may need to populate your world with characters before the plot comes to you, or perhaps your ideas will spring from your setting. The exact process doesn't matter. What's important is having a methodical way of working that takes you from idea to finished draft.

Many writers learn the importance of process the hard way. Take, for example, the award-winning mystery novelist Elizabeth George, whom we've already heard from in previous chapters. Her books sell a million copies and get translated into twenty languages. "I knew from the age of seven that I was meant to be a writer," she says. But before George broke in as a successful writer, she put in a stint teaching English at El Toro High School in Orange County, California, and collected rejection slips on five novels.

What made the difference between being unpublished and becoming a best-selling author? Process, says George: "I wish that I had known back then that a mastery of process would lead to a product. Then I probably wouldn't have found it so frightening to write." Her breakthrough book, *A Great Deliverance*, took her just three and a half weeks to write—once she found a writing process that worked for her.

George's process for novel writing today is as complex but ultimately as clear as her plots. It's crucial for this self-confessed "left-brained" writer to unleash her creative right brain. She puts in an enormous amount of work upfront, before she ever starts to write, in order to reap the dividends of that preparation at the keyboard. (Sound familiar?) "I have to know the killer, the victim and the motive when I begin," she explains. "Then I start to create the characters and see how the novel takes shape based on what these people are like."

Each character she creates must have what she calls a "core need," part of a complete psychological profile George creates for every person in her story. (George's own core need, for example, "is that I'm dominated by the need to be really competent at what I do," she says.) Each character also gets a physical description, a family history, and what George calls a "pathology," which she defines as "a particular psychological maneuver that he engages in when he's under stress." Much of this material, which she bangs out in stream-of-consciousness form, never makes it into print, but it helps her discover the truth about her characters. When she gets it, George says, she feels something right in her solar plexus.

"Creating the characters is the most creative part of the novel except for the language itself," she says. "There I am, sitting in front of my computer in right-brain mode, typing the things that come to mind—which become the seeds of plot."

George's plotting process is equally detailed. "I outline the plot beginning with the primary event that gets the ball rolling. Then I'll list the potentials that are causally related to what's gone before. I continue to open the story and not close the story, putting in dramatic questions. Any time the story stalls out on me, I know I've done something wrong—generally, I played my hand too soon, answered a dramatic question in a scene without asking a new one."

Her running plot outline might cover up to the next fifteen scenes. "The plot outline doesn't forbid the inspiration of the moment, but it does prevent a wild hare, something out of character that drags the story off in a wrong area."

For each scene, the outline notes what George calls her "THAD," short for "Talking Head Avoidance Device." The THAD that animates each scene, she says, springs from her prep work of getting to know her characters.

The outline also notes the point of view for each scene. Unlike many mystery writers, George shifts her point of view among multiple characters—rather than, say, sticking with the detective's viewpoint. "In any given scene, I ask, 'Whose story is being advanced here?'" she explains. "I can usually tell the point of view by which character's part in the narrative I've gotten to."

I've gone into George's process in such depth, not because you should necessarily imitate it, but because her thinking so clearly demonstrates a methodical approach to the elements of fiction: characters, setting, plot, scenes, and point of view. You need to find your own process, which may be very different from hers—because your brain works differently, or because you're tackling something different from George's psychological mysteries.

Focusing Your Fiction

Developing your own process begins with deciding what sort of fiction you're setting out to write—which brings us back to our old friend, focus. You must focus your efforts long before the first word hits the page. Obviously, a novel means greater scope than a short story; a movie script brings larger challenges than a half-hour television comedy. But more length doesn't necessarily mean more of everything. It might mean a longer time span in which your story unfolds—but not necessarily: James Joyce's mammoth *Ulysses*, after all, takes place in a single day. It probably does mean more variations on your theme, which means you'd better be darn sure of what your theme is.

Focusing demands an awareness of what you're writing and why: how the pieces work together to create a greater whole. How many times have you heard, in advice about fiction writing, to put in only what advances the story? That's focusing.

Since you're *inventing* what happens rather than picking and choosing strictly from the real world, focusing can be especially difficult. With infinite possibilities at your keyboard, you may find yourself trying to explore them all—and wind up not doing a good job at any. That way, too, lurks writer's block. Since you can write about anything, it's all too easy to wind up writing nothing. Should your story be a mystery? A romance? A romantic mystery set on Mars? The possibilities are endless!

Take the question of setting, for example. Sure, why not Mars? You can set your story anywhere (and anywhen) you want: in your hometown, in Paris, in second-century Rome, in an alternate universe in which Genghis Khan conquered Europe. Or all of the above.

But if you want to write faster, you'd be wise to restrict your possibilities to those closer to home, to your own experiences, or what you can readily research and extrapolate. That's not merely a recipe for speedier writing; "write what you know" is also sound advice for authentic, believable fiction. Not only is it easier to set a scene in the neighborhood McDonald's than it is to conjure up the frigid steppes of Siberia—you'll also write better about Big Macs than about, um, frozen food.

Remember: Find the story that only you can tell, and write it.

This doesn't mean that you ought to spend your whole fiction career penning epics set in your backyard and at the local Jiffy Lube. It does mean that you should paddle awhile in your own pond before trying to swim the Atlantic. And when you do dive into a more exotic setting, remember my rapid-research tips and don't bite off more than you can chew. If you're writing a short story set in Australia, for example, focus on the theme, the characters, and the plot; keep the setting a secondary or tertiary focus unless you've spent a lot of time there. Don't go overboard on description of things you've only seen in *National Geographic*!

Elizabeth George is, again, a good example. She sets all her novels in England, half a world away from her home in Huntington Beach, California. That means spending weeks at a time in England, which George first visited and fell in love with on a summer Shakespeare course. She keeps a flat in South Kensington, London, her home base for research excursions armed with camera and tape recorder. For *Well-Schooled in Murder*, for example, she visited a half dozen schools and created architectural plans and a brochure for her fictional British school setting. "I want to ground myself in specifics, not generics," she says. "I want to force myself to deal in details. I can't make these up, that's not my talent."

Maybe you can get away with setting your novel in England even if you don't keep a flat in London to use as a research base. But it will be a different sort of novel, less steeped in place and British culture, than what George writes. That's part of finding your focus, of setting achievable goals for yourself.

Creating Quick Characters

At least with settings you have something real to start with (even in science fiction you know that Mars is red); with characters you've got *terra incognita*. Sure, you can base them on people you know, or on aspects of your own character—but there's no encyclopedia you can turn to for quick facts about your characters. ("Let's see, I'll look under 'E' for 'Emotions' . . .")

And yet how many times have you heard that "you can never know too much about your characters"? That's where preparation pays off. Look at George's meticulous investment of time in her characters, which are the impetus for everything else in her writing process. When you reach the climax, you have to know whether your hero will run or make a stand. With properly prepared characters, a story begins to write itself once you turn them loose.

That's why the Gordons, the mystery-writing team (a.k.a. Mildred and Gordon Gordon) who also co-wrote *That Darn Cat*, used to write biographies of their principal characters before starting a new puzzler, much as George does today. If they didn't develop a "feel" for the key characters, they'd abandon the whole novel. Or why Barbara Taylor Bradford, author of *A Woman of Substance*, details each character on index cards. She'll note their fictional backgrounds, ages, motivations, even sketch family trees.

Not only do you need to know the intimate details of your characters; you should also think about how you plan to reveal what makes them tick. You're not going to write simply, "Janet was a nervous woman, probably because she'd had an unhappy childhood." No, you'll *show* her biting her nails and have a picture of her mother turned to face the wall. (You'll come up with much better stuff than I'm whipping out here!) Whatever specifics you plan to use to bring your characters to life, the magic word is *plan*.

How do you keep this preparation from eating up all your creative time—so you wind up with a villageful of imaginary people but no story? Again, you've got to focus. Develop the characters that will drive your story, whose decisions will make your tale twist and turn. Don't waste equal time on minor characters—those that are mostly functionaries in your saga. Yes, know everything you can about your photographer-turned-secret agent hero. But settle for quick strokes about the woman behind the camera counter who passes him the crucial film (and never appears again in your story), the taxi driver who speeds him to the airport, and the airline agent who takes his ticket. Besides, telling too much about minor characters gives your readers the wrong impression: that these are major characters who will turn up again later (Surely you wouldn't flesh out that ticket agent so thoroughly if she's not going to return as the spy's love interest?).

Even characters who play a major, yet purely functional role can be treated as stereotypes, or variations on a type. It's probably not necessary, for example, to create a family tree for the ex-marine who gives your spy hero his orders. He's an ex-marine, okay, and you know what he looks like and talks like, and maybe just to make him more interesting he's a ballet fan to boot. Chances are that's preparation enough to make him come alive (enough) on the page.

Your focus should be on your major characters, because they must change from your first page to "The End"—and that change becomes the motivating force for your story. Remember *Casablanca*? Rick (Humphrey Bogart) starts the story as an aloof bystander, content to cope with whatever hand the war deals him. As the closing credits roll, however, he's ready to join the French Resistance. Or think of Don Quixote and Sancho Panza. Don Quixote's faith gets shaken—doubt replaces his tilting at windmills—while his companion makes the opposite transformation, from realist to idealist.

Those transformations form the foundation of your plot. So before you send anybody off to save the world, or to tilt at windmills, you'd better know all you can about him or her.

Hatching Your Plot

How many times have you heard, "I have a great idea for a story"? Ideas are a dime a dozen, as we've already seen. But an idea does not equal a plot, and a plot is what you need to make a story.

At the Maui Writers Conference every year, suspense writer John Saul and his writing partner Mike Sack dramatize the difference between an idea and a story you can actually write, by putting participants through a grueling, even humiliating process they call "What If." Their challenge: Express your idea in twenty-five words or less, beginning with "What if . . ." It's much tougher than it sounds, and would-be writers who can't master it come away having been "Saul and Sacked"—but with much more clearly focused stories than they started with.

Try it yourself with your own novel idea. Then challenge yourself to sharpen your "What If," over and over again, until you have the perfect capsule of your plot. You might start with, "What if a man thinks he sees a murder?" A little more thought and that becomes, "What if a man thinks he's seen a murder but can't prove it?" Okay, but *why* can't he prove it? Why doesn't he just walk over and investigate? Maybe he's got a broken leg and is confined to a wheelchair—in his apartment. Okay, so then how can he see a murder? Through the window, of course, where he's become sort of a Peeping Tom, stuck in his room and bored. "What if a wheelchair-bound man thinks he's seen a murder out his apartment window, where he's been spying on the neighbors, but can't prove it?" That's twenty-five words—and that's the plot of Alfred Hitchcock's movie *Rear Window*, written by John Michael Hayes and Cornell Woolrich.

Successfully plotting your fiction demands putting your vague, general idea into focus: What ought to happen to bring this idea to life and (just as important) what should you leave out? As Richard Martin Stern, author of *Tsunami!*, once observed, fiction writing is largely a process of selection—choosing what's necessary and having the willpower to omit what isn't. To take an obvious example, *Rear Window* doesn't begin with the childhood of the Jimmy Stewart character. He breaks his leg while photographing a race, but the movie doesn't spend an hour showing us the race (Stewart loads film in his camera, Stewart drives to the race, the race begins, Stewart takes some pictures, Stewart takes some more pictures . . .) before getting to the point. The focus is on Stewart stuck in his apartment, becoming a bit of a voyeur—and the sooner we get him there, the better.

Plotting also involves deciding what you're going to tell the reader about what's going on—and when. Techno-thriller writer Tom Clancy has said that the way he tells his stories springs largely from a ninety-minute documentary he once saw on PBS about none other than Alfred Hitchcock and his films. What Clancy learned from that documentary is that suspense is achieved by "information control": "What you know. What the reader knows. What the characters know. You balance that properly, and you can really get the reader wound up." In *Rear Window*, if we know right away—or Jimmy Stewart knows right away—what's become of the neighbor's invalid wife, and why the neighbor is cleaning knives and a saw at the kitchen sink, there'd be no story.

Decisions, decisions! If this is all beginning to sound suspiciously like the process of focusing and organizing your *non*fiction writing, you're right. Just as with nonfiction, you can work through that process of selection and revelation in advance—or you can write a lot of pages that wind up in the trash. The fastest approach to plotting is to maximize your self-confidence and minimize wasted writing by deciding where your story is going and how you'll get there.

We've already looked at the debate—not to be so much of a debate, after all—over outlining, especially when it comes to fiction. For beginning novelists in particular, though, let me make one more pitch for outlining your work at least in some fashion. Actually, let me allow fantasy author Terry Brooks, who has more than fifteen million books in print worldwide beginning with *The Sword of Shannara*, to make the case for me:

"I happen to favor rather strongly the process of outlining a book before trying to write it, and I would recommend it to beginning writers, in particular, for two reasons," Brooks says. "First, it requires thinking the story through, which eliminates a lot of wasted time chasing bad ideas. Second, it provides a blueprint to which the writer can refer while working on a story over the course of months or even years. Use of an outline is not a popular practice because it is hard work. It isn't easy thinking a story through from start to finish. But writing a hundred pages that have to be discarded because they don't lead anywhere is a whole lot more unpleasant."

But it's not just Brooks who thinks it's a good idea to know where you're story's going before you and your characters head out. Barbara Taylor Bradford, for example, not only plans her characters, but also creates a ten-to-twenty-page outline of her plot. For his circus novel *Spangle*, Gary Jennings diagrammed his story on a twenty-foot sheet of brown wrapping paper, using different-colored inks to track his multitude of characters through the twists and turns of sixteen years. He further divided the sheet by date and location, and scribbled his research notes on what was going on in the real, historical world vertically along his timeline. Even Sidney Sheldon, who dives into his own books with only a character and no plot in mind, dictating to a secretary as the story strikes him, once said that any beginning writer ought to use an outline.

These are blockbuster sagas, multi-hundred-page books where you can't tell the characters without a scorecard. What about a frothy little humor book, maybe two hundred pages—surely you don't need a plot outline for a frolic like that? P.G. Wodehouse, the master of the brief humor novel, would disagree. Humor, Wodehouse once told a *Paris Review* interviewer, requires perhaps the most careful planning of all forms of writing: "For a humorous novel you've got to have a scenario, and you've got to test it so that you know where the comedy comes in." Before he'd start one of his romps, Wodehouse would pen four hundred pages of notes, then build an outline that would make your old grammar-school teacher beam with pride ("A. Bring in Florence's husband . . ."). All this planning paid off, Wodehouse insisted: "You can more or less see how it's going to work out. After that it's just a question of detail."

You can choose or adapt any of an endless series of schemes for the actual planning of your plot, depending on your needs and the nature of your story. For example, mystery writer William J. Reynolds—author of the "Nebraska" series, including *Things Invisible* and *The Naked Eye*—relies on what he calls "a kind of free-form stream-of-consciousness document, a 'road map' of how I see the story going." Parts of this free-form road map are quite detailed, he says, right down to bits of dialogue that may actually end up in the finished book. Other parts he leaves as vague as can be ("Somehow he finds out that . . ."), meaning Reynolds must work out the details later.

Even if you opt for letting the muse guide you through the specific twists and turns of your tale, at minimum you should write down your beginning and ending and what changes in-between. You wouldn't, after all, set out on a safari without at least knowing where to start and where you're hoping to go. Reynolds, for example, admits he seldom consults his outline once he's made it, and sometimes doesn't even create his outline until he's a few chapters into the book. ("But I need to have that outline before I feel comfortable really getting into the book," he says.) Nonetheless, his stories always *begin* and *end* at the points indicated on his "map."

So make sure you know at least how your story will start and where it will wind up. Your whole outline might be no more than this: "Chapter 1: Norbert sets out to find his true parents . . . Chapter 22: Norbert finds his true parents, but decides his adoptive parents are his 'real' parents after all." That's not much, but it's better than plunging into a first draft without knowing whether "Norbert" will succeed in his fictional quest or exactly what that quest will be.

For a surer "safari," you'll want to know a little bit more about the journey before you step into the jungle. For example, screenwriters say that Paramount Studios sometimes uses the plot of *The Bad News Bears*, of all things, as its model of a successful screenplay. It couldn't be much simpler, but it does show how a well-planned plot hooks readers and keeps them until the credits roll. It's a couple of steps more complicated than simply beginning-and-end, going on to sketch out the fundamental reversals along the way. You can "analyze" the plot of *The Bad News Bears*—or a zillion other successful stories—this way:

The hook: A lousy Little League team suddenly starts winning.

The complication: The team starts losing again.

The response: The team begins the difficult journey back to victory.

The conclusion: The team triumphs.

Your own story—whether screenplay, short story, or novel—might be drafted along similar lines, to give yourself a guide to the key plot points:

The hook: Norbert discovers that he's adopted.

The complication: But his true parents vanished in Alaska thirty years ago.

The response: Norbert begins a long and difficult journey to learn the truth about his heritage.

The conclusion: Norbert learns that "there's no place like home"—that is, that the parents who raised him are his "real" parents.

Perhaps his birth parents turn out to be rotten criminals, while something his adoptive parents taught him saves his life in Alaska. (Incidentally, unless you recently took a lengthy vacation in Alaska, this frivolous example is even more unlikely than it seems—because it would shatter the rule about "writing what you know" that we just learned a few paragraphs ago.)

To take your plot-planning one step further, you might detail how your story develops over a series of chapters—breaking the action down into, say, twenty pieces instead of just these four. Not that the plot should be distributed evenly, five chapters per story element. Rather, your hook and conclusion might each be no more than a chapter or two; your complication not much more. The bulk of your chapters will be devoted to the response to the main complication, and to the mini-responses to the mini-complications (Norbert is attacked by a polar bear . . .) along the way.

For this level of detail, you might use a simple notebook, one page per chapter. Then on each page you could write a sentence or two telling what each chapter is supposed to accomplish. (If it doesn't accomplish anything, don't write it!) You could note which characters will be introduced in which chapter. (Generally, it's a good idea to get all your major characters introduced within the first quarter of your story—but not to bring them in all at once, confusing the reader.) You might also note each character's reaction or response to the events in the chapter. Then rough in your time span: When does each chapter take place?

Finally, consider what screenwriters call the "backstory"—what has gone on before your story opens. What elements of the backstory will you inject, when and where? How does the backstory affect your characters, their motivations, and the complications of your plot? Part of the backstory in Norbert's saga is the truth about what happened to his parents before our story opens. Another part might be some key lesson Norbert learned in his pre-chapter-one childhood, which comes into play just in the nick of time to save him from that polar bear.

You could accomplish much the same as this chapters-and-notebook scheme with a combination of index cards and manila folders. If you take your research notes on index cards, say, you could then distribute them into folders so they're ready when you need them: Your notes on the structure of an Eskimo village should go in the folder for chapter seventeen, when Norbert wakes up in one after being dragged off the ice floe by his loyal sled dogs. Ditto for your cards on characters, in the chapters where they'll be introduced, and your cards on conflicts, plot twists, setting, and so forth. The key is to arrange your pages, or cards, or whatever to make sure that you are constantly giving the readers something new, something to hold their attention and advance the action toward your ultimate goal in the final chapter.

Storytelling by Scenes

However many chapters you have—and it really doesn't matter—your story will ultimately be composed of a series of scenes. (This is an important lesson, by the way, for nonfiction writers to learn as well if you're writing a narrative.) These scenes, in turn, add up to your chapters or acts. By thinking in terms of scenes, you can break your writing task into more fundamental building blocks. As we've already seen, that compartmentalizing—cutting your story into bite-sized chunks—is crucial to achieving both the organization and self-confidence necessary to write faster and better. If you think in terms of scenes, you can concentrate on writing each scene at hand, on making it the best you can. Then move on to the next scene, and the next. Before you know it, you're typing "The End."

For a one-hundred-minute feature film, you'll probably need about twenty-five different scenes. For a novel, you might have several scenes per chapter, or you might label each scene a chapter. A short story might be no more than a handful of scenes.

As we saw in Elizabeth George's writing process, each scene brings a sampling of your characters together for some sort of interaction that advances the plotline. You can think of your scenes as miniature stories: Each must "work" as a dramatic unit—with a beginning, middle, and end. Within each scene, just as with your overall story, you might start with some goal that your protagonist wants to achieve. (Norbert wants to charter a plane to fly into the Alaskan wilderness.) Then you'll introduce your mini-complication, which might not seem so "mini" to your hero. (The only available plane must first deliver a vaccine to an even more remote outpost.) And then you can mix in some twist—logical but unexpected—that throws your main character for a loop, that seems to send him even further from his primary goal. (The plane runs into a blinding blizzard en route.)

But of course your story can't be just a jumble of unconnected scenes. Each scene has to lead into the next—which is the point of the twist, or hook, or outright disaster at the end of each scene. Between scenes you need a sort of mortar, stuff that holds the bricks of your story together. These transitions must do the basic business of sequencing and pacing your story (jumping ahead five minutes or five years). They summarize and condense the narrative that's not worth developing into a full-fledged scene. (Norbert's uneventful flight from Seattle to Fairbanks, where he tries to charter the plane that turns into an event.) Most important, they have to link the turnabout at the end of one scene to a new goal at the start of the next. (Norbert wants to survive the blizzard.)

The principle that links your scenes, one to the next, is causality. Not only should each scene advance the plot; it should also have consequences for subsequent scenes. In the movie *High Noon*, for example, based on John W. Cunningham's short story, "The Tin Star," ex-marshal Will Kane learns that a killer he sent to prison has been pardoned and is coming on the noon train to get revenge. (Here's the backstory, by the way, informing the main narrative: Before our story opened, Kane was a marshal who sent killer Frank Miller to the slammer.) As a result (another scene), Kane's pacifist Quaker bride tries to convince him to leave town with her rather than fight. When he decides to stay and face Miller, the consequence is that his bride decides to leave him. And so on. Cause, effect, another cause, another effect—your scenes run one into the next like falling dominos.

What scene should start this chain reaction? How should your story begin? With a bang, of course—a bang that, as we've already explored in the chapter about openings, doesn't stand alone but rather flows naturally from and into the rest of your tale. Don't waste time—yours or the readers'—penning many scenes of what should properly be relegated to your "backstory." Instead, start with a scene that introduces some change into your hero's life, a change that triggers all the toppling dominos that are ahead. As confession-magazine editors used to advise, "Start on the day that's different." Open with a discovery, an arrival, or a conflict. If you're writing a suspense thriller, launch your story with a battle or a bomb: Tom Clancy, for example, opened his blockbuster *Red Storm Rising* with a fiery scene of sabotage at a Soviet oil refinery; all the suspense that follows is triggered by this scene. If you're writing a murder mystery, get that corpse onto page one. If you're telling of a tangle of interpersonal relationships, start with a phone call, the return of an old flame, or the day he walks out on her.

In our imaginary story about Norbert, we wouldn't fritter away a half dozen scenes on Norbert's ordinary life: Norbert goes to the grocery store, Norbert watches television, Norbert mows the lawn. No, let's open with Norbert making the stunning discovery that everything he thought he knew about himself is wrong. If our story is a ski slope, let's skip the long, boring ride up the lift. We'll start, instead, with our hero poised for a long, thrilling ride—and then we'll give him a push.

Making Your Fiction Flow

So your story is mapped out and you're ready to write your first draft. If you were paying attention in the previous chapter, you already know how to write faster, smoother, more polished first drafts in your fiction—for the psychological principles are the same whether you're pounding out an article or a novel.

Start with creative pressure. It's important not to write your novel, short story, or screenplay until you can't stand *not* to write it. William Faulkner once said that his novels began with an image that "haunted" him until, finally, he had to write the novel to answer the questions that materialized around this haunting image. Your first draft must be a sort of exorcism, transforming those creative ghosts inside you into scenes on the page.

All your preparation—researching your setting, getting to know your characters, outlining your plot—can almost be thought of as a productive way of delaying your actual writing. To write an effortless first draft, you have to build the creative pressure through these "delaying tactics." Start too soon and you'll run out of steam before "The End."

Once you're finally ready to start, don't fall into the trap of thinking that because this is fiction, make-believe, your writing can be any less precise. "I'll fix it later" is even more tempting if you're a fiction writer who must spin all the solutions out of your own head. Indeed, because fiction often requires a greater emotional involvement on your part, "later" is even less likely to provide answers. Later, you will be less "hot" on your story, more bored with your characters; your emotional involvement will be at a lower ebb. So write it right—right now, not later, because you'll never be better suited to do it than at your first, most intense draft.

Today's computer technology can make it seem too easy to write sloppily, to take that "fix it later" mentality. Sometimes it's best to pretend you don't have that word-processing flexibility. Novelist Matt Ruff, author of *The Fool on the Hill* and *Set This House in Order*, told an Amazon.com interviewer that he learned to write on his mother's IBM Selectric typewriter: "Though the Selectric had a limited ability to correct mistakes, and would forgive minor typos and misspellings, it couldn't erase whole paragraphs at a keystroke—so you had to think long and hard about what you wanted to say, or waste a lot of time retyping whole pages." Though he finally switched to a computer in college, Ruff says that his "apprenticeship" on the Selectric taught him a compositional discipline he might not otherwise have had.

"I don't do drafts," says Reynolds. "I think they're a waste of time. I try to be satisfied with any given section—page, chapter, paragraph, whatever—before I move on to the next bit. The idea of producing four or five hundred pages of 'rough draft,' then going back to page one and revising into a second draft, then going back again, etc., etc., sounds so tedious that I doubt I'd ever get past the first draft." (He does, of course, go back over previous work as he progresses, and polishes the whole manuscript—"dotting the i's and crossing the t's, not wholesale revision"—before dropping it in the mail.)

Because you're making it up, fiction first drafts are also particularly prone to "lard" words. If the rain is only in your imagination, it's too easy to make it a "driving" rain—like a zillion other fictional rainstorms. Those stars that only your characters see are probably going to be "twinkling," the fog "thick as pea soup," and the stairs "steep." But don't just replace these tired words with odd new words you've plucked out of the thesaurus: If they don't serve your story (don't *all* stars twinkle?), don't waste time writing them in the first place. Save that thesaurus time to spend on nouns and verbs, instead of pondering whether to write "old" or "aged" to describe a ninety-year-old character.

Ah, the temptations of the thesaurus. Fiction writers may be even more prone to perfectionism than their nonfiction kin. If you're aiming for Art, the desire to make your fiction perfect can be so strong as to keep you from writing anything at all. Such pressure, to follow in the footsteps of Shakespeare and Tolstoy, Austen and Proust! Keep in mind, when perfectionism starts putting the brakes on your productivity, that much of what today we revere as great literature was written under deadline pressures for commercial purposes. The giants of literature had to eat, too. Whether you write a novel that endures for the ages has far more to do with how large your soul and talent may be, and little to do with one more trip to the thesaurus.

Finally, for the fiction writer no less than for a newspaper reporter on deadline, getting it written demands discipline: putting your seat on the chair and your fingers on the keyboard. Even as daunting a project as a novel can be reduced to willpower and mathematics: If you can write just two to four pages a day of exceptionally good prose, remember, you'll finish a novel in one hundred days. If you can manage ten pages a day, five days a week, as the prolific novelist Dean R. Koontz says he does, you'll produce ten novels a year and be considered a phenomenon of productivity. Frederick Faust, who wrote literally hundreds of westerns under the pen name

"Max Brand," used to write only two hours a day. His secret? He wrote two hours every day, and he wrote fourteen pages in each two-hour session.

Steven Saylor, author of a mystery series set in ancient Rome, approaches his writing pretty much like a regular job. Though he could work any time, any day he chooses, Saylor opts to write from Monday through Friday, and take weekends off. He starts around ten o'clock in the morning, and stops about four in the afternoon, with other chores of his writing business filling the other "nine to five" hours. The discipline of a regular workweek, Saylor says, keeps him on track.

Other novelists, such as science fiction and fantasy writer Greg Costikyan, discipline themselves by word count rather than hours. Costikyan says that when going all-out on a novel he shoots for 2,500 words a day. Some days that may take him just two hours; other days, it may take twelve.

Writing regularly, Reynolds notes, not only makes the words add up faster but also makes it easier to slip into the harness at each writing session. When he made himself keep to a schedule on his first novel, *The Nebraska Quotient*, he soon discovered "it took less and less time to get back into the groove when I began each evening's session. Pretty soon I could just sit down and pick up where I left off the previous evening, with little or no warm-up."

Suddenly, he adds, a project that had kicked around in his ambitions for years was on its way to reality. You get into a groove and the pages start to pile up. You keep at it, and pretty soon there's a book sitting there.

But you must approach your fiction writing as *work*, the same as anything else worth doing in life. Having a story that you're burning to tell isn't enough, or there'd be successful novelists and screenplay writers on every block. Like any other work, fiction writing requires preparation, planning, discipline, and drive. That's the bad news. The good news, as we've seen, is that it does not require anguish, hair-pulling, alcoholism, or long nights staring at an empty page.

Go on, start filling those pages. Get to work.

Exercises

1. Try summarizing the plot of a favorite movie in twenty-five words or less, beginning with "What if . . ."

2. Now try summarizing your current writing project in a "What if . . . ?" of no more than twenty-five words.

3. Flesh out your current writing project in a mini-outline consisting of brief descriptions of the beginning, ending and what changes in-between.

4. Write a brief statement of how your protagonist changes from the start of your story to the end.

5. Using the *Bad News Bears* formula in this chapter, sketch a four-step outline of your story (or of a favorite movie or novel).

6. Expand your mini-outline to a list of about twenty key scenes.

CHAPTER 14

HOW TO FINISH WHAT YOU START

Did your mother ever tell you to make sure you leave a good last impression? You know what I mean: Polishing your heels, checking the line of your haircut in back in a mirror, making sure your shirt is tucked in behind you. Moms worry about that sort of thing.

As a writer, you need to take a mom-like attitude toward the parting impression you leave with readers. A good ending can pull your story all together for readers, making the whole more than the sum of the assembled parts. The right ending can leave readers with a gasp or a smile, can lock your message in their heads with stunning force or near-subliminal subtlety. Or, as William Zinsser aptly put it: "The perfect ending should take the reader slightly by surprise and yet seem exactly right to him."

Conversely, a bad ending can ruin all your hard work in leading readers from there to here. Just as your opening is important for drawing the reader into a story, the ending goes a long way toward determining its ultimate impact. Think of endings in the movies: What if Thelma and Louise had decided instead, what the heck, let's just give ourselves up? What if Charlton Heston hadn't stumbled across the Statue of Liberty at the end of *Planet of the Apes*? (Sorry, did I just spoil it for you? See how important endings can be?)

Structurally speaking, your ending is the other side of the bridge that began with your opening, got supported by your thematic development, and takes readers to—where? It's essential that your ending makes the journey seem worthwhile and brings readers to a satisfactory destination. That destination must deliver on the promise made through your focus and angle. All of which is no mean feat: "Great is the art of beginning," Thomas Fuller once observed, "but greater the art is of ending."

Like your beginning, the ending must spring naturally from the heart of your story. A tacked-on ending not only cheats the reader, but also leaves a bad taste in the mouth that you have no opportunity to wash out. The ancient Greeks and Romans could get away with *deus ex machina* endings, in which a "god out of a machine" unexpectedly descends to resolve all the story's problems and wrap things up in a tidy package—but today's toga-less audiences won't sit still for such trickery. A kindly uncle, never before alluded to, cannot suddenly show up on your hero's doorstep and pay off those crushing debts. A secret message from the Kremlin, utterly unprepared for in previous chapters, cannot call off what seemed to be the brink of World War III. And your heroine cannot wake up to discover, on the last page, that "It was all just a dream."

Your endings should be as seamless a part of the fabric of your story as you can weave. So your ending will be only as good as what you've built so far. "What's wrong with my third act?" an aspiring playwright once asked George S. Kaufmann. To which Kaufmann archly replied, "Your first."

But endings don't have to put you in a panic. The key to successful endings, not surprisingly, lies in the homework you do before you sit down to write your first words. Just as your outline leads you safely and sanely through your opening, theme, chronology, exposition, and other essential elements, so too can advance planning create a safe landing for your story.

As you map out your writing and the bits and pieces fall into place, keep in mind some possible strategies for organizing your ending. These structural secrets—which are not mutually exclusive but may be creatively combined for truly satisfying conclusions—are just a sampling of the many options for wrapping up your story. But having a few such possibilities in your writer's bag of tricks can take some of the fear and trembling out of finishing what you've started.

Coming Full Circle

The first finishing strategy you may want to try looks back toward your opening; we've already seen several examples of how this can make a satisfying closing. In your opening, after all, you set out a problem, introduced a novel situation, popped a surprise, posed a challenge, or asked a question. So in your ending, it's only natural to look back to where you started and resolve the problem or answer the question with which you began. Has the situation changed, for better or worse? Was your initial impression accurate? What have you and the readers learned along the way? How have your characters grown?

In a story that offers some new solution to the problems of life, for example, you likely opened by dramatizing the problem. Whether you're tackling household clutter, depression, the challenges of traveling with kids, acne, or sexual dysfunction, the point of your piece is to lead the reader down some possible avenue of help. At the end of the road, it's not surprising that you should wind up back where you started—but with the problem solved.

Even if your approach is more anecdotal, you can use some element of your opening scene or story to bring readers full circle at the end. For example, I started a story on planning a family-history vacation, for *Family Tree Magazine*, with this anecdote:

> Genealogy tour guide James Derheim and his clients, who were following their roots back to Germany, were expecting to stop in for coffee with some shirttail relatives and visit for an hour, no more. Instead, at 9:30 in the morning, they were greeted by the smell of roasting wild pig. The clients' distant German cousin had shot the pig himself on the ancestral family lands. Quick morning coffee turned into a luncheon feast, where tourists and kin formed lifelong bonds spanning not only the Atlantic but genealogical gaps.

That set up a simple little gag at the end, which I led into by bringing back Derheim via a quote:

> "Be prepared to be treated like visiting royalty, invited into people's homes and treated to meals," Derheim adds. After all, your family history vacation, if you do your homework, can be an exciting experience for your distant relatives as well.

> Just in case, you might want to start developing a taste for roasted wild pig.

On a more serious note, go back to chapter eleven and see how the opening of my story on the soldier killed in Grenada set up my ending, and how this "coming full circle" created a resonance for readers.

The same sort of approach can work for fiction. In a memorable story entitled "There Will Come Soft Rains," Ray Bradbury depicts a completely automated house of the future continuing to function long after its occupants are gone. He opens with this benign morning ritual: "In the living room the voice-clock sang: *Tick-tock, seven o'clock, time to get up . . ."* Two paragraphs later, a second automated voice chimes in: "Today is August 4, 2026." At the end of the story, after most of the automated house has been consumed by a fire that no one's home to put out, only one wall remains standing in the ruins. But that wall contains a lonesome automated voice that dutifully calls out, the next morning, "Today is August 5, 2026," over and over, though no one is there to hear it.

Problem Solved, Question Answered

Many stories are built around a question: Will Melissa ever find true love? Can computers in the classroom someday replace teachers? Will the dashing hero find the microfilm before it's too late? Did the celebrity fall from grace because his career grew too far too fast, or does the blame lie with his agents and managers? If your theme and focus boil down to this sort of question, the natural solution to your finishing woes is simply to end by answering the question posed by this "hook." Not only does this strategy show you a way out of your writing project—it also, of course, fulfills an essential obligation to your readers! Your job is to satisfactorily answer the story's central question or deliver on its thematic promise by your final page; if the ending itself forms or sums up the answer, so much the better.

That story on computers in the classroom, for instance, might build to a quote (often an effective tool to end a story) from a teacher whose credibility you've already established:

> "Sure, computers can help kids learn," Smith says, surveying the rows of blinking screens in her classroom, "but I'd take a good teacher without computers over a poor one with computers, every time."

That's it. End it. You've presented the pros and cons, the facts and figures, and competing points of view. You've found a quote (or it might be an anecdote or some telling detail or scene) that perfectly encapsulates your bottom-line answer to the question posed by your hook.

Similarly, a profile ought to have a focus that gives it a greater reason for being than just "Meet so-and-so." Powerful profiles may probe the subject's character, asking a fundamental question whose answer becomes the substance of the article. The profile's conclusion, then, begs for some summation of that answer. You the author can do it, but it's more effective to cast it in the subject's own words or actions. This closing bit can be subtle, even symbolic.

Suppose that your profile of the burned-out celebrity posed the question of who was really in charge of his career. The answer your article develops is that overeager, greedy agents and managers were really responsible for the star's meteoric rise and fall. If then in your research you were lucky enough to get this little scene, you'd have a ready-made ending:

> A knock on the door signals that the ex-teen idol's time for talking is up. He manages a parting flash of that famous smile, then climbs into a waiting cherry-red Corvette to make his big entrance for the auto show.
>
> The drive onto the auditorium floor is only a few hundred feet. But this time, at least, he's the one in the driver's seat.

That probably seems contrived after the fact, but if you had your focus firmly in mind at some point the aptness of that scene would leap out at you. It's a bit of business you could have left out. Or you could have used it without wringing any symbolic import from the scene. But the writer alert to nuances of structural strategy would spot the scene as a perfect answer to the story's essential question.

In fiction, you have the freedom to make up such an evocative answer to your story's essential question. You can craft the moving final scene where, yes, Melissa finds true love or the hero snatches the microfilm away just in time. This isn't just a handy way out of an ending dilemma: It's part of your job as the writer.

Your fictional answering finale doesn't have to take the form of a scene (though that's always a good bet). Think of the closing paragraphs of F. Scott Fitzgerald's *The Great Gatsby*, surely among the most memorable endings in all of literature. While such a complex novel can't readily be boiled down to a single question, one question the story poses is whether Gatsby will "get the girl," Daisy, whom he first saw years ago when he was a poor army lieutenant and now reconnects with after he's become wealthy. Tragically, as the story unfolds, the answer turns out to be no. Despite what Gatsby believed, no, you can't repeat the past. No, money can't buy happiness. Nick, the narrator, ponders this at the end of the book, how the distance between Gatsby and Daisy proved as unbridgeable as the water separating Gatsby from "the green light at the end of Daisy's dock": "He had come a long way to this blue lawn and his dream must have seemed so close that he could hardly fail to grasp it. He did not know that it was already behind him . . ." That sets up the book's unforgettable closing lines:

> Gatsby believed in the green light, the orgastic future that year by year recedes before us. It eluded us then, but that's no matter— tomorrow we will run faster, stretch our arms farther. . . . And one fine morning—

> So we beat on, boats against the current, borne back ceaselessly into the past.

Fitzgerald answers the question he posed in the novel when he reunited Gatsby and Daisy. The green light blinks, far away across the water, but we can't reach it any more than Gatsby could.

Living Happily Ever After

What happened to the surviving characters after the end of *The Great Gatsby*? Fitzgerald could have gone on and on—detailing, say, Nick's experiences through the Great Depression and the early years of World War II. But he didn't. Though *The Great Gatsby* has a variety of chronological twists and turns, it knows when to stop—at the end of the story.

Our made-up closing scene with the ex-teen idol happens also to be at the chronological end of our made-up story. And that's certainly one way chronology can help you find your story's conclusion: End it where the story ends. The interview is over, the race is won, the patient comes out of her coma, or the heroine reunites with her lover (or fails to). They all live happily ever after, or they don't.

Some stories, alas, are not so neat, particularly in nonfiction. The problem may not be solved, the scientists' work goes on, the debate continues.

Still other stories—and this may be the most common situation you'll face—have natural chronological endings, but you must agonize over whether this is indeed to best place for your writing to end. The life of Nick the narrator, after all, did not end at the close of *The Great Gatsby*; the ending is merely where Fitzgerald realized his story needed to wrap up. Or imagine writing a travel article: You could end almost every travel piece with getting on the plane to go home, with one last look at the lovely island or sparkling city from the air before clouds and distance sweep it into memory. But is that really the best way to end a travel story? *Every* travel story?

You can build your endings on chronology, but you don't have to limit yourself to chronological endings. It's more important for your ending to reflect your focus and angle than the clock or calendar. Part of your task as a writer is to select the cut-off point for your own work: Should it end with you getting on the plane—or with the scene the evening before, sipping a tropical drink while watching the sun go down? If the focus of your story is on the island as the ultimate place to get away from it all, go with the sunset.

Given that you have the ultimate control over presentation and selection, how then can you use chronology to help find your endings? The key is finding a cut-off point that has more than merely chronological importance, an ending that resonates with the reader and reflects your angle and focus.

To pick this cut-off, you might try sketching key points in your chronology in a rough outline. For our imaginary travel piece, this might look like:

A. Historical background of Bora-Bora
B. Arrive on Bora-Bora
C. Spectacular island views
D. Encountering the charming people

. . .

M. Tropical sunset
N. Goodbye to the island

Of course, for dramatic effect you would probably write it more like this:

B. Arrive on Bora-Bora
C. Spectacular island views
A. Historical background of Bora-Bora
D. Encountering the charming people

. . .

and so on, flashing back to the historical background only after you've caught the reader's interest.

So where's the best spot to chop off this chain of events? We've already agreed that the tropical sunset makes a better cut-off point than the flight home. But you don't need to be bound by A-B-C chronological order in your endings any more than in your openings. Suppose your focus is something like, "The people of Bora-Bora turn out to be even more beautiful, in their kindness and respect for tradition, than their lovely island." Then you might prefer to extract part of "D. Encountering the charming people" (let's call this second anecdote or whatever, D2) and save it for the ending.

Your actual outline might then look like this:

B. Arrive on Bora-Bora
C. Spectacular island views
A. Historical background of Bora-Bora
D. Encountering the charming people
   . . .
M. Tropical sunset
D2. Final remembered encounter with the charming people

While a lengthy chronological twist, such as a full-bore flashback, would be confusing at the end, you could introduce this brief detour as a remembrance:

> The gentle splash of the waves in the sunset reminded me of the soft laughter of two little native girls I met the day before . . .
>
> [anecdote]
>
> . . . More so even than the beauty of the sunsets, their smiles— and those of the other Bora-Borans I met—are what will draw me back to this enchanted place.

You can certainly write less labored endings than I can make up here (although now at least I can take that trip to Bora-Bora off my taxes . . .). The point is that you should consider your whole chain of events, fictional or non-, as you seek the perfect ending. Finding your ending may be as simple as stopping where the story stops, or it may require a last little backtrack.

Your chronology, like your opening and your thematic development, should feed into your ending until it seems—to readers, at least—as perfect and inevitable, yet surprising, as a tropical sunset. When you and the reader arrive there together, you'll know that, yes, this is the place to stop.

Getting to the Finish Line

But even once you've figured out what your ending is, getting there can sometimes be a challenge for writers. Much like mom's reminder to leave a good last impression, "Finish what you start" is one of those admonitions we all heard from our mothers. It's easier said than done, however, as any writer knows. You've crafted a solid opening, you're steaming through your first (almost final) draft, and then . . . Well, somewhere between that initial burst of creativity and enthusiasm, and typing "The End," you run out of momentum. You can't quite wrap it up. The art of writing becomes the drudgery of writing, and you begin to wonder if maybe you should have followed some of mom's *other* advice and become a doctor instead.

You're not alone in struggling to finish what you've started. Virgil, it's said, took a decade to complete *The Aeneid*—and still thought it needed another three years' work when he gave it up. Sinclair Lewis spent seventeen years laboring to bring his best-known novel, *Main Street*, to fruition. And Katherine Anne Porter needed more than two decades to finish *Ship of Fools*.

But it's not only writers who have such a hard time finishing what they start; nearly everybody does, to some degree. Psychologists say we all have a built-in drive to complete what we've begun—it's not just mom making us feel guilty—but some of us seem to be better at harnessing that innate force. Learning to make the most of your inborn "completion drive" is critical to getting things done. You can write as fast as your keyboard can handle, but if all you have to show for it is a pile of half-written first drafts you're not really *writing* anything; it's just typing practice.

"Know thyself" is probably the first step in getting your completion drive into high gear. Imagine that you're typing along on your laptop and your battery suddenly starts to die. What do you do? Do you calmly plug in your laptop or switch batteries and get right back to work? Or do you decide that, gee, now's a good time to go shopping for a new battery, or maybe a whole new laptop? Or perhaps, in the search for a battery, you get distracted and end up sorting through stuff in the closet for the rest of the afternoon. The rest of that chapter can wait, sure, while you clip and file those really important back issues of *Procrastinator's Digest Magazine*.

If that latter putting-it-off persona sounds like you, then you might have a completion drive in need of revving up. To see if you suffer from "finish-phobia," try answering this quick completion quiz:

1. Look around your house. Is it packed with half-completed projects you can't throw out? I'm not talking about only writing chores here, but also about that afghan-in-progress, the DVD player you bought but never finished hooking up or learning to use, and the Christmas cards from two years ago that you never finished addressing.
2. Try listing the major projects—again, not just writing work—you've started and finished in the past six months. Now make a list of those you've begun that are still "pending." Is the latter list a good deal longer than the first?

3. Would you describe yourself as "impulsive" rather than "driven," "impatient" more so than "stubborn"?
4. In a typical week, do you often find yourself coming back to tasks or chores you've already picked up and abandoned once or more?

If most of your answers were "yes" or "yeah, I guess so" (or if you couldn't even finish this little quiz!), then you probably need a completion-drive tune-up. If none of these quiz questions sounded like you, your completion drive is likely working fine. It's even possible that you're one of those rare individuals whose completion drive works overtime—who suffers from a compulsive "finish mania" and needs to learn to slam on the brakes. Moderation in all things, after all. You can skip the rest of this chapter, in that case, and get an entirely different kind of help. (Of course, the really compulsive completer won't be *able* to skip the rest of this chapter; once begun, the finishaholic has to read through to the last page.)

For the vast majority of writers who daily struggle with finishing what they start, don't despair. Force yourself to read on. No, no, don't wander away now and work on that half-completed needlepoint you started three years ago. Stay with me here; there's help for you yet.

Closing in on Closure

To a Gestalt psychologist, your drive to finish what you start is more than merely good advice from mom. It's a real psychological drive experts call "closure," as basic as "waiting for the other shoe to drop." The more you really don't care whether that other shoe drops, the more your completion drive needs revving up.

Here's a little exercise that can show you how closure works—and that demonstrates how, even if you're a "finishphobic," your mind still has a natural need to finish things, a need you can put to work to finish your writing projects. Try sketching a circle, but leave the last little bit of the loop unconnected. Now take another look at your almost-circle. See? Your brain fills in the blank, completing the circle so it almost seems that the final arc is there after all. Kurt Koffka, a pioneer of Gestalt psychology, explained this trick of perception as the tensions of "imperfectly formed neural patterns . . . leading inevitably to their own completion."

What do "imperfectly formed neural patterns" have to do with getting that story done? Well, put yourself in the place of the composer who (as the story goes) loved to sleep late. To get him out of bed and down to breakfast, the great composer's clever wife would play the first three chords of a series on the piano downstairs. One . . . two . . . three . . . But where was the fourth and final chord? The composer would toss and turn upstairs until finally he could stand it no longer. Downstairs he'd come to finish the chord series and, by the way, to eat breakfast.

Just as closure worked like an alarm clock for this sleepyhead composer, you can program yourself to "wake up" and finish your writing. Learning to use closure can pay dividends beyond finally learning whodunit in a murder mystery or getting your Christmas shopping done before New Year's. After all, it doesn't do much good to write fast for three-quarters of a story if the final fraction comes agonizingly slowly, far after deadline, or not at all.

So how do you exercise your "closure" muscles and build the mental biceps it takes to finish fast? We're getting to that. First, though, there's another little psychology lesson. Welcome to the "Zeigarnik Effect," named after a Russian psychological researcher, Bluma Zeigarnik, who discovered it in a 1927 experiment. Zeigarnik's subjects were a group of 138 children, whom she gave a series of simple tasks to perform. With half of the tasks, she let the children work straight through to completion. With the other half, however, Zeigarnik interrupted the children partway through and made them move on to something else. Then she quizzed the children an hour later to see what they recalled of the work they'd done. She found that 110 of the 138 children remembered more of the *interrupted* tasks than they did the completed ones.

Zeigarnik concluded that we tend to forget completed tasks because the motivation to finish them has been satisfied. Unfinished tasks, however, stay fresher in the memory because the original motivation behind them remains unsatisfied.

So when you're writing a story, it's not just the piles of notes and the image of an angry editor (or mom) that nag you to finish: The Zeigarnik Effect keeps the memory of your work-in-progress fresh in your mind. Once you've tucked that story into a manila envelope and licked the flap, however, the Zeigarnik Effect lets the memory of that writing task fade into a dim glow of accomplishment.

Or at least that's how it's supposed to work. A writer with a healthy sense of closure and a fully functioning Zeigarnik Effect ought to zip through to the final page without a hitch. Indeed, you should hardly be able to stop yourself from finishing!

Alas, countervailing psychological forces sometimes keep your natural completion drive from doing its job. You may think of these counterforces as "writer's block," just plain laziness, or inefficiency. But understanding the *real* causes of your failure to finish is crucial to conquering them and getting your story in the mail.

Every writing project has its share of frustrations. The secret to keeping up your pace until the finish line is how you handle these rough spots. "Low frustration tolerance" is what psychologists label the problem of quitting too quickly, of not sticking with a task. Sports stars have a simpler phrase: "no pain, no gain."

Remember all our talk early on about the d-word, discipline? You may not like it any better now, but it remains a key to overcoming your low frustration tolerance and seeing your writing projects through to completion. You've got to have the discipline necessary to keep writing even when you hit a roadblock. Instead of getting detoured and distracted—"discomfort dodging," as some psychologists dub this trick of steering clear at the first sign of frustration or difficulty—you've got to stick with it.

Low frustration tolerance, however, isn't the only explanation for failing to finish what you set out to write. Unrealistic expectations, a related foible, can also short-circuit your best intentions. I don't mean simply that you set your sights too high; it's fine to have ambitious goals. But unrealistic expectations can trip you up when you forget about all the steps between the present reality and your dreams. If you don't have the discipline to "pay your dues" en route to the top, you'll have a harder time staying the course.

You can't expect to write the Great American Novel, in other words, the first time you sit down at the keyboard. You can't give up just because your first story doesn't wind up in the *New Yorker*. And that principle holds not only for your writing career but for each writing task you tackle. Having a bunch of ideas isn't enough; you've got to follow through on them. Thinking that ideas, even talent, are enough to make your story succeed—in the absence of plain old hard work—is a classic sign of a noncompleter.

Fear of failure can also lead you to put off finishing what you start. That may sound contradictory—failing because you're afraid of failing—but it's a common cause of procrastination. If you never finish anything, your work can hardly be criticized, can it? And there's always the will-o'-the-wisp that if only you fiddle with your story a little while longer, if only you put off finishing it, you can still somehow make it perfect. If a story is done, you have to send it out into the hard light of day that will reveal its flaws. A work forever in progress, however, is a work forever straining for perfection.

You may even fail to complete your writing projects because you're afraid of *success*. Deep down, you may feel you really don't deserve to succeed as a writer. So you subtly sabotage yourself, short-circuiting stories before the final chapter. Maybe succeeding as a writer would mean you would quit your day job as an accountant or a public-relations executive—a job that, gosh darn it, you actually enjoy.

A fear of completion may even be linked to fear of that ultimate finish, death. Do you know the old superstition that if you complete your life's work, you'll die? Finishing an important writing project can seem like a little death.

With all these powerful reasons not to finish what you've started writing, it's perhaps a wonder that anything ever gets written at all. But some lucky souls simply have an equally powerful innate completion drive, pushing them along to the final word. What about the rest of the world, the not-so-lucky and not-so-driven ones? You've got to build up your mental muscles. Once you begin to grasp why it's often so difficult for you to complete a story (at least in time to meet that deadline), you can "pump iron" to overcome those obstacles.

Turbocharging Your Completion Drive

Time-management experts are full of suggestions for planning and organizing your working life to increase your odds of finishing what you start; we've already seen a lot of these ideas as they apply to writing. But conquering your "finishphobia" goes beyond time management. (For one thing, you're likely to keep procrastinating on all those good time-management ideas, just like everything else.) The best tactics for turning yourself into a writer who completes work promptly combine traditional time-management with smart psychology.

The basic principle is to train yourself to finish things by helping yourself to finish small tasks, or pieces of tasks. Once you get in the completion habit and see how good it feels, you'll be motivated to finish ever-larger projects. So, if you're a finishphobic, do not, for example, start by tackling a blockbuster novel or a lengthy non-fiction exposé. Write some smaller things—a short story, an op-ed essay, a simple profile—that you have a better chance of seeing to completion.

In other words, develop will power in small doses. By forcing yourself to complete something, even a small story or "fluff" article, you'll gradually strengthen your inborn completion drive—just as a weight lifter builds his muscles by repeated use. Each time, try something a little bit lengthier or tougher, a longer sprint; eventually you'll be writing marathons.

Your initial completion exercises can even be smaller than a whole story. Break your projects down into their component parts, and reward yourself for finishing each section. Did you finish a page? Terrific. Did you make it to the end of the scene? Wonderful. Do it again tomorrow. Pretty soon you'll be *really* finished.

Think in terms of a writing *schedule*. How long will each part of the project take you? Don't fool yourself here—it's important, if you're not to fall victim to unrealistic expectations, to develop a realistic sense of how long writing chores really take. If you can break the job down into finite, finishable parts, and figure out about how long each part will take you, you can apportion the time between now and the deadline.

Let's say you're writing a four-thousand-word article for a magazine, and the editor has given you a month in which to work. You estimate (honestly, now) that researching and interviewing will take you two weeks. Organizing your notes and getting ready to write, you think, will eat up another week. That leaves you just over a week to write your first draft, polish it, and get the manuscript in the mail. In order to leave a margin for error and revision, you'll probably have to write about a thousand words a day once you start at the keyboard. That's not nearly as hard as it sounds: Remember, you'll have done all the hard work of planning and organizing before you ever write word one.

The same principle applies to longer works. As we saw in the previous chapter, mystery writer William J. Reynolds labored in fits and starts for a couple of years on his first novel, *The Nebraska Quotient*. He'd write a bit one Saturday but not the next and, ultimately, didn't seem to be making much progress towards getting the book done. Then he says he "got serious" about finishing and made himself write every single day for one hour. "An hour was a manageable time," he says, "not so long as to be daunting after a full day at my regular job, so brief that I didn't dare waste any of it sharpening pencils or unhooking paper clips, and yet significant enough that I made real progress if I shoulder-to-wheeled it." An hour at a time, the book marched along to completion—and publication, which launched a whole career as a mystery novelist.

Whatever daily quota you set for yourself, and whether it's weighed in words or minutes, once you've finished (yes, *finished*) what you set out to do for the day, resist the urge to keep on going and gain a little extra ground. Rest on your laurels for today, so tomorrow you'll have the self-confidence and creative energy to do it again. Successful speedy writers are like the tortoise in the race with the hare: Slow and steady finishes fastest.

Only hares, by the way, think of themselves as "thriving on deadline pressure." Do not only your editors but yourself a favor and plan to finish your story a little *before* it's due. Scheduling your time otherwise is a plan for failure, and that's exactly what we want to avoid here. You're seeking to build a sense of success—so give yourself a little leeway in which to succeed.

Another way in which you should give yourself a little leeway is your own attention span: Work *with* it rather than against it. When I was a columnist, really having to crank out copy, the newspaper kept a big pot of coffee—free!—down the hall in the cafeteria. Whenever I felt my attention begin to wander as I wrote, or reached a point where I knew the story would benefit from a few moments' extra cogitating on my part, I'd get up from my desk and wander down the hall. I'd get a cup of coffee. I'd slowly walk back to my desk. And by the time I sat down again I'd be ready to work some more.

You don't have to single-handedly support Juan Valdez and his family, of course. When your attention wanes, you could hop up and walk around the house, do a couple of pushups, jump up and down, try some isometrics, or go get a glass of water. It was the stroll, really, rather than the free coffee that made my trips to the cafeteria a handy break.

The key is to limit your interruptions—allow them, since you're only human, but keep them in check. Some people, when their attention begins to wander during a writing stint, let themselves get so distracted that they never come back to the keyboard. If your "coffee break" turns into a couple of hours of puttering around the house or watching the Game of the Week, you'll never finish your writing chores. Conversely, if you force yourself to sit at the keyboard for hours without a brief respite, you'll soon turn your writing into drudgery. Don't fight that limited human attention span; fool it.

Think of this working pattern in terms of simple mathematics: If your attention span is about fifteen minutes and you take a one-minute mini-break whenever you start to flag, in an hour you'll squeeze in fifty-six minutes of work and "waste" just four minutes. Those four minutes represent a worthwhile investment in keeping fresh.

Finally, to finish what you start to write it's important to keep your goal in mind. Keep reminding yourself what you're trying to accomplish: a lively article, a moving short story, an amusing screenplay, or a mystery novel that will keep the world on the edge of its collective chair. This is a principle that applies to almost any human endeavor, from writing to sports. When Billie Jean King was turning the tennis world topsy-turvy, for instance, she would spend twenty minutes several times each week just staring at a tennis ball. That odd-sounding exercise, she said, helped build her concentration for the game situations when she had to keep her eye on the ball.

Learn to keep your eye on the ball. You'll find it helps along the way to game . . . set . . . and match.

Exercises

1. Find an example of a published story or article whose conclusion "comes back around" to its opening. Try writing a different conclusion that doesn't refer to the lead.

2. Chart the chronology of your current writing project or a published story with a chronological narrative, as shown in this chapter. Experiment with changing the chronology to end at a different place. What happens if the story ends earlier or later chronologically?

3. Write a summary of how a favorite novel or movie might have ended if the storyline had been allowed to continue to a more "natural" (but probably less effective dramatically) conclusion (e.g., the hero grows old and dies).

4. Take the "completion quiz" in this chapter. How do you rate on the scale from "finishphobic" to "finishaholic"?

5. Try flexing your completion muscles: Write a letter to yourself describing your current writing project in five to six hundred words. Finish writing the entire letter before allowing yourself to take a break or get up from your chair. Don't let yourself write more than six hundred words or fewer than five hundred.

6. Compute a simple schedule for your current writing project. Allowing for research and planning time, how many words a day over how many days do you need to write to get it done?

CHAPTER 15

FROM FIRST DRAFT TO FINAL DRAFT

Arthur C. Clarke, one of the planet's most prolific writers of both science and science-fiction, nonetheless once conceded, "Sometimes it is as hard to *stop* work on a piece as it was to start in the first place." The lesson that Clarke said he'd learned over the years was that "you must learn to recognize the point of diminishing returns, and send your 99.99 percent completed masterpiece out into the cruel hard world."

Literature is full of authors who had a hard time recognizing that point of diminishing returns. How many more great novels might Thomas Wolfe have written if he could have mastered the work of revision? As he wrote to his editor, Maxwell Perkins, "Revision is simply hell for me. My efforts to cut 50,000 words may sometimes result in my adding 75,000." In the phrase of his contemporary, F. Scott Fitzgerald, Wolfe was "a putter-inner." He kept putting more into his books, taking more out, then putting more back in again. Wolfe no doubt put in and took out enough to make several good-sized novels, which the world will never get to read.

Even Ernest Hemingway, known for his ability to "go for the kill" as a hunter, had a hard time finishing some of his novels. He rewrote the last page of *A Farewell to Arms*, it's said, nearly forty times.

The modern record for compulsive revision, though, has to be held by Harold Brodkey. His novel, originally titled *A Party of Animals*, was first contracted for in 1960 but didn't materialize until 1991, several zillion revisions and a new title (*The Runaway Soul*) later. Brodkey, according to his publisher (which at one point, eighteen years into the process, gave up on him, only to pick the novel up again a few years later), would change his thinking, axe a chapter, and then add several more—until "the novel became sort of a life in progress."

These revisionaholics are hardly alone. If you've ever sat around listening to writers talk about their work, and stayed awake long enough to remember any of the conversation, you probably heard some sort of exchange along the lines of, "How many drafts do you do?" Some writers even take pride in the vast number of versions of the same story that they churn out on the road to supposed perfection. Jerzy Kosinski, for example, would do more than a dozen drafts of his novels. Even that wasn't enough tinkering for him, though: To the dismay of his publishers, Kosinski would rewrite the typeset galleys a couple of times—and then rewrite again when he got the page proofs.

As the saying goes, "No work of art is ever finished; it is only abandoned." But if you want to write both faster and better, you need to learn to recognize Clarke's point of diminishing returns and move on to the next project. So how many drafts *should* you do? Assuming you've been paying attention to the previous chapters, you know by now that, if you're properly prepared, your first draft can be pretty close to your last draft. You should always go through it at least once more, for a light polish. On really big or complicated stories, it couldn't hurt to revise a little harder on the second run-through, then add a third, light polishing draft. (If this is starting to sound too much like a car wash and wax, console yourself by remembering how rapidly cars move through one of those gadgets!) How many drafts should you do? Let's say no more than three. Sorry, Jerzy. (Oh, and don't try Kosinski's correcting-on-galleys trick, either, unless you're eager to lose your publisher.)

But "how many drafts?" isn't really the right question. Revising the right way isn't about counting drafts. Better to ask *when* in the process you should revise, and *how much.*

Although you might want to change a word here or there, fix a typo, or adjust a comma if you read through what you've written the day before, in order to recapture your writing momentum, that doesn't really count as another draft or as genuine revision. For your first serious look at what you've written, I'm of the school that advises waiting until you get all the way to the end. For one thing, you may stumble over some problem in chapter ten that requires you to fix something way back in chapter three. (Remember the movie *Bill and Ted's Excellent Adventure,* and how those time-traveling dudes must keep reminding themselves to go back—later— to a point earlier in time and "plant" a way out of their present jam?) Best in that case to go all the way through to the end and know everything that needs doing in chapter three *before* you spend time revising it; otherwise you might have to fix it more than once. Also, interrupting the forward progress of your story to tinker with what you've already written is asking for completion-drive trouble. Once you start looking backward instead of forward, the temptation to endlessly revise instead of finishing what you've started can be irresistible.

And how much should you revise? While every writer and every story will be different, as a general rule it's better to err on the side of restraint. Don't forget that you wrote your first draft (after careful preparation) at the peak of your writing momentum and emotional involvement with your subject. Here is probably when you were speaking most "truly" as a writer. When you revise, that creative drive is history. You're thinking more dully and routinely; if you're overzealous, you might revise your story's emotional vigor, freshness, and originality right into oblivion.

Over-revising can put over worked prose in place of the freshness of your first draft. Rewriting—as opposed to careful self-editing—can lead to precious writing that smacks of a thesaurus overdose. If you find yourself thinking, "What more colorful or unusual adjective could I use here instead?"—you're revising too much. If you start replacing every instance of "he said" or "she said" with "he ejaculated" or "she tittered," try a walk around the block. Then get that story in the mail before it's too late!

A further peril of relying too much on revising and rewriting is becoming *too* familiar with your own material. Soon you know your story so well that you lose perspective. *You* know what you mean. You can no longer tell what readers need to know. You cease being able to judge what will interest readers who, unlike you, come to the material fresh. At some point, even the most skillful writer loses touch with what ought to stay and what ought to be cut; it's all the same.

Some writers grapple with this challenge of perspective by what's been called the "refrigerator" system: They put a completed first draft in the refrigerator—or, more likely, a bottom drawer—to "cool" for several weeks or even months. This sounds promising, but you can never really attain the complete objectivity of someone—like an editor—seeing your story for the first time. And putting a story in the "fridge" too long can cause you to lose all your original creative drive, and even your interest. How many stories have languished indefinitely in the metaphorical refrigerator, wilting like old lettuce?

Bare-Minimum Revision

As I warn against the dangers of too much revising, though, I should confess to a prejudice: Revision just doesn't interest me very much, and I don't like doing it. If a big fat contract landed in my mailbox with the chance to earn millions writing a whole book on revising (a sure bestseller, say, "Valley of the Rewrites" or "Sex and the Second Draft"), I'd have to pass. It's not that I don't believe in polishing your writing, or think it's unimportant. I just don't find the need to spend much time or creative energy on revising—because, frankly, my first drafts come out darn near ready for the typesetter.

That's not bragging: My first drafts are better than many writers' third drafts because, as we've seen throughout this book, I prefer to invest my time and creativity up front rather than after one whole set of words has been committed to paper. You can make the same boast if you do your homework before you start writing and then pay attention to your plan when you're at the keyboard. If you find yourself tearing up your work and reassembling it after it's written, you don't need a chapter on revising—you need to go back to the start of this book.

Moreover, in the grand scheme of things, getting your writing organized right—what interests me the most, what we've spent most of this book on—is simply more important than polishing each sentence a dozen times. It's like the difference between building a house from a good blueprint and making sure that the paint in your living room precisely matches the roses on your bathroom wallpaper; both are desirable, but if the roof falls down the wallpaper hue won't much matter. Or consider that old saw about "rearranging the deck chairs on the *Titanic*"—if your story is headed for an iceberg, no amount of fine-tuning the adjectives is going to save it.

Don't believe me? Listen to Pulitzer Prize-winner Jon Franklin: "The brutal fact is that structure is far more fundamental to storytelling than polish. . . . Readers will buy story without polish, but I defy you to find a best-seller that has polish without story." And even when revising, the most important work comes down to questions of structure and organization. Your first job in taking a hard look at your first draft has to be making sure the roof won't fall down on the reader's head. As William Zinsser says about his own work, "My revisions aren't the best ones that could be made, or the only ones. They're mainly matters of carpentry: fixing the structure and the flow. . . . Most rewriting is a matter of juggling elements that already exist. And I'm not just talking about individual sentences. The total construction is equally important."

Not surprisingly perhaps, that's also what editors concentrate on when revising your work. They might let a poor word choice slip through, or a run-on sentence, but the first priority has to be making sure your story works as a whole for readers, leading them clearly and irresistibly from start to finish. Trust me on this: In the days before computers entirely replaced typewriters, when I was an in-flight-magazine editor, I used to literally cut and paste pieces of writers' stories, and Scotch tape and scissors were my most important tools.

Editors also have intense deadline pressures and other members of the production team breathing down their necks ("When's that story going to be ready to lay out, Dave?"). So they learn the hard way to concentrate their efforts where it will make the most impact for the readers. Most editors have a sort of mental checklist they run through—and it always starts with organizational questions.

Revision—the Big Picture

We've talked before about learning to "think like an editor," and revision is another point in the process where that editor's mind-set really pays dividends. You need to develop your own checklist—whether written or just in your head—to stay one step ahead of the editor's blue pencil, tape, and scissors. Just as an editor would do, let's start with the big picture, those questions of organization and reading flow that must be answered before we worry about the commas:

• **Does the opening grab the reader and flow smoothly into the rest of the story?** Editors are obsessed with openings, and good editors rarely let a bad opening slip past. All too aware of how busy and fickle readers are these days, editors also know the opening is the key opportunity—maybe the only opportunity—to "sell" the story to potential readers. Don't forget that your opening may in turn be your only chance to "sell" an editor: Many editors, confronted with a mountain of "slush pile" manuscripts, read only the opening paragraph or first page—unless something grabs them and makes them keep reading.

Try to read your opening paragraphs with fresh eyes: Are they crafted to intrigue someone coming to this subject without your passion or acquired expertise? Then make certain that the attractive road you've started the reader down doesn't lead off a cliff—your lead has to lead somewhere, seamlessly flowing into the body of the story. If there's a sharp drop-off where the opening ends and the "real" story begins, you need to do some repairs. It's even possible that your opening doesn't spring naturally from the focus of your story, that it's one of those tacked-on come-ons we warned against back in chapter eleven. If so, go back to the heart of your story and look again for your real opening: It may be buried in the body of your article and need only to be promoted to the beginning.

- **Are your focus and theme clearly encapsulated in some sort of "hook"? Is your hook high enough?** Don't make readers wonder for pages on end what the heck this story is about and why they should care. Particularly in nonfiction, if your story lacks this essential "who cares?" section or it's buried too deep in your text, you and it are in trouble. Beat the editor to the punch and fix it now.

Make sure, too, that you've stuck to the focus you set out with. Does your story still fit the "Hollywood high concept" that you developed, or the mock headline and subhead you crafted to summarize it?

- **Is your story logically organized?** Does it flow logically from point to point or scene to scene, with all the appropriate material grouped together in each point or scene? Try thinking in subheads, and make sure that what follows each possible subhead belongs there. Remember the editor with the scissors and tape, or the modern-day word processor. Editors are more likely than anybody—writers and readers included—to be finicky about organization, because their ultimate goal is clarity of communication. Of course, that should be *your* goal, too.

Similarly, though your writing doesn't have to pass a logician's inspection, now is the time to make sure your arguments hold water and your assertions are properly supported. Examine each point you make with these questions in mind: Does what comes next logically follow (the dreaded non sequitur)? Does the evidence you present actually support your point? Look for logical leaps and factual holes, for what lawyers call "assuming facts not in evidence." Have you left out something that "everybody knows" when "everybody" really doesn't? Do you introduce new terms and ideas at the proper points, or must the reader read backwards to understand what you're saying?

- **Is everything that belongs together placed together?** If you're covering points A, B, C, and D, do you say everything you need to say about C in one spot, or are little bits of C scattered throughout the story? Would your organization hold up under the close scrutiny of a fifth-grade teacher bent on impressing students with the holy obligations of outlining? Putting all the stuff that belongs together under the same organizational umbrella is one of an editor's most common and burdensome tasks. Your outline, if you built it right and stuck to it, should have eliminated most of these editing sore spots; now's the time to make sure.

Some bits of your main points will wind up elsewhere in your story, of course, to do the work of your opening, "hook," and even ending. You might need to use an example from C in your opening and another in your hook. But everything else about C belongs in your C section—not scattered here and there in the A, B and D portions.

- **Does each paragraph or section flow easily into the next?** Here's the time to test all your transitions. Seek out and destroy any interruption in the flow of your story. Rough transitions may be simply a sign of poor linking between paragraphs—fixable by tweaking a few words or switching a phrase—or they may be a red flag signaling something's out of place. If you can't make a chunk fit smoothly into your flow at a given point, maybe it doesn't belong there. See if the sore-thumb section fits more naturally and logically elsewhere in your story. And check it against your focus: Maybe the right cure is surgery—just cut it out.

- **Does your chronology track?** Test your first draft to see how many twists and turns in the sequence of events you force readers to follow. If you have more than one flashback, more than a single loop in time, you're probably asking for trouble—and confusion. Review the tenses you employ in each stage of the story, looking for elements out of sequence. Be ruthless with unnecessary backtracking. Try charting your chronology as it happened in time, then comparing this list to the order of events in your story: A story that begins *in medias res* and then catches up to itself (E-F-G-A-B-C-D-H . . .) is okay—just don't risk a second loop in time. But seemingly random insertions of elements out of chronological order (A-B-C-H-D-E-Q-F . . .) are pure poison to reader flow.

- **Does your ending tie it all together?** Some stories can just stop, but only when all that's come before leads to a conclusion that's not only natural and logical, but that supports the story's focus. Other stories demand a more overt ending strategy that hammers home your main theme. Some can even have surprise endings—though the surprise should never be truly out of the blue, but rather a revelation that makes all the previous material more meaningful and whole.

Check your ending against your focus: Have you delivered what you promised? Test the ending, too, against your opening: Have you brought readers to a destination that fits with the start of your journey together?

- **Are there unanswered questions?** This is particularly important in revising fiction. Suspense novelist Phyllis Whitney, for instance, once said that whenever she rereads one of her pages, she notes questions that must be answered in subsequent chapters. If those questions aren't resolved, the whole plot chain breaks and readers are left miffed and frustrated. As you read over your first draft, look for gaps and holes; then plug them.

- **Have you written to the right length?** In the publishing world, pages equal dollars. Editors frown on writers who regularly turn in copy that's the wrong length (usually too long, seldom too short), and keep coming back to those who consistently deliver the goods as ordered. Rigorous pruning of extraneous material at every step of the writing process, plus regular counting of words-so-far as you write the first draft, will help you finish your first draft within striking distance of your desired length. But often you'll still wind up a little long. Surgical removal of extra adjectives and adverbs and general tightening of your prose can usually solve the problem, but sometimes you need to tinker with the big picture of your structure to reach the right length.

If you've followed your outline, it should be easier to identify which chunks can be removed or radically condensed without damage to the whole. You may even need to reshuffle a few pieces to make sure they fit your altered organizational scheme. That's okay—your outline is a map, not a straitjacket.

Little Things That Mean a Lot

Editors in general and copy editors in particular empathize with an often-quoted axiom of architect Mies van der Rohe: "God is in the details." You may think that paragraphing, sentence structure, careless word choices, misspellings, and grammatical lapses are just "picky details," but editors won't. That's the second "lens," if you will, through which they examine a manuscript, after the big picture.

Again, though, it's possible to get bogged down in honing the fine points of your manuscript. You can spend hours debating whether you should use "compose" or "comprise" (or maybe "constitute"?). You could go over your manuscript a dozen times, on each pass trying to eradicate a different compositional or grammatical sin.

Obviously, editors don't have the time to tackle a manuscript this way, and neither do you. So they've also got a system for this level of revising (typically called "line editing"). From experience, most editors develop a mental checklist of points they watch for in all manuscripts—"pet peeves" might be a less-charitable label. Each sentence, each paragraph, gets scanned with this checklist in mind. Sure, a few things that are so uncommon they're not on the list might slip through—though their sheer oddity is likely to call attention to them. Once an editor has run a manuscript through his checklist, he can pass it on, secure in the knowledge that he's made it 95 percent perfect.

If you, as a writer, can learn to revise your manuscripts to the point where, from an editor's point of view, they arrive 95 percent perfect, you'll get more work than you can handle even with your new, speeded-up writing habits. Over time, you'll develop your own checklist for this level of editing your own work, but here are some points to start with:

• **Paragraph breaks.** Check each time you begin a new paragraph to make certain the break is logical and (the heck with logic!) that it helps to keep the reader reading. While you needn't be a slave to grammar-school notions of topic sentences, each paragraph should have some clear reason for being and for being a distinct unit. See if the two strongest sentences in each paragraph are the first and the last—where they carry the most weight with readers; if not, maybe your paragraphing needs reshuffling. Paragraphs must also march the story along: If you have a lot of long paragraphs in succession, you might need a shorter one for a change of pace.

• **Sentence rhythm.** Watch out for short sentences. Watch out for long sentences. Consider your use of clauses. Is there a sameness like this? As you revise, try to "hear" your sentences in your head, almost like music. Powerful prose contains a powerful rhythm within it, a variation of short and long, simple sentences and complex ones, just as great music waxes and wanes, races and slows. Listen to the music of your writing without regard to the actual words: Does it go *dum-dum-dum* or *di-dum/di-dum/di-dum*? Or does it achieve a more elegant and interesting rhythm, a *di-dum/dum/ di-dum-di-dum/dum*? Read great writers until the sound of their writing fills your head, then create your own symphony of sentences.

• **Passive voice.** Remember that the Bible opens, "In the beginning, God created the heavens and the earth"—*not* "In the beginning, the heavens and the earth were created by God." A symptom of our bureaucratic, responsibility-avoiding society, passive voice runs rampant in feeble writing: "Thousand-dollar toilets were purchased by the department . . ." instead of "The department bought thousand-dollar toilets." "Cost-overruns were incurred by this office . . ." instead of "This office spent too much." As you scan your own sentences, watch for that telltale "object . . . were + past tense verb . . . by . . .

subject" construction. Question every sentence that has something being done *by* somebody. Shouldn't the somebody come first, as in: "subject . . . action verb . . . object"? Instead of "The ball was hit by the girl," write "The girl hit the ball."

Not every instance of passive voice must be hunted down and destroyed. (The nitpickers among you, I know, are already combing through this book to find passive-voice examples of not practicing what I preach. Cut it out!) But if a manuscript that is turned in by you seems to be all effects and no causes, soon the editor's patience will be exhausted. (Now go back and revise that last, flat sentence to: "But if you turn in a manuscript that seems to be all effects, no causes, soon you'll exhaust the editor's patience.")

- **Backwards sentences.** A close kin of passive voice, backwards sentences likewise shun the powerful "subject-verb-object" sentence structure that makes your prose run like a locomotive. Critiquing the stilted "Time-ese" of Henry Luce's *Time*, *Life*, and *Fortune* magazines of the 1950s, Wolcott Gibbs wrote, "Backward ran sentences until reeled the mind." (And he wrapped up his critique with the equally arch, "Where it will all end, knows God!") Scout your stories for similarly convoluted prose. Ask yourself, "Does this sound natural? If I were telling this story to a friend, is this how I would say it?" If the answers are *no* and you seem to be writing the way *Star Wars'* Yoda in talks, forwards turn your sentences so convoluted they will not be.

- **Present participles.** Yet another way of avoiding direct writing, present participle-itis isn't as grammatically fancy as it sounds. It's simply the padding out of otherwise straightforward verbs: "The car was driving over the bridge" instead of "The car drove over the bridge." "He was running the bases" instead of "He ran the bases." Unless you've got a good reason for using the present participle—"He was running the bases when the ball hit him"—avoid it.

- **Wimpy verbs.** If you've noticed that verbs dominate this checklist so far, good—you're catching on. Verbs are the fuel of the English language. You could toss all your adjectives in the trash and still be able to say something, but without verbs you have no writing, only collections of words. Verbs make things happen. That's why it's crucial to use the strongest, most concrete verbs you can muster. When you revise, watch out for sentences that begin with "There is . . ."—a sure sign of wimpy verb use. But also revise back to life sentences that use mushy, non-specific verbs: "She showed unhappiness" instead of "She sobbed," "The plane abruptly descended" instead of "The plane crashed." Check whether your verbs are hidden in a thicket of excess words: "have a need for" instead of "need"; "make a requirement for" in place of "require." Warning bells should go off when you come upon words such as "take," "have," and "make" clogging up your verbs.

Speaking of verbs, make sure your tenses match throughout. Few things drive editors crazier faster than stories that begin in the present tense and then slide into the past, or vice versa. A tip-off for trouble can be found in your labeling of quotations: See if you start off with "he says" and then somewhere switch to "he said."

- **Other vague writing.** Weak writing doesn't infect only verbs, of course; it's a plague on all aspects of prose. As Strunk and White succinctly advise in *The Elements of Style*, "Prefer the specific to the general, the definite to the vague, the concrete to the abstract." As you check over your first draft, look for instances where you say nothing instead of something, where you write around a subject instead of through it. If you catch yourself sounding like a bureaucrat or one of those overwrought academics sometimes dubbed "educationists," pare your prose back to the essentials.

To illustrate how much more powerful are the specific and definite than the general and vague, Strunk and White cite an experiment by George Orwell, who rewrote this passage from Ecclesiastes in the King James Bible: "I returned, and saw under the sun, that the race is not to the swift, nor the battle to the strong, neither yet bread to the wise, nor yet riches to men of understanding, nor yet favor to men of skill; but time and chance happeneth to them all." Here's Orwell's bloodless translation of that passage: "Objective consideration of contemporary phenomena compels the conclusion that success or failure in competitive activities exhibits no tendency to be commensurate with innate capacity, but that a considerable element of the unpredictable must inevitably be taken into account." Get the point?

- **Avoid clichés like the plague.** Some of what might be called "clichés" will inevitably sneak into your prose, since after all what makes a phrase a cliché is its common use—even in the prose of careful writers. In revising, you need not chop or change every single phrase that sounds familiar; too much of that approach will make your writing sound like it's written by a Martian or a machine, alien to common idiom. You can even brighten up your writing with deliberate clever turns on familiar phrases. But do watch out for the easy, lazy use of clichés where a fresher phrase could do more. Don't let clichés substitute for specifics or familiar phrases squeeze out original thinking. "The scene at the gallery was as colorful as a rainbow" tells the reader nothing more than it was, well, colorful. But if you replace the cliché with a simile suited to the occasion, you can both paint a more vivid picture, and increase the thematic unity of your writing: "The scene at the gallery was as colorful as a Jackson Pollock painting" (suggesting both color and a busy, buzzing scene).

- **Mixed metaphors.** And scrambled similes and metaphors that just plain go on too long, for that matter. If, in revising your stories, you run across phrases like "As captain of the corporate ship, the CEO has to get his team across the goal line and into the end zone while dodging the tomatoes and brickbats so often hurled by the 'audience' of investors," a screaming red danger signal ought to go off. One metaphor or simile per sentence, please, and don't stretch any metaphorical structure so long that it collapses into silliness.

- **Excess verbiage.** Oops! Make that just plain "verbiage." If you paid attention when I harped on "lard words," you should already be on the alert for the extraneous words that weigh down your writing. Again quoting Strunk and White: "A sentence should contain no unnecessary words, a paragraph no unnecessary sentences, for the same reason that a drawing should have no unnecessary lines and a machine no unnecessary parts." In addition to the wasteful words warned about above, be on the lookout for:

Overloaded adjectives—Be wary of nonspecific, content-free adjectives. If you can eliminate an adjective without any loss of information, do so: "The beautiful sunset filled the sky with reds, pinks, and purples" works just as well without the self-evident and nonspecific "beautiful." Keep in mind the "nice" test: Adjectives such as "nice" (or "interesting," or "meaningful") add nothing to your writing; if you can't say something more specific than "nice," don't say anything at all. Also keep an eye out for adjectives trying to do the work of verbs. If an adjective can be replaced with a verb by switching the sentence around, try it: "The intense sunlight was painful" can become "The sunlight hurt my eyes," losing two adjectives and no information.

Adverbs—Reading most writing these days, you'd be tempted to conclude that English would be better off without adverbs. See? I could have written, "better off without adverbs entirely," but what would I have gained? Look out for adverbs that are empty intensifiers: "very," "extremely," "especially," "particularly," "totally," "absolutely," "unusually," and their meaningless ilk. Ditto for wishy-washy qualifying adverbs: "ordinarily," "generally," "fairly," "rather," "somewhat." When revising dialogue, check for spots where you gave in to the temptation to tack an adverb onto every "said": "he said eagerly," "she said lustily," "he added forlornly."

Redundancies and tautologies—Don't repeat yourself unnecessarily by saying the same thing twice without cause. (Now try taking the redundancies out of *that* sentence!) Warning flags to watch for when revising include adjectives that duplicate the meaning of the nouns they're attached to ("old antiques," "new innovations," "noisy cacophony," "excess verbiage") and words followed by synonyms ("each and every," "separate and distinct," "wild and unruly").

Circumlocutions—Don't use a wagonload of words when one will do. Watch out for mouthfuls such as "at this point in time" ("now"), "in advance of" ("before"), "in the event of" ("if"), and "as to whether" ("whether").

If you've made it this far, successfully juggling the big picture and the details as you revise your first draft, you're almost home. You've almost succeeded in "thinking like an editor" and giving your manuscript the quick polish it needs. Now there's just that little matter I mentioned before, those additional "details" of grammar, punctuation, and spelling.

Sharpening Your Basic Tools

Wait, come back! Don't panic! I know, ridiculous as it sounds, many writers can't spell. Others don't know—or care about—the essentials of grammar and punctuation. Often they even build up a phobia about these basic tools of writing to the point where they can't cope with this fundamental aspect of revision. You don't need to panic, however, when confronted with grammar quandaries or spelling mysteries; all it takes is a willingness to look things up and an efficient approach to doing so.

Admitting your ignorance, as Socrates once observed, is the first step toward knowledge. So don't try to bluff your way through grammar, punctuation, and spelling. Keep a handful of essential reference works at your side when you're revising and consult them whenever you're in doubt. You can also speed up this process by recognizing some common trouble spots and memorizing their solutions.

Ready for the world's quickest course in English grammar, punctuation, and spelling? Here goes:

- **Grammar and usage.** Start with the slim but invaluable *The Elements of Style*, often referred to as "Strunk and White." Add one of the hefty usage tomes such as *Fowler's Modern English Usage* and a standard stylebook (I recommend either *The New York Times* or the AP style manuals). That's all you really need in your grammar and usage arsenal. Any question you can't settle by checking one of these books is probably too obscure to worry about; leave it for the editor, so at least he can feel useful.

While English usage has a zillion twists and tricks, if you can keep a few quick-and-dirty rules in mind you'll save a lot of time looking up answers to common quandaries. Here's one editor's top ten grammar and usage traps to watch for in revising your writing:

1. *Among vs. between*—Use "among" for more than two, "between" for two.
2. *Compose vs. comprise*—The whole "comprises" the parts; the parts "compose" (or "constitute") the whole.
3. *Farther vs. further*—"Farther" refers to actual, measurable distance—yards and miles; otherwise, use "further."
4. *However*—Avoid using at the beginning of a sentence.
5. *Importantly*—Instead of "most importantly" or "more importantly," write "most important" or "more important." Ditto for "first" instead of "firstly," and so on.
6. *It's vs. Its*—"It's" means "it is." The possessive is "its."
7. *Less vs. fewer*—"Less" refers to quantity, "fewer" to number. If you can count them, use "fewer."
8. *Literally*—Don't use "literally" in combination with a metaphor, since it means that something is actually the case. "He ate so much that he was literally bursting" means the poor guy was coming apart at the seams and spilling his entrails into the dining room.
9. *Unique*—Never modify "unique" with an adverb, as in "very unique" or "somewhat unique." "Unique" means "one-of-a-kind," and is not a synonym for "unusual."
10. *Which vs. that*—If the sentence would make sense without the clause, use a comma and introduce it with "which." Otherwise, omit the comma and opt for "that."

- **Punctuation.** The above-mentioned references will mostly address your punctuation woes as well, and most good dictionaries include a quick reference to punctuation. Some issues of punctuation (commas before "and" in a series or the niceties of plural possessives, for example) are more matters of editorial style than right or wrong, so don't sweat them too much. Just try to be consistent (that style manual will help here).

The punctuation problems that give editors fits are actually relatively few and simple:

1. Commas vs. semicolons—If you could substitute a period and have two sentences, use a semicolon; otherwise, opt for the comma.
2. Exclamation points—Use with discretion! Don't make everything an exclamation!
3. Hyphens—Topic number one for editorial catfights. In general, hyphenate compound adjectives if the hyphen aids clarity. Omit the hyphen after "ly" adverbs ("solidly built").
4. Quotation marks—In American writing, commas and periods go inside quotation marks; semicolons and colons go outside. Question marks go outside unless the quotation is a question (*What do you mean by "rewrite this"?* vs. *"How long should the story be?" he asked.*).

- **Spelling.** This is the easiest one, of course, yet somehow the aspect of writing that gives more folks the heebie-jeebies. Get a dictionary and look it up, for gosh sakes, the way I just looked up "heebie-jeebies." Keep a hand-sized, abridged dictionary close enough to consult without getting up from your chair. You'll also want an unabridged dictionary somewhere in your office or work area, to check more obscure or technical terms. Specialized dictionaries are a must as well if you often write about technical fields such as medicine, law, or science.

  Your word-processing program can help catch most slips of the fingers and simple misspellings. But don't forget that if your misspelling accidentally spells some other word, the computer won't catch it. Don't rely on the spell checker as your only spelling tool.

The Grammar Black Hole

Having laid it on pretty thick about put-upon editors and the divinity of details, I'd like to add a quick cautionary note. Don't let concern over the details of grammar, usage, and the like become an obsession. Here's yet another trap for the time-pressed writer: You might end up becoming a darn good copy editor, but never getting anything written. Get it right. Be careful. But rely on the sort of systematic approach I've laid out in this chapter to get your revising done without letting the quest for correctness erode your efficiency.

Proper writing, as important as it is, can also be a breeding ground for pedantry. A glance through *Fowler's* will reassure you that many of the "errors" your grade-school teachers browbeat you about aren't worth worrying about. Don't lose sleep, for example, over split infinitives or sentences that end in prepositions. Allow yourself to begin occasional sentences with "But" or (more sparingly) "And." Sentence fragments can be a powerful device. When used in moderation. Not overdone. Like this.

Make the language work for you. It's a wonderful, versatile thing, this language of ours. Learn to get the most out of it.

Get Me a Rewrite!

Okay, you've written a solid first draft and polished it to (what seems to you) 95 percent perfect. What do you do when the editor calls and says, gee, he or she doesn't think your story is so perfect after all? Just when you thought it was safe to move on to your next writing project, the (blankety-blank) editor wants you to do some more revising.

Go ahead (after you say, "Sure, no problem," through gritted teeth and carefully set the phone down instead of hurling it across the room), rant and rave about tyrannical, stupid, insensitive editors who wouldn't know great writing if it bit them on the nose. Take a deep breath. Then go back to your desk and *do exactly what the editor wants—but no more.*

Leaving aside whether the editor is right or a demented idiot who should switch to a more suitable line of work, like operating a jackhammer, the editor is the one you've got to satisfy to get your work into print. Unless you have the clout of Stephen King and can storm off to a new publisher, it's best to play ball.

In fact, it's best to pay close attention to what the editor asks you to do. Take notes on your phone conversation. If the editor sends your manuscript back, with notes or a separate letter, resist the urge to tear it into teensy pieces and stomp on it. Follow the editor's instructions as precisely and literally as possible: If the editor wants more of X but less of Y, give him more X and less Y. If in doubt, just as with an initial assignment, ask. Feed back the editor's words as you understand them: "So, Sally, you want more X and less Y, right?"

Ah, but resist the temptation to also take this second chance to fiddle around with *Z*! Don't waste time and court trouble by spinning out a whole new draft if you don't have to, or changing things the editor didn't mention. Heck, you might inadvertently alter something the editor *liked*. No, leave well enough alone.

Editors will appreciate writers who take their suggestions seriously—and who get the revised manuscript back to them promptly. Few editors have lengthy author-revision times built into their schedules. They know what they want, and they want it now. Or yesterday, if possible.

So give it to them. Get that manuscript back in the mail—and hope it's the last you see of it until it's printed with your byline attached.

Now What?

Now you've got to put it into practice, of course. If you've been following along with the exercises at the end of each chapter, you've already got a great start on writing your next project not only faster but better. You've seen that "writer's block" is, well, all in your head. You know that by clearing away the clutter—both physical and mental—that keeps you from writing efficiently, you can free yourself to become the best writer you're capable of being.

But writing faster and better is a habit that must be practiced every day of your writing life. Don't let yourself think, "Oh, yeah, I know how to do this more efficiently, but just this once . . ." You've got to make the habits of focus, organization, and self-discipline as much a constant in your life as brushing your teeth.

One of the appeals of being a writer, I think, that draws so many people to it as either a dream or a career is that writing is ultimately up to the individual. It is not a team sport. Writing is just you, alone in a room with your inspiration and imagination, doing something only you can do exactly that way. Only Jane Austen could have written *Pride and Prejudice*. Only Arthur Conan Doyle could have created Sherlock Holmes. No one but Mark Twain could have made us chuckle at that jumping-frog contest—or follow Huck and Jim on that raft. It took F. Scott Fitzgerald's singular vision to see Daisy's green light at the end of the dock.

But unlike *The Great Gatsby*, the light that beckons you is not unreachable. You can create the works of reporting and make-believe, of comedy and tragedy, that will be your unique gift to the readers of the world.

Isn't it time you got started?

Exercises

1. Pick a short story or magazine article and go through the revision checklists in this chapter. Mark it up as if you were editing it.

2. Using another published piece, go through it and highlight any examples of passive voice. Try rewriting those sentences in active voice.

3. Take several paragraphs of your current writing project and try rewriting them without using any adverbs at all.

4. Compare a passage by a writer you admire with a passage from an ordinary story of a similar type. How do the passages differ in how they use parts of speech? Calculate the percentage of adjectives and adverbs in each (number of adjectives or adverbs divided into the total number of words).

5. Go through chapter one of this book and revise it using this chapter's checklists. Please do not share your results with the author!

Appendix: Essential Web Sites for Writers

Search Sites
Google (www.google.com)
AltaVista (www.altavista.com)
HotBot (www.hotbot.com)
Yahoo! (www.yahoo.com)
Internet Archive (www.archive.org)

Reference Sites
Encyclopaedia Britannica (www.britannica.com)
Bartleby.com (www.bartleby.com)
The Internet Movie Database (www.imdb.com)
Switchboard (www.switchboard.com)
Maps on Us (www.mapsonus.com)
HowStuffWorks (www.howstuffworks.com)

Finding Resources
Association of College and Research Libraries of the American Library
    Association (www.ala.org/acrl)
Special Libraries Association (www.sla.org)
LibDex (www.libdex.com)
LibrarySpot (www.libraryspot.com)
refdesk.com (www.refdesk.com)
Library of Congress (www.loc.gov)
Amazon.com (www.amazon.com)
Barnes and Noble (www.bn.com)

Finding Experts
ProfNet (www.profnet.com)
Yearbook.com (www.expertclick.com)
Expert Source (www.businesswire.com/expertsource)
FACSNET (www.facsnet.org/sources/newssources)
Experts.com (www.experts.com)
MediaResource (www.mediaresource.org)
Bznet USA (www.gehrung.com/biznet/biznet.html)
AllExperts (www.allexperts.com)

Writers Organizations

American Society of Journalists and Authors (www.asja.org)
National Writer's Union (www.nwu.org)
Science Fiction and Fantasy Writers of America (www.sfwa.org)
Society of Children's Book Writers and Illustrators (www.scbwi.org)
Writers Guild of America (www.wga.org)

Writing and Selling Your Work

Preditors & Editors (www.anotherealm.com/prededitors)
WritersDigest.com (www.writersdigest.com)
WritersMarket.com (www.writersmarket.com)

Index